"objective" psychology, 29-55

VOLUME TWO

Psycho-Myth, Psycho-History:

Psycho-Myth, Psycho-History:

Essays in Applied Psychoanalysis

By
Ernest Jones, MD

HILLSTONE
A DIVISION OF STONEHILL PUBLISHING
New York

*This collection of essays first published
in Great Britain under the title of*

ESSAYS IN APPLIED PSYCHO-ANALYSIS

ISBN 0-88373-015-4

Library of Congress Catalog Number: 74-76611

Manufactured in the United States of America

CONTENTS

I

PSYCHO-ANALYSIS AND FOLKLORE[1]

THE very extensive and original contributions that psycho-analysis has made to the science of folklore in the past twenty years have passed almost entirely unnoticed by folk-lorists. That the present is the first occasion on which the matter has been brought to their direct attention cannot, I think, be the main explanation of this remarkable neglect. I should regard it rather as one more manifestation of the anti-psychological bias that prevails among scholars and men of science. In their laudable endeavour to emerge from the subjective pre-scientific era they have naturally tended to confound objectivity with the study of the outer world, and to identify contemplation of the mind with subjectivity. This attitude has proved eminently successful in so far as the investigation of physical phenomena that are unin-fluenced by mental processes is concerned, or at least the drawbacks attaching to it have hitherto been relatively in-considerable and are only now beginning to be perceived, but the limitations it imposes on the study of phenomena which are the product of mental processes are so grave as to confine such studies to a preliminary charting out of the ground. This is evident when we consider the material studied in folklore, whether it be customs, beliefs, or folk-songs, for without exception it is the product of dynamic mental processes, the response of the folk soul to either outer or inner needs, the expression of various longings, fears, aversions, or desires. Indeed the only reason why

[1] Read before the Jubilee Congress of the Folk-Lore Society, Sept. 25th, 1928.

I

what I have just said escapes being a platitude is that, in providing explanations for any of this material, folklorists have necessarily forged a psychology of their own or else taken a commonly accepted one for granted. When they explain certain customs as having been motivated by the desire for more food or better crops they are justified in assuming such desires as common human attributes and experience no need to investigate their nature any further; that, they would say, is the business of the psychologist or physiologist. This attitude, however, has many pitfalls, for modern psychology has indubitably shown that the human mind is a far more complex apparatus than is commonly supposed, and that many motives which appear simple enough on the surface prove on examination to have a much more elaborate substructure.

Another consideration comes into play here. Psychology itself has in the past been singularly unhelpful to ancillary sciences such as folklore. What is known as academic psychology—and I am leaving philosophy quite out of account here—has found itself in an unprecedented situation, the nature of which is not at all generally appreciated. In approaching its subject-matter it finds insuperable barriers almost at the entry. In investigating the genesis of any given mental processes it has, necessarily, to make halt whenever thoughts are approached which are of too intimate a nature to be disclosed, or else a point is reached when the subject himself is unable to provide any further data—a state of things which we now know to be due to the confines having been reached between the conscious and the unconscious mind. The psychologists had perforce to content themselves with relatively superficial mental processes, such as the data of sense physiology or the rapidity with which various objects could be committed to memory and the like. It was only when the science of clinical psychology was born that a motive, namely, mental suffering, was furnished powerful enough to overcome a person's natural objection to laying bare the secrets ot his soul, and it was only when Freud provided the special technique of psycho-analysis for the exploration of the unconscious that it became possible to trace any mental process to its ultimate source. The discoveries thus made have, as is well known, proved to be startlingly revolutionary, and have led to a fundamentally new conception of the mind. This in its turn was bound to have repercussions in all the sciences, including folklore, that are concerned with the products of mental activity. Contributions from this point of view have in fact been made to a number of such sciences, such as anthropology, mythology, philology, pedagogy, and—last but not least—to folklore. It is the object of the present paper to present to you some of the points of view in question, and to illustrate a few of the bearings they have on the study of folklore material.

Perhaps the most important conclusion reached by psycho-analytic work is that what we call our mind, i.e., the mental processes known to consciousness, is only a transformed selection of the whole mind, derived from its deeper and absolutely unconscious layers and modified by contact with the stimuli of the outer world. The deeper unconscious layer, originating in our organic instincts, is mainly composed of wishes which are actively striving for expression. They come into conflict with opposing forces, especially those relating to fear and guilt, the nucleus of what later will become the moral conscience. What is allowed to seek expression by entering consciousness represents a compromise between the two groups; the wishes achieve fulfilment only in a modified and disguised form. In our judgements and beliefs about the outer world far more contributions from the obscure inner world of the mind are to be found than is commonly supposed, and it is particularly with those subjective and less rational contributions to

3

thought and conduct that folklore is concerned. When prominent they often produce a quaint or even comical effect, and elicit the disdain to which folklorists are accustomed in regard to the material of their work, but when traced to their origin they prove not only to have a perfectly intelligible logic of their own, but to be derived from the most fundamental sources of our being.

Psycho-analysis has produced much evidence to show that all our conscious ideas, feelings, interests, and beliefs originate in the unconscious; the conscious mind originates nothing, its functions being confined to criticism, selection, and control. Unconscious impulses may be called primitive both as being earlier in development in time, thus being nearly synonymous with "infantile", and as representing a lower stage in mental evolution, one out of which more highly differentiated forms of mental activity develop. Now these primitive impulses may come to expression in consciousness in, broadly speaking, one of two ways. Normally they undergo a process of transformation and adaptation in accordance with external reality; in this process they become adjusted both to the claims of reality and to the demands of inner conscience (what is nowadays called the "super-ego"). The other way in which they may come to expression is through the formation of complicated forms of compromise which act in effect as disguises, the impulses themselves remaining in their unaltered form and undergoing none of the transformation characteristic of the first mode. The former thus gives rise to what may be called the normal interests, ideas, and occupations of mankind. It is the second class that is of special interest in the present connection. They represent relics of the primitive mental state, fragments left over in the process of evolution. In the language of folklore they would be termed survivals. The value of them to the psychologist is the direct light they throw on the primitive mind before it has undergone evolu-

4

tion. To the ancillary sciences they are of value because through this knowledge they can be interpreted and thus throw light on the context in which they occur. Now the important point is that the material we have termed survivals is to be met with in very similar form in extremely diverse fields. To give a few examples of this: neurotic symptoms, the field in which these discoveries were first made, are all survivals of this nature, and represent part of the infantile life that has resisted the process of normal growth. The phenomena of dream life, the understanding of which has exercised the imagination of so many generations, have proved to be of the same nature and, as you probably know, the elucidation of them plays an extensive part in the modern treatment of neurotic symptoms, to which they afford a close parallel. To come to our present subject, many savage beliefs and folklore customs can be shown to be closely related, in both form and content, to the other phenomena that I have just classed under the same general heading. They show the same peculiar mental mechanisms characteristic of unconscious products and, what is perhaps even more important, they reveal the same underlying content and are derived from the same sources. This sentence, which contains the gist of my whole thesis, I shall presently have to amplify at some length, for to do so is to discuss the relationship between psycho-analysis and folklore. To put the whole matter in another way, what we maintain is that there is a far-reaching parallelism between survivals of primitive life from the racial past and survivals from the individual past. The practical value of this generalization is that the study of survivals in folklore can be usefully supplemented by the study of survivals in living individuals, where they are far more accessible to direct investigation.

One little point may be mentioned at the outset. As you all know, a controversy has raged for many years among folklorists over the very definition of their subject-matter; the question was admirably summed up by our last President, Mr. A. R. Wright, in his valedictory address. The point at issue was whether folklore should be confined to the study of survivals from the past, to phenomena which in the nature of things are approaching exhaustion, or whether it should also include the new manufacture of a certain class of data possessing the same characteristics as the familiar survivals. Mr. Wright quoted the following passages from previous presidential addresses: "But folklore, being what it is, namely the survival of traditional ideas or practices among a people whose principal members have passed beyond the stage of civilization which those ideas and practices once represented, it is impossible for it to have any development";[1] "One advantage possessed by our inclusive science is that the evidence which it presents is not disturbed by the intrusion of unsuspected elements. It is a science of survivals, not of discoveries";[2] and he then proceeded to make a vigorous defence of the opposite point of view. "The old tree of folk thought and practice has life not only in its *surviving* branches, on which there are both withered twigs and fresh buds, but also in new and vigorous shoots which are being put out from the old trunk."[3] Now psycho-analysis would certainly support this more comprehensive view of the subject, the one vigorously defended by Mr. Wright, laying stress, as it does, on the dynamic and spontaneous aspects of these survival products and regarding them as efforts on the part of the unconscious to find expression; it would point out not only that the impulses that generated these products are a permanent part of man and are still as actively at work as ever, but also that the differences between the new products and the old can be

[1] G. L. Gomme, *Folk-Lore*, Vol. IV, p. 6.
[2] Edward Clodd, ibid., Vol. VI, p. 75.
[3] A. R. Wright, ibid., Vol. XXXVIII, p. 24.

shown to be more superficial than essential. Mr. Wright takes as an example of the former the war superstition that to use a match to light three cigarettes portended the death of the third smoker. Folklorists cannot fail to be reminded at once of the great part played in superstition by the idea of death following a third act or process, e.g., a third stroke of apoplexy and so on. Psycho-analysis would go still further, and would be able to correlate the form of this belief with certain unconscious ideas concerning the number three, and it would in practice be able to show that just these unconscious ideas have been operative in the case of any particular person who was seriously influenced by the cigarette superstition. In doing so it would establish a continuity between the old and the new products, and would thus justify the inclusion of both in the same region of scientific study. I might illustrate the same point from another example which will also illuminate the connection between psycho-analytical and folkloristic data. In Sir Laurence Gomme's study of anthropological survivals in these islands he comes to the conclusion that "the whole associated group of customs received adequate explanation only on the theory that it represented the detritus of a once existing totemic system of belief".[1] Now in the psycho-analysis of individuals we have in a number of cases been able to demonstrate that ideas closely parallel to totemistic beliefs had been cherished during infancy, partly consciously, partly unconsciously, and, what is even more interesting, that survivals of this primitive period had been left in later life in the form of particular neurotic symptoms such as animal phobias. In other words, we have before us in the individual the whole evolution of beliefs, and customs or rituals based on them, which is parallel to what in the field of folklore has run a course of perhaps thousands of years.

[1] G. L. Gomme, *Folklore as an Historical Science*, 1908, p. 276.

The unconscious mind has a considerable number of characteristics which distinguish it from the conscious mind, and indications of many of these can often be traced in the phenomena that I have here grouped as unconscious survivals. I shall not take up your time by enumerating them here,[1] but should like to mention one or two of them with which you will be specially familiar in the field of folklore. In psycho-analysis we refer to it by the name of "omnipotence of thoughts", implying thereby the unconscious belief that the thoughts, or rather wishes, of the person in question possess a magical power of reaching fruition in the outer world. The elucidation of mental processes of this kind plays a large part in daily psycho-analytic work, and as to folklore I am at a loss to choose an illustration of it, for the vast majority of folkloristic data are based on this principle. Every custom or ritual or formula designed to bring about results in the outer world, preservation from sickness, improvement in the crops, and so on, is based ultimately on the idea that the human mind possesses the power to influence the course of nature in the outer world, a power which religion deputes to Deity and achieves by the more indirect technique of prayer.

The characteristic just mentioned may perhaps be regarded as a special example of a more general one, namely the disregard of reality. In its extreme form this can attain quite delusional dimensions, and, in fact, emerges into consciousness among the insane as actual delusions. Most often, however, the tendency to ignore reality is not absolute, at least in its conscious manifestations. It is this attribute that confers on so much of folklore material its apparent irrationality. I use the word "apparent", for the process in question is not really irrational, once one grants its premises; but the premises are often enough not in accord with the facts of external reality. If, for example, peasants

[1] *See* Freud, "The Unconscious," *Collected Papers*, 1925, Vol. IV, Ch. VI.

beat a saucepan during an eclipse of the sun, the procedure is not so senseless if one admits the presence of a wolf who is trying to devour their hero. Speaking still more broadly, we are concerned here with the part the imagination plays in the vast majority of folklore phenomena, and psycho-analysis can trace the workings of the imagination back to the internal phantasies that precede interest in the outer world and which take their origin in unconscious interests and impulses. Imagination can, of course, be generated in response to an inner need, i.e., act "spontaneously", or be stirred from without. External influences can do nothing except affect the form assumed by the imaginative act. It is through discounting this consideration that certain members of the "diffusionist" school of anthropology have invented an antinomy between the psycho-analytical and the anthropological points of view which does not, in my opinion, really exist. The all-embracing explanation they find in demonstrating the spread of a given belief or custom reminds me of the similar attitude in psycho-pathology of those who are satisfied by ascribing every neurotic symptom to "suggestion" from without, and the criticism one would make is the same in the two cases. With neurotic symptoms one can prove that, where outside suggestion has played a part, it has done so only by stirring internal impulses that were ready enough to be stirred, and that its influence is confined to determining in some degree the form taken by the product of the internal impulse. I am persuaded that much the same must be true of the mass as of the individual, for the forces at work are of the same psychological nature with both. It is not a valid argument against this to point out that the original meaning of a custom is sometimes lost in its new setting, and can be discovered only by tracing historically its spread from its place of origin, or even that the meaning may change as the result of the transplantation. To this I would reply that the "meaning" here referred to is rarely more than the rationalistic façade given by the people to the belief or custom, and that behind this façade and quite unknown to them lies the real deeper motive. If the deeper motivation be investigated it will be found to be very similar in the two cases, i.e., that the belief before and after transplantation is often the expression of the same underlying impulse.

I will now consider one of the most puzzling and important features of unconscious mentation, namely symbolism. A great part of the confusion on this subject arises simply from the fact that many quite disparate processes are often described by the same term.[1] Metaphors, emblems, similes, and so on, in fact almost any process in which one idea stands for another, have had the name "symbolism" applied to them. In psycho-analysis the word is employed in a much more restricted and defined sense, to designate a peculiar process whereby an idea or process represents an associated one which is in a state of repression in the unconscious mind. The number of possible symbols is countless, whereas the number of ideas in the unconscious that can be symbolized is very limited indeed, only those referring to the immediate blood relatives, various parts of the body, and the phenomena of birth, love, and death. Actually the large majority of symbols represent some half-dozen unconscious ideas. It follows that the interpretation of symbols displays a somewhat depressing monotony, though it is not true to say, as is sometimes done, that it is stereotyped. One is often less depressed than amazed by this monotony, though both emotions are obviously irrelevant to the more important question of the truth of the interpretations, a matter I have not the opportunity to discuss here. I would only point out that the data of folklore are replete with examples of symbolism in the psycho-analytical sense, and

[1] *See* "The Theory of Symbolism," Ch. VIII of my *Papers on Psycho-Analysis*, 1923.

that the interpretation of such symbols not only illuminates the inner meaning of the data but can constantly be confirmed by comparative study of allied material.

In the following example I would call special attention to the fact that a symbol always represents a concrete idea, never a general or abstract one. Let us take for instance the custom of throwing rice at weddings, which used to be general in the days of my youth, but which has now been replaced by the use of confetti. It would doubtless be agreed that the rice in this context represents the idea of fertility, and the act of throwing it the corresponding wish in respect of the bridal couple. Psycho-analysts would say that the rice is an *emblem* of fertility, but a *symbol* of seed; and they would mean by this that investigation of the unconscious would show that it was the idea of seed there from which all the other acts and thoughts proceeded. I have published an exhaustive study[1] of the beliefs and customs surrounding the idea of salt, one which has the same symbolic meaning, and have there discussed the relation of symbolism to superstition.

It will be seen that the unconscious ideas are not only more concrete but also cruder than the ideas represented in metaphorical processes, and this crudity and simplicity of unconscious ideas is a matter on which it is necessary to insist. In the allied, but now obsolescent, custom of throwing an old slipper or shoe after the departing couple, a custom which has more than one meaning in different layers of the mind, one would regard the object thrown as a symbol for the (fruitful) female organ itself, an interpretation that may be supported by quoting the decidedly broad saying that used to accompany it—"May you fit her as well as my foot fits this old shoe"—or by the Bohemian custom of getting hens to lay more eggs by feeding them with peas in a

---

[1] "The Symbolic Significance of Salt in Folklore and Superstition," Ch. IV in my *Essays in Applied Psycho-Analysis*, 1923.

shoe on a holy eventide.[1] To take off the bride's shoe has the same defloration significance as to tear through the bridal wreath or loosen her girdle. Symbols with the same meaning that play a very considerable part in folklore are the cowry shell, the crescent moon, innumerable cups, goblets, cauldrons, and caskets, and almost any object with an opening, from door portals and snake-stones to hollow trees or even the opening under a leaning ladder. Perhaps the most familiar example of all is the inverted horseshoe still to be seen over most stable doors. This is the descendant of the actual genital organ of the mare or cow displayed in Eastern countries to ward off the Evil Eye, just as the Shela-na-gig did that used to be found outside the door of Irish churches. It is the counterpart of the numerous forms of Asherah with its usual accompaniment of male symbols such as the arrow, cross, palm tree, star, etc., facing its concavity.

These few examples alone raise a host of problems. I intend to mention only two of them, and indeed shall have to postpone consideration of these until something has been said about the content of the unconscious. The first problem is, how comes it that the very same symbol can be used now as a sign of bad luck and now as a sign of good luck, and that the ideas symbolized are constantly changing in their relation to good and bad luck? An even prior question is, what is the real meaning of good and bad luck, terms which play such an enormous part in folklore beliefs and customs? The second problem concerns the place occupied by the subject of sexuality. Although no one has suggested that all unconscious symbols are sexual, which would be an entirely false suggestion, we have to face the fact that an astonishing number, certainly the large majority, are of this nature, and we cannot refrain from inquiring into the meaning of this unexpected finding. Now it would be quite wrong to ascribe a merely lascivious motive to the occurrence of

[1] Aigremont, *Fuss- und sehuh-Symbolik und Erotik*, 1909, S. 54.

sexual symbols, and if this were more generally recognized there would perhaps be less prudishness in dealing seriously with the problem. The circumstances that such symbolism pervades all religions, even the higher ones, should in itself be enough to make us regard the matter more soberly. I hope to show presently that the two questions just raised are intimately connected and that they are concerned with the most fundamental issues of life and death.

I think it is fair to say that the phenomena studied in folklore relate for the most part to simple or even lowly themes. The same is true *a fortiori* of the unconscious mind. In folklore we have to do with the simple wishes and fears of the people and very little with elaborate philosophical, spiritual, or artistic preoccupations. We find the people concerned with such matters as the preservation of health, the warding off of danger and death, the hopes of fortune, and the desire for happy marriage and the blessing of children. The unconscious is similarly engrossed with such topics and in even more primitive terms. I will illustrate this by laying before you two broad generalizations about its content. The first is that it is mainly concerned with the themes of birth, love and death. These are the springs of life, and psycho-analysis would go so far as to maintain that all our manifold imaginative interests originate there, and consist only in ramifications of these themes modified by the influence of two other factors, the defensive reactions against certain dangers inherent in them (the moral "super-ego"), and contact with outer reality. These two influences exercise a constantly moulding effect on the primitive impulses that are striving for expression in their naked form. They control them, thwart them, select from them, and modify them to such an extent that in the final forms in which they emerge they are mostly transformed or distorted out of recognition. From time to time, of course, they emerge in ruder forms in various contexts. If, for instance, myths and nursery tales were taken seriously and not as a form of entertainment, we should doubtless be horrified at the recurring evidences they present of barbarous and loutish impulses. Sir Laurence Gomme is assuredly right when he says that "it is not accidental but persistent savagery we meet with in the folk-tale"[1]. Further, as might be expected, the orientation of these impulses is decidedly egocentric; the unconscious, like charity, begins at home.

The second generalization about the unconscious is that primarily it recognizes no human beings except the immediate blood relatives; parents, siblings, and children. Attitudes and feelings about other people are all developed by either transforming or directly transferring those belonging to the relatives. This finding has tremendous import, but first I should like to make it a little more intelligible by reminding you of the banal fact that an infant's feelings and reactions are of necessity displayed first in respect of the persons in its immediate environment. The generalization I have just enunciated is by no means identical with this banal fact, though it has much in common with it. It illustrates the genetic aspects of the unconscious, and shows how nearly akin it is to the infantile. The really important feature of it is that, since the unconscious is composed of our most primitive impulses, we have to face the conclusion that in that region of the mind the relationship to other members of the family far transcends the conventional ones of piety and affection. It does this in both directions, i.e., it is both more and less affectionate than one would infer from conscious manifestations. By less than affectionate I mean the jealous and hostile attitudes inherent in the family relationship, which regularly culminate in death-wishes. By more than affectionate I mean sexual, and in saying this I reach the hotly contested doctrine of psycho-analysis on the subject of infantile sexuality. This is not the place either to

[1] G. L. Gomme, op. cit., p. 82.

expound or to defend the doctrine, and I can only express my personal conviction of its truth. The only possible alternatives are that psycho-analysts are entirely mistaken in maintaining the existence of infantile sexuality, or, on the other hand, that, as they assert, powerful motives of repression are generally operative in leading people to overlook or discount the signs of it that exist all around. Those who have seriously examined the mass of evidence that has been adduced can, I think, hardly remain long in doubt between these two alternatives.

The aspect of this subject that most concerns us here is the relationship of infantile sexuality to other members of the family, the so-called incest trends. According to psychoanalysis every child goes through a period in the first few years of its life where its development is dominated by unconscious conflicts relating to these trends, and very much of its future will depend on how it copes with them. Powerful barriers of fear and guilt are constructed against the forbidden and dangerous trends, and these barriers from the nucleus of what later becomes morality, conscience, and much of religion. I cannot describe here the complicated ways in which the two sets of forces in this conflict result in various compromises, out of which much of our conscious mind emerges; what interests us here is the less satisfactory products of the conflict. By these I mean the relics of the primitive state, what I termed "survivals" in the earlier part of my paper, and, as I then pointed out, they are very nearly synonymous with much of the data investigated by folklorists. The most typical group is that which in its psychological structure can be likened to neurotic symptoms. An example would be the averting of "ill-luck" by a magical gesture, incantation, or amulet. There is an interesting group, however, which is intermediate between this one and the quite normal transformation of the primitive impulses into daily activities. This intermediate one may, in a broad sense, be called artistic. The prominent part in it that phantasy plays allies it to the last group, from which it is separated, however, by a certain deference to reality. At the present Congress we have had several attractive presentations on the matter of folk-songs and folk-dance, but there are two topics even more familiar to us all in this connection. I refer to fairy tales and children's games. It has long been surmised, and in part demonstrated, that both these prerogatives of childhood have more to do with adult life than might at first sight appear. It seems clear, for instance, that the building and defending of castles and the use of bows and arrows must be traditionally handed down from times when these were serious occupations in adult life. In some cases, as in the doctor game and the preoccupation with dolls, the relation to the sexual life of adults is unmistakable, but it will surprise many of you to be told that there is good reason to suppose that sexual elements are to be traced in most of these youthful interests. Symbolism plays an even larger part in the mentality of children than in that of adults, and the actual psycho-analysis of young children has shown that both their spontaneously invented games and the traditional ones they adopt so eagerly are often the symbolic expression of the infantile sexuality I mentioned earlier. The same is true of fairy tales. Let me illustrate this by the familiar example of the frog-prince type of tale, in which the frog through repeated pleadings is gradually admitted to increasing intimacy with the maiden and is finally unspelled on being admitted to her bed. We learn from the sequel that the frog was all the time a prince in disguise, but to this we have to add the fact that the frog is in the unconscious a constant symbol of the male organ when viewed with disgust. So we have to complete the interpretation by saying that the story represents the maiden's gradual overcoming of her aversion to intimacy with this part of the body.

This leads me to say a word about the part played by animals in phantasy, in children's games, in nursery tales, in legends, and, last but not least, in dreams. The simple fact that these animals, in spite of their frequently objectionable behaviour, surprise us by displaying peculiarly human characteristics should provide a hint to their real meaning. This is no more and no less than that they represent particular human beings, most often the parents, especially the father, less often brothers or sisters or children. In many fairy tales, e.g., *The Twelve Brothers*, *The Seven Ravens*, etc. (Grimm), this is explicitly stated, and, incidentally, we get a hint of the motives behind such transformations, since it is clear that in these instances the father has cast the spell from jealousy of his daughter's fondness for the brothers. It is noteworthy that the father-animal identification is usually much more disguised than the other forms, indicating that the repressed thoughts about the father are in a corresponding state of inhibition. The animals of heraldry, however, might be quoted in this context, for the connection between heraldry and ancestry is evident enough as is that between the worship and taboos about snakes and piety for ancestors. Again, there are the numerous beliefs of tribes and nations being descended from particular animals, as the English are supposed to be from horses. Ancestor worship and the numerous beliefs about ancestors are but a displacement of similar attitudes concerning the father. The animals may of course be actual or imaginary ones, such as unicorns, dragons, etc., and in the latter case indicate a further stage in the disguise of the repressed idea. For the reason of the disguise is certainly repression. If one asks why should not the actual persons intended appear in the story or dream, the answer we get from investigation of the data is always the same, namely, that the theme that has given rise to the phantasy contains elements that are unacceptable to consciousness, and so are

17

allowed to emerge only when they have been changed into an unrecognizable form. The various elements in question fall into two groups, sexual and hostile, a rule to which I know no exception, and the incompatibility of these attitudes with the piety due to one's family is obvious.

These human animals remind us of the other figures of phantasy, giants, dwarfs, fairies, and ghosts, about each of which very much could be said. It is generally recognized by now that the conception of giants, with their clumsy stupidity and their alternation of kindliness and ogrish devouring of children, is a projection of various infantile thoughts about grown-ups, particularly the parents, and perhaps one might say the same as regards the sexual significance of jesters, and dwarfs, of which Thumbkins and Rumpelstiltskin serve as typical examples. The belief in ghosts is one which has naturally attracted much attention from folklorists, and here again I would suggest that much advantage may accrue from co-operation between their work and that of psycho-analysts. It is surely clear that a limit is soon reached if we confine our investigation of ghosts (and allied spiritistic phenomena) to examination of the purely objective aspects, without taking into account the subjective state of the witnesses. In such studies we cannot distinguish between the parts played by the inner world and the outer world so long as we attend, as is nearly always the case, to the latter only. Psycho-analysis is naturally concerned with the former problem and often enough has to investigate the fear of ghosts, the proneness to see them, and so on. After unravelling and curing such mental states, it is possible to say something pretty definite about the genesis and meaning of them, and a great deal of evidence has accumulated to show that this is intrinsically connected with unconscious death wishes relating to one or both of the parents, the strength and ramifications of which are difficult to overestimate.

After making this wide excursion let us return to the two questions I raised earlier in the paper, namely, the problem of luck and the problem of why it is that sexual symbolism occupies such an unexpectedly large part in the unconscious processes from which folklore survivals are derived. Curiously enough, the answer to these questions is substantially the same. Both subjects have to do with certain fears and wishes dating from a particularly difficult phase in development which everyone goes through, which everyone forgets, and of which there is therefore no conscious knowledge. It is perhaps the outstanding discovery attaching to the name of Freud that every young child goes through a stage of intense incestuous attachment which leaves an ineffaceable mark on all its later development. In connection with it two invariable reactions occur, fear and hate, and, soon afterwards, guilt. The dread of punishment, as distinct from the normal fear of punishment or enmity, is in the unconscious always associated with this primary theme, whatever be the context in which it occurs consciously. The sense of sin is born in connection with incest wishes, all sin is apprehended as incest by the unconscious, and therefore all guilt and moral punishment remain throughout life inextricably intertwined with these primary ideas. The very word "incest" is derived from a Sanskrit word signifying "undisciplined", "unpunished". Another remarkable ramification is the way in which the concept of punishment is in the unconscious extended to that of misfortune in general. Here, as in so many other respects, Christian theology follows closely the prototype of the unconscious, for it, too, regards the misfortunes that befall humanity as Divine punishment for our sins. The practical corollary from all this is that exactly in proportion to the difficulty an individual has experienced in overcoming this early phase in development will he tend to react to the misfortunes of life as if they were punishments for sin. He will try to ward them off by measures which may be purely magical in nature, or may assume the religious form of penance and propitiation.

The next point is that the punishment for sin is always the same in the unconscious. It appropriately takes the talion form of deprivation of sexual capacity, this being most typically expressed in men as impotence—which is the conscious equivalent of castration in the unconscious—and in women of sterility. Often enough this finds directly conscious expression, as in the endless superstitions and practices to do with fertility and sterility on the one hand, and the manifold dread of what was called the "ligature" on the other hand, the dread which is the secret of the witchcraft epidemic. Usually, however, the dreads and defensive measures are expressed in various symbolic guises that need to be interpreted before their meaning becomes clear. Two vast subjects in this connection are those of ill-health and death, which is natural enough when one reflects how largely they bulk among the misfortunes of humanity. Hypochondriacal concern about health and a disproportionate apprehension of death always, as I have expounded elsewhere in a similar connection,[1] prove when investigated to be the manifestations of unconscious guilt with dread of the punishment of impotence.

I come last to what, I think, is the most interesting point of all in this complicated subject. It is that, just as the punishment for forbidden sexuality (incest) always takes the talion form of a veto on sexuality, so do the apotropæic measures designed to ward off evil seek to achieve their aim by means of the same talion, or what might perhaps be here better termed homœopathic, principle. The underlying idea appears to be that if only the person could dare to prove to himself that he could commit incest, symbolically of course,

---

[1] "Psycho-Analysis and Anthropology," *The Journal of the Royal Anthropological Institute*, Vol. LIV, 1924.

without the dreaded punishment ensuing, that very impunity would be the best reassurance imaginable against his fears. This is the reason why sexual symbolism plays such an astonishing part in the customs and beliefs that make up so much of folklore. As I indicated above, it would be both superficial and erroneous to regard these findings as simply indications of lasciviousness. They are dictated by the desire to free the personality from guilt, from danger from punishment, and from misfortune, and thus to restore the innate faculty of potency and fertility, in short, to ensure happiness. We have here the explanation of how it is that the idea of incest signifies both the maximum of danger and the maximum of security. And that is the reason why the same act, the same object, the same belief can at one moment or in one place represent the idea of good-luck and at another that of ill-luck.

If this Congress were entirely devoted to the relation of psycho-analysis to folklore, it would be able to deal with only the fringe of such a vast subject. I have singled out, however briefly and inadequately, what I consider to be a few of the most vital points of connection, and will express the hope that future co-operation between workers in what are apparently very different fields will be equally fruitful to both.

II

THE SYMBOLIC SIGNIFICANCE OF SALT IN FOLKLORE AND SUPERSTITION[1]

I

I n the course of some highly suggestive remarks on the subject of superstition Freud[2] writes: "I take it that this conscious ignorance and unconscious knowledge of the motivation of psychical accidents is one of the psychical roots of superstition." He maintains in general that the undue significance attached by the superstitious to casual external happenings arises from associative connections that exist between these and important thoughts and wishes of which the subject is quite unaware, and that it constitutes a projection of the significance really belonging to these unconscious thoughts: the feeling of significance, therefore, is fully justified, though it has been displaced into a false connection. The object of the present communication is to examine in the light of this thesis one of the most familiar and wide-spread of superstitions—namely, the belief that it is unlucky to spill salt at table. In doing so the endeavour will be made to use the inductive method only, that is to say, to construct hypotheses only when they appear to be legitimate inferences from definitely ascertained facts and then to test them in their capacity to resume the whole range of accessible evidence.

Two primary considerations may be mentioned at the outset. First that in all ages salt has been invested with a

[1] Published in *Imago*, 1912, Bd. 1, S. 361 and 454.
[2] Freud, *Zur Psychopathologie des Alltagslebens*, 1904, S 82.

significance far exceeding that inherent in its natural properties, interesting and important as these are. Homer calls
it a divine substance, Plato describes it as especially dear
to the Gods,[1] and we shall presently note the importance
attached to it in religious ceremonies, covenants, and
magical charms. That this should have been so in all parts
of the world and in all times shows that we are dealing
with a general human tendency and not with any local
custom, circumstance or notion. Secondly, the idea of salt
has in different languages lent itself to a remarkable pro-
fusion of metaphorical connotations, so that a study of these
suggests itself as being likely to indicate what the idea has
essentially stood for in the human mind, and hence perhaps
the source of its exaggerated significance.

We may begin by considering the chief characteristic
properties of salt that have impressed themselves on popular
thought and have in this way become associated with more
general ideas of an allied nature. Perhaps the most prominent of these is the *durability* of salt and its *immunity against
decay*. On account of this property salt was regarded as
emblematic of durability and permanence,[2] and hence of
eternity and immortality;[3] in the Middle Ages it was
thought that the devil for this reason detested salt.[4] In
connection with eternity is also mentioned the idea of
wisdom, which salt is likewise supposed to symbolize,[5]
though Pitré[6] says that this comes merely from a play on
the words *sedes sapientiæ* and *sale e sapienza*. Brand,[7] how-

---

[1] Plutarch, *Morals* (Goodwin's English Edition), 1870, Vol. II, p. 338.

[2] Lawrence, *The Magic of the Horse-Shoe: with other Folk-Lore Notes*, 1899.
Ch. III, "The Folk-Lore of Common Salt," p. 157.

[3] Seligmann, *Der böse Blick und Verwandtes*, 1910, Bd. II, S. 33.

[4] Bodin, *De la Démonomanie des Sorciers*, 1593, p. 278.

[5] Collin de Plancy, *Dictionnaire Infernal*, 1818, t. II, p. 278; Lawrence, ibid.

[6] Pitré, *Usi e costumi, credenze e pregiudizi del popolo Siciliano*, 1889, Vol. III,
p. 426.

[7] Brand, *Observations on the Popular Antiquities of Great Britain*, 1849,
Vol. I, p. 433.

ever, quotes an introductory address delivered at a German university in the seventeenth century that seems to show an intrinsic connection between the two ideas: "The sentiments and opinions both of divines and philosophers concur in making salt the *emblem of wisdom or learning*; and that not only on account of what it is composed of, but also with respect to the several uses to which it is applied. As to its component parts, as it consists of the purest matter, so ought wisdom to be pure, sound, immaculate, and incorruptible: and similar to the effects which salt produces upon bodies ought to be those of wisdom and learning upon the mind." This explanation of the association between the ideas of salt and wisdom sounds a little too strained to be altogether convincing and suggests that perhaps there may be other determining factors besides those just mentioned. Wisdom was frequently personified holding a salt-cellar, and the bestowal of *Sal Sapientiæ*, the Salt of Wisdom, is still a formality in the Latin Church. The heavenly Sophia appears in mystical science as sodium, and her colour is yellow, the colour of burning salt.[1]

The idea of durability in regard to salt is evidently an important cause of the old association between it and the topic of *friendship* and *loyalty*.[2] Owing to its lasting and incorruptible quality it was regarded as the emblem of perpetual friendship,[3] and from this several secondary meanings are derived. One corollary, for instance, is that the spilling of salt is supposed to involve a quarrel or breaking of friendship.[4] Salt has played an important part in matters of *hospitality*. Stuckius[5] tells us that the Muscovites thought a prince could not show a stranger a greater mark

[1] Bayley, *The Lost Language of Symbolism*, 1912, Vol. I, p. 228.
[2] *See* Victor Hehn, *Das Salz. Eine kulturhistorische Studie*, 2e Aufl., 1901, S. 10-12.
[3] Brand, op. cit., Vol. III, p. 162; Lawrence, op. cit., pp. 169, 171.
[4] Wuttke, *Der deutsche Volksaberglaube der Gegenwart, Dritte Bearbeitung*, 1900, S. 211; Brand, loc. cit.
[5] Stuckius, *Antiquitatum Convivialium*, 1690, S. 17.

of affection than by sending to him salt from his own table. In Eastern countries it is a time-honoured custom to place salt before strangers as a token and pledge of friendship and good-will,[1] and in Europe it was usually presented to guests before other food, to signify the abiding strength of friendship.[2] When an Abyssinian desires to pay an especially delicate attention to a friend or guest he produces a piece of rock-salt and graciously permits the latter to lick it with his tongue.[3] In the most diverse countries and at all ages, from Ancient Greece to modern Hungary, salt has been used to *confirm oaths and compacts*;[4] according to Lawrence, "in the East, at the present day, compacts between tribes are still confirmed by salt, and the most solemn pledges are ratified by this substance." Such compacts are inviolable, and in the same way "to eat a man's salt", a phrase still in current use, carries with it the obligation of *loyalty*; during the Indian mutiny of 1857 a chief motive of restraint among the Sepoys was said to have been the fact that they had sworn by their salt to be loyal to the Queen.[5] Byron, in "The Corsair", refers to this group of beliefs as follows:

> Why dost thou shun the salt? that sacred pledge,
> Which, once partaken, blunts the sabre's edge,
> Makes even contending tribes in peace unite,
> And hated hosts seem brethren to the sight!

Closely allied to the preceding feature of incorruptibility is the capacity salt possesses of *preserving other bodies from decay*. It is generally supposed that this is the reason for the power salt has of warding off the devil and other

---

[1] Lawrence, op. cit., p. 156.
[2] Lawrence, op. cit., p. 169.
[3] Lawrence, op. cit., p. 188.
[4] Schleiden, *Das Salz. Seine Geschichte, seine Symbolik und seine Bedeutung im Menschenleben*, 1875, S. 71-3; Lawrence, op. cit., pp. 164-6.
[5] Manley, *Salt and other Condiments*, p. 90.

malignant demons, who have a horror of it.[1] The same
property has also greatly aided in establishing the association between salt and immortality; the connection is plainly
seen in the Egyptian custom of using salt for embalming.
It is one reason for the custom, obtaining until recently in
every part of Great Britain, of placing salt on a corpse;[2]
usually earth was added, "the earth being an emblem of
the corruptible body, the salt an emblem of the immortal
spirit." In later years this was said to be done so as to
prevent decomposition,[3] an idea probably akin to the
original one. A Welsh elaboration of the custom was to
place a plate of bread and salt over the coffin (the combination of bread and salt will be discussed later); the professional "sin-eater" of the district then arrived, murmured
an incantation and ate the salt, thereby taking upon himself all the sins of the deceased.[4]

An important conception of salt is that of its constituting
the *essence* of things, particularly of life itself. This seems
to include two sub-ideas, those of necessary presence and
of value respectively. The idea of ultimate essence no doubt
underlies the Biblical phrase (Matthew v. 13) "Ye are the
salt of the earth", and in many other expressions it is used
in the sense of aristocratic, quintessential, and the like.[5]
In alchemy salt was considered to be one of the three
ultimate elements out of which the seven noble metals were
generated. Mercury symbolized the spirit, sulphur the soul,
and salt the body; mercury represented the act of illumination, sulphur that of union, and salt that of purification.
Herrick, in his *Hesperides* (p. 394), ranks salt even more
highly:

[1] Conway, *Demonology and Devil-Lore*, 1879, Vol. I, p. 288; Moresin, *Papatus*,
etc., 1594, p. 154; Bodin, loc. cit.
[2] Dalyell, *The Darker Superstitions of Scotland*, 1835, p. 102; Sikes, *British
Goblins*, 1880, p. 328; Brand, op. cit., Vol. II, pp. 234, 235.
[3] Brand and Sikes, loc. cit.
[4] Sikes, op. cit., pp. 324, 326.
[5] *Oxford English Dictionary*, Vol. VIII, p. 59.

The body's salt the soule is, which when gone,
The flesh soone sucks in putrefaction.

In Ancient Egypt salt and a burning candle represented
life, and were placed over a dead body to express the ardent
desire of prolonging the life of the deceased.[1] The following
argument was employed by Latin writers, e.g., Plutarch:
"After death all parts of the body fall apart. In life the soul
maintains the parts intact and in connection with one
another. In the same way salt maintains the dead body in
its form and connection, thus representing—so to speak—
the soul."[2] The culmination of eulogies, in which the idea of
value is also prominent, is to be found in a treatise on salt,
published in 1770, where the writer launches forth in im-
passioned style the most extravagant encomiums upon this
substance, which he avers to be the quintessence of the
earth. Salt is here characterized as a Treasure of Nature, an
Essence of Perfection, and the Paragon of Preservatives.
Moreover, whoever possesses salt thereby secures a prime
factor of human happiness among material things.[3]

Salt is closely associated with the idea of *money* or
wealth, and indeed this is one of the connotations of the
word. Nowadays the implication is even of excessive or
unfairly high value, as in the colloquial phrase "a salt or
salty price"; similarly in French "il me l'a bien salé" means
"he has charged me an excessive price". In commercial
circles the expression "to salt a mine or property" means to
add a small quantity of some valuable substance to it so as
artificially to raise its selling price. In Ancient Rome
soldiers and officials were paid in salt instead of money,
whence (from salarium) the modern words "salair" and
"salary" and the phrase "to be worth one's salt" (=to be

[1] Moresin, op. cit., p. 89.
[2] Ibid.
[3] Elias Artista Hermetica, *Das Geheimnis vom Salz*, 1770.

capable, to earn one's salary). A salt currency was in vogue in Africa in the sixth century, and in the Middle Ages this was so also in England,[1] as well as in China, Tibet, and other parts of Asia.[2] The name of the Austrian coin "Heller" is derived from an old German word for salt, "Halle."[3] The Montem ceremony at Eton,[4] which consisted in collecting money in exchange for salt, was continued until 1847. Salt-Silver was the term used to denote the money paid by tenants to their lord as a commutation for the service of bringing him salt from market.[5] In parts of Germany the game is played of placing some sand, some salt, and a green leaf on the table and making a blind-folded person grope for them; if he seizes the salt it denotes wealth.[6]

These and other considerations have invested the idea of salt in the popular mind with a sense of *general importance*. Waldron[7] states that in the Isle of Man "no person will go out on any material affair without taking some salt in their pockets, much less remove from one house to another, marry, put out a child, or take one to nurse, without salt being mutually exchanged; nay, though a poor person be almost famished in the streets, he will not accept any food you will give him, unless you join salt to the rest of your benevolence". To carry salt with one on moving to a new dwelling is a very wide-spread custom;[8] it is related that when the poet Burns, in 1789, was about to occupy a new house at Ellisland, he was escorted there by a procession of relatives in whose midst was carried a bowl of salt.[9] The Arabs of Upper Egypt, before setting out on a

[1] Brand, op. cit., Vol. I, p. 436.
[2] Schleiden, op. cit., S. 68-70, 82.
[3] Hehn, op. cit., S. 90.
[4] Brand, op. cit., pp. 433-40.
[5] Brand, op. cit., p. 403.
[6] Wuttke, op. cit., S. 233.
[7] Waldron, *Description of the Isle of Man*, 1725, p. 187.
[8] Wuttke, op. cit., S. 396.
[9] Rogers, *Scotland, Social and Domestic*, 1869, Vol. III, p. 288.

journey, burn salt to prevent ill-luck.[1] The laying of salt at the table was in the Middle Ages a tremendous ceremony. The other implements were disposed with minute care in their relation to the salt, which throughout was treated with special deference.[2] With the Romans it was a matter of religious principle that no other dish was placed upon the table until the salt was in position. Rank and precedence among the guests were precisely indicated by their seat above or below the salt and their exact distance from it. Schleiden[3] remarks: "How great was the importance attached to salt is also seen from the fact that hardly a place existed in which salt was produced where this was not expressed in the name of the place, from the Indian Lavanápura ('Salt-town') and the Austrian Salzburg ('Salt-town') to the Prussian Salzkotten and the Scottish Salt-coats."

The high importance attaching to salt led to various *magical powers* being ascribed to it, and it has been very extensively employed in magical procedures. It could be used for these and other purposes by placing it on the tongue or by rubbing the body with it, but the favourite method was to dissolve it in water and bathe the person with this. The principal function of salt in this connection, like that of most other charms, was to ward off harm, chiefly by averting the influence of malignant spirits. Salt is almost universally thought to be abhorrent to evil demons,[4] the only exception I know of being in Hungarian folk-lore, where on the contrary evil beings are fond of salt.[5] Salt was always missing from the devil's and witches' banquets.[6] Salt has therefore been one of the staple charms

[1] Burckhardt, *Travels in Nubia*, 1822, p. 169.
[2] Lawrence, op. cit., pp. 197-205.
[3] Schleiden, op. cit., S. 70.
[4] Bodin, loc. cit.; Collin de Plancy, op. cit., pp. 277, 278; Schleiden, op. cit., S. 78.
[5] Lawrence, op. cit., p. 159.
[6] Wright, *Sorcery and Magic*, 1851, p. 310.

against the power of the devil,[1] of magicians,[2] of witches,[3] of the evil eye,[4] and of evil influences in general:[5] such beliefs are found in countries so far apart as Arabia[6] and Japan.[7] Cattle are also protected against witchcraft in the same way.[8] In India and Persia one can even determine by means of salt whether a given person has been bewitched or not.[9] Salt will also protect the fields from evil influences.[10] It was further used to prevent the souls of the dead from returning to earth and to secure them peace in Purgatory.[11]

These practices were performed with especial frequency with *children*. The custom of rubbing new-born infants with salt is referred to in the Bible (Ezekiel xvi. 4). The use of salt to guard the new-born against evil demons and evil influences, either by placing a little on the tongue or by immersing the infant in salt and water, was in vogue throughout Europe from early times, and certainly ante-dated Christian baptism;[12] in France the custom lasted until 1408 of putting salt on children until they were baptised, when it was considered no longer necessary.[13] At the present day it is still placed in the cradle of the new-born child in Holland.[14] In Scotland it was customary to put salt into a

[1] Bodin and Collin de Plancy, loc. cit.

[2] Grimm, *Deutsche Mythologie, Vierte Ausgabe*, 1876, S. 876.

[3] Krauss, *Slavische Volksforschungen*, 1908, S. 39; Mannhardt, *Germanische Mythen*, 1858, S. 7; Seligmann, op. cit., Band II, S. 33; Wuttke, op. cit., S. 95, 258, 283; Grimm, op. cit., Nachtrag, S. 454.

[4] Seligmann, op. cit., Band I, S. 312, 313, 320, 331, 344, 346, 365, 377, 389; Band II, S. 73, 144, 220, 376.

[5] Lawrence, op. cit., p. 177.

[6] Burckhardt, loc. cit.

[7] Bousquet, *Le Japon de nos jours*, 1877, t. I, p. 94; Griffis, *The Mikado's Empire*.

[8] Seligmann, op. cit., Band II, S. 104, 241, 329; Wuttke, op. cit., S. 40, 435, 438; Krauss, loc. cit.

[9] Seligmann, op. cit., Band I, S. 262, 264.

[10] Seligmann, op. cit., Band II, S. 374.

[11] Wuttke, op. cit., S. 465, 472.

[12] Conway, op. cit., Vol. II, p. 217; Lawrence, op. cit., pp. 174, 175; Seligmann, op. cit., S. 34; Wuttke, op. cit., S. 382, 387.

[13] Schleiden, op. cit., S. 79.

[14] *New York Times*, November 10, 1889.

child's mouth on entering a stranger's house for the first time.[1] Salt was also placed in the mouth of a new-born calf for similar purposes as with children.[2]

Salt has been extensively used for *medicinal purposes*. It was believed to have the function of both preventing[3] and curing[4] diseases, as was already commented on by Pliny, particularly those caused by occult influences. It is possible that the Latin word "salus" (=health), the earliest connotation of which was "well-preserved", was originally related to the word "sal".

Another important function of salt was its use in furthering *fecundity*. As this obviously cannot have been derived from any natural property of the substance, it must represent some symbolic significance in harmony with the general importance attached to it. Schleiden[5] makes the following interesting remarks in this connection: "The sea was unquestionably the fructifying, creative element. Leaving aside the few marine mammals, the offspring of sea creatures are to be counted by thousands and hundreds of thousands. This was all the more easily ascribed to the salt of the sea, since other observations believed to have been made were connected with it. It was recalled that in dog-breeding the frequent use of salt increased the number of the progeny, and that on ships carrying salt the number of mice multiplied to such an extent as to give rise to the idea of parthenogenesis, i.e., to the view that mice could beget young without the co-operation of a male. The conviction was thus formed that salt must stand in a close relation to physical love, so that salt became the *symbol of procreation*." It was used in this connection in two ways, to promote

---

[1] Dalyell, op. cit., p. 96.
[2] Seligmann, op. cit., S. 58; Wuttke, op. cit., S. 436, 443.
[3] Wuttke, op. cit., S. 374.
[4] Dalyell, op. cit., pp. 98, 99, 102; Lawrence, op. cit., p. 180; Seligmann, op. cit., Band I, S. 278; Wuttke, op. cit., S. 336.
[5] Schleiden, op. cit., S. 92, 93.

fecundity and to avert barrenness or impotence. The latter is illustrated by Elisha's action of throwing salt into the fountain of Jericho (2 Kings ii. 21): "Thus saith the Lord, I have healed these waters; and for the future they shall not be the occasion either of death or barrenness." Gaume[1] states that salt has the specific function of promoting fecundity, and its symbolic significance in this direction is seen in the following Indian practice:[2] A woman who wishes for a child, particularly for a son, fasts on the fourth lunar day of every dark fortnight and breaks her fast only after seeing the moon. A dish of twenty-one balls of rice, one of which contains salt, is then placed before her, and if she first lays her hand on the ball containing the salt she will be blessed with a son. In this case no more is eaten; otherwise she goes on until she takes the salted ball. The ceremony may be observed only a limited number of times; if in these she fails altogether to pick out the salted ball first she is doomed to barrenness. In Belgium salt is mixed with the food of a pregnant mare or cow so as to make the birth easy;[3] in Normandy it is given to cows so as to ensure plenty of butter.[4] In East Friesland[5] and Scotland[6] salt is put into the first milk after calving with the object of securing a plentiful supply of good milk. In Bohemia a special cake containing salt is given to a pregnant cow so that she may bear a choice calf and yield plenty of milk.[7] In Ireland when the seed is being sown the mistress of the house first puts salt into the field,[8] and a similar custom exists in East

---

[1] Gaume, L'Eau Bénite au Dix-neuvième Siecle, 1866, Cited by Conway.

[2] Indian Notes and Queries, Vol. IV, p. 106.

[3] Von Reinsberg-Düringsfeld, "Volksgebrauche in Kempen," Ausland, 1874, S. 471.

[4] Kuhn, Märkische Sagen und Märchen, 1843, S. 388.

[5] Wuttke, op. cit., S. 446.

[6] Dalyell, op. cit., p. 101.

[7] Wuttke, op. cit., S. 442.

[8] Gough's Edition of Camden's Britannia, 1789, Vol. III, p. 659 and Vol. IV, p. 470.

Prussia.[1] In Bavaria to obtain a rich harvest the first load is sprinkled with salt and water.[2]

It is only natural that the general importance attached to salt should have been reflected in the sphere of *religion*, and we find that this was so in a remarkable degree. Salt was an essential constituent of sacrificial offerings in Ancient Egypt,[3] as well as in Greece and Rome;[4] Brand says of the latter: "Both Greeks and Romans mixed salt with their sacrificial cakes; in their lustrations also they made use of salt and water, which gave rise in after times to the superstition of holy water." In Judaism we find descriptions of three different usages taught by the Bible. As in other countries, salt formed a necessary part of sacrificial offerings: "Every oblation of thy meat offering shalt thou season with salt; neither shalt thou suffer the salt of the covenant of thy God to be lacking from thy meat offering: With all thine offerings thou shalt offer salt" (Leviticus ii. 13).[5] A covenant, especially a religious covenant, was ratified by means of salt: "It is a covenant of salt for ever, before the Lord" (Numbers xviii. 19); "The Lord God of Israel gave the kingdom over Israel to David for ever, even to him, and to his sons, by a covenant of salt" (2 Chronicles xiii. 5). The idea of a bond of loyalty through eating salt also occurs: the passage "we have maintenance from the king's palace" (Ezra iv. 14) means literally "we are salted with the salt of the palace".[6] The salt sources in Germany, which later became associated with the doings of witches, had a considerable religious significance;

---

[1] Seligmann, op. cit., Band II, S. 34; Wuttke, op. cit., S. 419.
[2] Wuttke, op. cit., S. 423.
[3] Arrian, *De Expeditione Alexandri*, lib. iii, cap. 1.
[4] Brand, op. cit., Vol. III, p. 161.
[5] In Job i. 22, the literal rendering of the passage "In all this Job sinned not, nor charged God foolishly" is "In all this Job sinned not, nor gave God unsalted". (Conway, op. cit., Vol. II, p. 150.)
[6] Lawrence, op. cit., p. 156.

Ennemoser[1] writes of them: "Their yield was regarded as a direct gift of the near Divinity, and the winning and distributing of the salt as a holy occupation—probably sacrifices and folk festivities were connected with the drying of the salt."

In the Roman Catholic Church salt was introduced for baptismal purposes in the fourth century[2] and has played a prominent part there ever since.[3] In St. Margaret's Church in Ipswich there is a font bearing the curious inscription "sal et saliva", which must go back to some fecundity rite, saliva being a typical unconscious symbol of the male fluid. According to Schleiden,[4] this idea was derived from the Jewish use of salt at the circumcision rite. The celebration of baptism in Scotland by a layman was afterwards confirmed by a priest administering a particle of salt.[5] Gratian, in his Decretalia, explains that the use of consecrated salt in the mouth of one about to be baptised is to render the rite more efficacious.[6] In the baptismal ceremonies of the Church of England in medieval times salt was placed in the child's mouth, and its ears and nostrils were touched with saliva—practices which became obsolete at the time of the Reformation.[7] As a rule, however, salt is applied in the dissolved state, the well-known "Salzstein",[8] composed of salt and water that has been separately blessed beforehand. The holy water thus constituted was extensively used in both Catholic and Protestant countries, and for the identical purposes for which simple salt and water had previously been used by the common people, the only difference being

---

[1] Ennemoser, *Geschichte der Magie, Zweite Aufl.*, 1844, S. 839.
[2] Pfannenschmid, *Das Weihwasser im heidnischen und christlichen Cultus*, 1870.
[3] See Lawrence, op. cit., p. 182.
[4] Schleiden, op. cit., S. 76.
[5] Dalyell, op. cit., p. 97.
[6] Cited by Dalyell, loc. cit.
[7] Lawrence, op. cit., p. 176.
[8] Seligmann, op. cit., Band I, S. 322; Wuttke, op. cit., S. 142.

that the latter was not quite so efficacious as the consecrated mixture. Thus it was officially employed by the
Roman Catholic Church for profiting the health of the body
and for the banishing of demons,[1] by the English Church
to prevent the devil from entering churches and dwellings,[2]
and by the Scottish Church for expelling demons, for
sanctifying religious rites, and to prevent new-born babies
from becoming changelings.[3] Holy water was also used, and
to some extent is still used, to avert the evil eye,[4] to prepare
for a journey,[5] to cure demoniac possession,[6] to make the
cattle thrive,[7] to prevent witches from turning the butter
sour,[8] and to ensure the fortunate delivery of a pregnant
cow.[9] In the same connection may be mentioned certain
African taboos concerning salt. A demon who inhabited a
lake in Madagascar was so averse from salt that whenever
any was being carried past the lake it had to be called by
another name, or it would all have been dissolved and lost.[10]
A West African story relates how a man was told that he
would die if ever the word "salt" was pronounced in his
hearing; one day the fatal word was pronounced, and he
promptly died.[11]

We may now consider another attribute of salt which
has given rise to many symbolic connotations—namely, its
peculiar *taste*. Seligmann[12] says: "Salt is on account of its
piquant power a life-furthering material", and he associates

---

[1] Gaume, loc. cit.; Moresin, op. cit., pp. 153, 154.
[2] Ady, *A Perfect Discovery of Witches*, 1661.
[3] Napier, *Folk Lore, or Superstitious Beliefs in the West of Scotland within this Century*, 1879.
[4] Seligmann, op. cit., Band I, S. 325; Band II, S. 315, 396.
[5] Wuttke, loc. cit.
[6] Reginald Scot, *The Discoverie of Witchcraft*, 1584, p. 178.
[7] Wuttke, op. cit., S. 439.
[8] Wuttke, op. cit., S. 448.
[9] Wuttke, op. cit., S. 142.
[10] Sibree, *The Great African Island*, 1880, p. 307.
[11] Nassau, *Fetichism in West Africa*, 1904, p. 381.
[12] Seligmann, op. cit., Band I, S. 278.

with this the beliefs in the influence exertéd by salt when it penetrates into other substances, e.g., bread, and also the belief in its capacity to cure disease. This property of salt has been especially connected with speech in various metaphorical ways. Lawrence[1] writes: "Owing to the importance of salt as a relish, its Latin name sal came to be used metaphorically as signifying a savoury mental morsel, and, in a general sense, wit or sarcasm. . . . The characterization of Greece as the 'salt of nations' is attributed to Livy, and this is probably the origin of the phrase 'Attic salt', meaning delicate, refined wit." A pungent or pithy remark or jest is termed salt,[2] as in such expressions as "there is no salt in his witticisms", though the use of the word in this sense is becoming obsolescent in English; in French a similar one obtains, in expressions such as "une epigramme salé", "il a répandu le sel à pleins mains dans ses écrits", etc. In the Biblical passage (Epistle to the Corinthians iv. 6) "Let your speech be always with grace, seasoned with salt" this connotation is probably present, as well as that previously mentioned of wisdom or sense. The same metaphor is also applied in a general way, apart from speech, as in denoting an insipid man as "having no sense or salt", lacking in piquancy or liveliness, just as in Latin the word insalsus (=unsalted) meant stupid. This metaphorical attribute of salt is evidently closely akin to the one previously mentioned of "essentialness".

A property of salt that has been extensively exploited by the popular imagination is the ease with which it *dissolves in water*. That a substance otherwise so durable should disappear when put into water and, though leaving no visible trace of its presence, should endow the water with its peculiar properties (capacity to preserve from decay, pungent taste, etc.) has always impressed the people as

[1] Lawrence, op. cit., p. 161. *See* also Schleiden, op. cit., S. 91.
[2] *See Oxford English Dictionary*, loc. cit.

being a remarkable characteristic, and is perhaps partly responsible for the mysterious significance attaching to holy water. One obvious practical application, of which frequent use has been made, is to estimate the amount of moisture in the atmosphere by the varying avidity of salt for it. It has thus been quite rationally used to *foretell the weather*.[1] From this have been derived the following symbolical uses of it for the same purpose.[2] An onion is cut into twelve pieces, which are strewn with salt and named after the twelve months; the piece that becomes specially moist denotes a wet month in the coming year. The same may be done with twelve nutshells, which have to be examined at midnight. Or a piece of salt is placed on each corner of the table to denote the four seasons of the year; the one that has collected most moisture by the morning indicates the wettest season. The last-mentioned practice is also used to find out if the coming harvest will be valuable or not.[3] This foretelling capacity of salt has naturally been generalized far beyond its original sphere. Thus, according as a particular heap of salt remains dry or not it is concluded that a corresponding person will or will not survive the coming year, that a given undertaking will be successful or the reverse, and so on.[4]

Water is not the only substance into which salt can be absorbed with the production of peculiar changes. Indeed, the capacity of salt to *enter into combination with a second substance* may be regarded as one of its most salient characteristics. The substance with which it is by far the most often associated in this way is *bread*. The combination of the two has been used for practically all the purposes enumerated above in connection with salt, and in folk beliefs the two are almost synonymous. Thus bread and salt are both

[1] Willsford, *Nature's Secrets*, p. 139.
[2] Wuttke, op. cit., S. 231.
[3] Wuttke, op. cit., S. 230.
[4] Wuttke, op. cit., S. 231.

absent from the devil's feasts;[1] the combination of them is
potent against witches,[2] and against the evil eye;[3] it guards
cattle against disease,[4] ensures a plentiful supply of milk,[5]
and removes obstacles to the churning of butter.[6] It is
equally efficacious with adults and infants. It is carried into
a new dwelling to avert evil influences and to bring good
luck;[7] in Hamburg nowadays this custom is replaced by
that of carrying at processional times a cake covered with
chocolate, in the form of a bread roll, and a salt-cellar of
marzipan filled with sugar. The combination of salt and
bread has also been extensively used to confirm oaths,[8] and
is still so used in Arabia at the present day.[9]

The mixture of *wheat and salt* was used for the same purpose as that of bread and salt. It was an important part of
the Roman propitiatory sacrifices,[10] and also of the Jewish
oblations.[11] In Russia it was offered as congratulatory to
strangers,[12] as we have seen salt alone was in other countries.
In Ireland women in the streets, and girls from the windows,
sprinkled salt and wheat on public functionaries when they
assumed office.[13]

Lastly may be mentioned the attribute of salt as a *means
of purification*. That salt water possesses this quality in a
high degree was observed at an early stage of civilization,

[1] Grimm, op. cit., S. 877.
[2] Seligmann, op. cit., Band II, S. 37, 52, 93, 94; Grimm, op. cit., Nachtrag, S. 454; Wuttke, op. cit., S. 129, 282.
[3] Wuttke, op. cit., S. 282; Seligmann, op. cit., Band I, S. 398; Band II, S. 37, 38, 93, 94, 100, 250, 334.
[4] Dalyell, op. cit., p. 100.
[5] Seligmann, op. cit., Band II, S. 38; Dalyell, loc. cit.
[6] Seligmann, loc. cit.
[7] Seligmann, op. cit., S. 37.
[8] Dekker's Honest Whore, 1635, Sc. 13; Blackwood's *Edinburgh Magazine*, Vol. I, p. 236; Lawrence, op. cit., p. 164.
[9] Lawrence, op. cit., p. 185.
[10] Brand, op. cit., Vol. III, p. 163; Dalyell, op. cit., pp. 99, 100.
[11] Dalyell, op. cit., p. 99.
[12] Dalyell, loc. cit.
[13] Brand, op. cit., p. 165; Dalyell, loc. cit.

and by Roman ladies it was actually regarded as a means of attaining beauty.[1] Especially in regard to the sea this feature has led to numerous poetical applications and also to the development of many superstitions. It is intelligible that this purifying attribute should have played an important part in the use of salt in religious cults, and this we find was so, notably in Egypt and Greece.[2] We shall return to the subject later on when discussing the relation of purification to baptism.

II

We may now survey the facts just related. While it has only been possible in the allotted space to give a relatively few examples of the numerous ways in which ideas concerning salt have played a part in folk belief and custom—it would need a special treatise to record them all—it is probable that the most prominent and typical of them have been mentioned; at all events no special selection whatever has been made, beyond relegating sexual ones to the background. It is hardly necessary to say that the grouping here adopted is unduly schematic, being one of convenience in presentation only; a given custom would mostly be dictated by interest in other properties of salt as well as the one under which it is here mentioned.

In regard now to the matter that formed our starting-point—namely, the superstitious fear of spilling salt—it is plain that here a significance is attached to an act which does not inherently belong to it, and it is equally plain that the same is true of most of the customs and beliefs related above. There are two possible explanations that may be offered for this state of affairs. The *first* would run some-

[1] Schleiden, op. cit., S. 84.
[2] Schleiden, op. cit., S. 84, 85.

what as follows. The present-day superstition has no meaning beyond an historical one; it is simply an instance of the tendency of mankind to retain traditional attitudes for no intelligible reason, and is an echo of the time when the idea of salt was properly invested with a greater psychical value than it now is. In former times the significance attached to the idea of salt that we now regard as excessive was not so, being justified in fact and to be accounted for quite naturally by the real importance of the substance. There is undeniably a certain amount of truth in this view. Salt, being a substance necessary to life and in some countries obtainable only with considerable difficulty,[1] was inevitably regarded as both important and valuable, though this consideration must lose much of its weight in regard to most parts of the world where the supply is plentiful. Again, the curious properties of salt, its preserving capacity, its power of penetrating other substances, etc., would naturally impress the primitive mind, and the view just described would doubtless try to account for the belief in its magical powers by pointing out that such minds work on a simpler plane of thought than do ours. To this argument, however, comparative psychology could object that, although this type of thought—just as that of children—certainly often differs from what we term rational thinking, careful investigation always shows that it is very far from being so bizarre and unintelligible as it may at first sight appear; the formation of illogical connections is not meaningless, but has a perfectly definite and comprehensible reason for it. The general criticism, therefore, that must be passed on this explanation is that while it adduces unquestionably important considerations these are only partly capable of accounting for the facts, and are inadequate as a complete explanation of them. Other factors must have been operative in addition to those just mentioned.

[1] Lawrence, op. cit., p. 187.

The *second* explanation would supplement the first by regarding the excessive significance attaching to the idea of salt as an example of what Wernicke called an *Überwertige Idee*, that is to say, an idea overcharged with psychical significance. Only some of this inherently belongs to the idea itself, the rest being of adventitious origin. Such processes are, of course, very familiar in daily life: a banknote, for instance, is valued not for the intrinsic worth of the paper but for the worth that extrinsic circumstances give it. Psycho-analytic investigation has shown on the one hand that such transference of affect from one idea to another allied one is much commoner than was previously realized, and on the other hand that very often the subject is quite unaware of the occurrence. Thus a person may experience an intense affect—fear, horror, etc.—in regard to a given idea or object purely through the idea having formed strong associative connections with another idea which is justifiably invested with this affect; the intrinsic attributes of the idea do not account for the strong affect attached to it, this being in the main derived from a different source. The most striking manifestations of this process are seen in the psychoneuroses; the patient has a terror of a certain object which is not customarily regarded with terror, the reason being that the idea of the object is unconsciously connected in his mind with that of another object in regard to which the terror is quite comprehensible. In such cases the secondary idea may be said to represent or symbolize the primary one.[1] The more bizarre and apparently unintelligible is the phobia or other symptom, the more strained is as a rule the connection between it and the original idea, and the stronger is the emotion investing the latter. Apart from the neuroses instances of exceedingly strained connec-

[1] On the precise distinction between symbolism and other forms of indirect mental representation see Ch. VII of my *Papers on Psycho-Analysis*, 1918, "The Theory of Symbolism".

tions are less common. What happens as a rule is that the affect belonging to the two ideas, the symbolized and the symbolizing one, is very similar, so that the affect transferred from the one to the other accounts for only part of the affect accompanying the secondary idea. In this case the intrinsic qualities of the idea account for some of the affect, but not for all; the affect is appropriate in quality, but disproportionate in quantity. Unless the cause of this exaggeration is appreciated there is an unavoidable tendency to overlook the fact itself on rationalistic grounds; then the intrinsic qualities of the secondary idea are erroneously regarded as constituting an adequate explanation of the affect in question.

The main difference, therefore, between the two explanations is this: the first assumes that the affect, or psychical significance, attaching to the idea of salt was once not disproportionate to its real value, whereas the second, regarding the affect as disproportionate, maintains that some of it must be derived from an extraneous source.

In seeking for this source we have two distinct clues to guide us. In the first place, the universality of the beliefs and customs under discussion, and the remarkably high and even mystical significance that has been attached to the idea of salt, indicate that any further idea from which this may have been derived must be both a general one, common to all mankind, and one of fundamental psychical importance. In the second place, the association between the idea of salt and any further one must have been formed through the resemblances, real or fancied, of the corresponding qualities of the two ideas. It becomes necessary, therefore, to consider with closer attention the popular conception of these qualities that was described above.

This conception may be summarized as follows. Salt is a pure, white, immaculate and incorruptible substance, apparently irreducible into any further constituent elements, and indispensable to living beings. It has correspondingly been regarded as the essence of things in general, the quintessence of life, and the very soul of the body. It has been invested with the highest general significance—far more than that of any other article of diet—was the equivalent of money and other forms of wealth, and its presence was indispensable for the undertaking of any enterprise, particularly any new one. In religion it was one of the most sacred objects, and to it were ascribed all manner of magical powers. The pungent, stimulating flavour of salt, which has found much metaphorical application in reference to pointed, telling wit or discourse, doubtless contributed to the conception of it as an essential element; to be without salt is to be insipid, to have something essential lacking. The durability of salt, and its immunity against decay, made it an emblem of immortality. It was believed to have an important influence in favouring fertility and fecundity, and in preventing barrenness; this idea is connected with other attributes than the one just mentioned, probably indeed with them all. The permanence of salt helped to create the idea that for one person to partake of the salt of another formed a bond of lasting friendship and loyalty between the two, and the substance played an important part in the rites of hospitality. A similar application of it was for confirming oaths, ratifying compacts, and sealing solemn covenants. This conception of a bond was also related to the capacity salt has for combining intimately with a second substance and imparting to this its peculiar properties, including the power to preserve against decay; for one important substance—namely, water—it had in fact a natural and curious affinity.

If we now try to discover what other idea these ideas could arise in reference to, besides that of salt, the task is surely not difficult. If the word salt had not been mentioned in the preceding description anyone accustomed to hidden symbolism, and many without this experience, would regard it as a circumlocutory and rather grandiloquent account of a still more familiar idea—that of human semen. In any case a substance possessing the attributes just mentioned would lend itself with singular facility to such an association. Indeed, the mere fact that salt has been regarded as the emblem of immortality and wisdom is in itself suggestive to anyone who is alive to such possibilities, for the other well-known emblem of these two concepts is the snake, which is in mythology and elsewhere the phallic symbol *par excellence*. The surmise that the idea of salt has derived much of its significance from its being unconsciously associated with that of semen fulfils at least one postulate of all symbolic thinking—namely, that the idea from which the excessive significance is derived is more important psychically than the idea to which this is transferred; the radiation of the affect, like that of electricity, is always from the site of more intense concentration to that of less.

At the present stage of our investigation it is plain that the inference just drawn cannot be regarded as being much more than a surmise, or at the most a working hypothesis, one which will appear more or less plausible according to the experience of unconscious symbolism by which it is viewed. It must next be tested by the ordinary rules of science—namely, by its capacity to predict and by its power of satisfactorily reducing to simple terms a series of disparate phenomena.

If the hypothesis is correct then one could foretell that customs and beliefs would be found showing a direct relation between the idea of salt on the one hand and such ideas as those of marriage, sexual intercourse, and potency on the other, as well as a larger number showing a plainly symbolical relation between the two sets of ideas; further, that the ideas concerning salt and water mirror similar, more primitive ones concerning semen and urine, and that the partaking of salt would be connected with ideas relating to sexual intercourse and impregnation. It will presently be seen that anthropological and folk-loristic material provides ample confirmation of these expectations.

The supposed action of salt in favouring fecundity and in preventing barrenness has been mentioned above. It was a classical belief that mice became impregnated through eating salt;[1] any objection to our hypothesis, therefore, that the connection between the ideas of salt and semen is too remote for them ever to have been brought together, except artificially, at once falls to the ground, for here we have a direct identification of the two substances. In the Pyrenees the wedding couple before setting out for church put salt into their left pocket to guard against the man's being impotent. In Limousin, Poitou, and Haut-Vienne the bridegroom alone does this, in Altmark the bride alone. In Pamproux salt is put into the clothes of the wedding couple with the same motive.[2] In Germany salt is strewn in the bride's shoe.[3] In Scotland on the night before the wedding salt is strewn on the floor of the new home with the object of protecting the young couple against the evil eye;[4] I have elsewhere[5] shown that the idea of maleficium, with which that of the evil eye is practically identical, mainly arises from the pervading dread of impotence, and Seligmann[6] actually mentions the use of salt to counteract the "ligature", i.e., the spell cast over the sexual functions by evil influences.

[1] Pliny, *Nat. Hist.*, X, 85.

[2] The preceding examples are all taken from Seligmann, op. cit., Band II, S. 35, 36, or from Schleiden, op. cit., S. 71, 79.

[3] Schell, "Das Salz im Volksglauben", *Zeitschrift des Vereines fur Volkskunde*, Jahrg, XV, S. 137.

[4] Seligmann, op. cit., S. 35.

[5] Ernest Jones, *Der Alptraum in seiner Beziehung zu gewissen Formen des mittelalterlichen Aberglaubens*, 1912, S. 107, 108.

[6] Seligmann, op. cit., Band I, S. 291.

Frobenius[1] relates a folkloristic story told with the direct-
ness of peasant thought. A penis and vagina once went
together on a journey to buy salt. Each carried its portion.
On the way back it began to rain. The vagina said to her
comrade: "Our salt will get wet if we carry it on our heads.
Let us put it in my opening; then it will keep dry." They
did this, and there we have the reason why the penis ever
seeks the vagina since it contains the daintiest delicacy
(i.e., salt), while the vagina always wants salt (i.e., semen)
from the penis.

Salt has often, especially in former times, been considered
to have an exciting influence on the nervous system, and it
was thus thought to possess the attribute of arousing
passion and desire.[2] Schleiden[3] writes: "The Romans
termed a man in love 'salax', (whence our 'salacious') and
this view still survives with us when we jokingly say that
the cook who has put too much salt into the soup must be
in love." In Belgium the custom of visiting one's sweetheart
in the nights after festivals is called "turning one's love
into salt".[4] Shakespeare evidently uses it in the same sense
in the passage "Though we are justices . . . we have some
salt of our youth in us".[5] In some stories collected among
African natives by Frobenius[6] salt is referred to as a direct
equivalent of semen. Paracelsus, in his *De Origine Morborum
Invisibilium*,[7] teaches that Incubi and Succubi emanate
from the sperma found in the imagination of those who
commit the unnatural sin of Onan, but that this is no true
sperma, only corrupted salt.

The following are two metaphorical applications of the

[1] Leo Frobenius, *Schwarze Seclen*, 1913, S. 433.
[2] Schleiden, op. cit., S. 92.
[3] Schleiden, op. cit., S. 93.
[4] Von Reinsberg-Düringsfeld, op. cit., S. 472.
[5] *The Merry Wives of Windsor*, Act II, Sc. 3.
[6] Frobenius, *Schwarze Seelen* (Privately printed), 1913, S. 433. Dr. Otto Rank
kindly informs me of this.
[7] Hartmann's *Life of Paracelsus*, 1667, p. 90.

46

same idea. Salt is used to keep the fire always burning,[1] and there are examples, which need not be quoted, of the combination of salt and fire being used for every purpose in regard to which salt alone has superstitiously been used. At the Osiris festivals in Egypt all those taking part had to light lamps the oil of which had had salt mixed with it.[2] The idea of fire, however, in poetry as well as in mythology,[3] is constantly used to represent the ideas of the fire of life and the fire of love. Again, lameness is often brought into symbolic association with impotence (incapacity, inability), and in Sicily salt is used specifically to prevent lameness.[4]

The initiatory ceremonies universally performed by ruder peoples at the age of puberty commonly include a sacrificial or propitiatory act; circumcision is a replacement of such ceremonies, having been put back to the age of infancy just as baptism has been by most Christian Churches. In Egypt salt is strewn when circumcision is performed.[5] In various initiations, both earnest and jocular, at universities and schools salt played a central part, and the phrase "to salt a freshman" is still in vogue.[6] Of late years it has been replaced in this respect by the more convenient alcohol, another unconscious symbol for semen,[7] but the feeling-attitude remains the same—namely, that the young man needs the administration of an essential substance before he can be regarded as having attained full virility.

It is known that there exists an intimate connection between extreme *abstinence* attitudes of all kinds and excessive sexual "repression"; over-great prudishness is apt to be accompanied by a desire to abolish all alcohol from the

[1] Mühlhauser, *Urreligion des deutschen Volkes*, 1860, S. 133.
[2] Schleiden, op. cit., S. 76.
[3] Cp. Abraham, *Traum und Mythus*, 1909, S. 31, etc.
[4] Pitré, loc. cit.
[5] Seligmann, op. cit., Band II, S. 37.
[6] Cp. Brand, op. cit., Vol. I, pp. 433-9.
[7] Abraham, "Die psychologischen Beziehungen zwischen Sexualität und Alkoholismus", *Zeitschrift für Sexualwissenschaft*, 1908, S. 449.

universe, as we see at the present day in America. In the same way salt has been brought into manifold relation with the idea of sexual abstinence. The workers in the salt-pans near Siphoum, in Laos, must abstain from all sexual relations at the place where they are at work, the motive being a purely superstitious one.[1] The celibate Egyptian priests had at certain times to abstain wholly from the use of salt, on the ground of its being a material that excited sensual desires too much.[2] Abstinence both from sexual relations and from the partaking of salt is enjoined for several days on men of the Dyak tribes after returning from an expedition in which they have taken human heads,[3] and for three weeks on a Pima Indian who has killed an Apache;[4] in the latter case the man's wife also has to abstain from salt during the same period.[5] The full account of these customs clearly shows that they constitute rites of purification and expiation. Abstinence both from sexual relations and from salt is also frequently prescribed during important undertakings or on weighty occasions: thus on Lake Victoria Nyanza while fishing,[6] and in the island of Nias while traps are being laid for wild animals.[7] In Uganda any man who has either committed adultery or eaten salt is not allowed to partake of the sacred fish-offering.[8] In Mexico the Huichol Indians undergo the same double abstinence while the sacred cactus plant, the gourd of the God of Fire,

[1] Aymonier, *Notes sur le Laos*, 1885, p. 141.
[2] Schleiden, op. cit., S. 93.
[3] Tromp, "Uit de Salasial van Koetei", *Bijdragen tot de Taal- Land- en Volkenkunde van Nederlandsch-Indië*, 1888, Vol. XXXVII, p. 74.
[4] Bancroft, *Native Races of the Pacific States*, 1875, Vol. I, p. 553; Grossman, in Ninth Annual Report of the Bureau of Ethnology, 1892, p. 475.
[5] Russell, "The Pima Indians", Twenty-Sixth Annual Report of the Bureau of American Ethnology, 1908, p. 204.
[6] Frazer, *The Golden Bough*, Third Edition, Part II, Taboo, 1911, p. 194.
[7] Thomas, "De jacht op het eiland Nias", *Tijdschrift voor Indische Taal- Land- en Volkenkunde*, 1880, Vol. XXVI.
[8] Roscoe, "Further Notes on the Manners and Customs of the Baganda", *Journal of the Royal Anthropological Institute*, 1902, Vol. XXXII, p. 56.

is being gathered.[1] Similar double observances obtain in other countries in connection with the promotion of fertility; in fact the last-named custom is related to this, for the main benefits that the sacred cactus is supposed to bestow are plentiful rain-supply, good crops, and the like. The Indians of Peru abstain for as long as six months both from sexual intercourse and from eating salt on the occasion of the birth of twins; one of the twins was believed to be the son of the lightning, the lord and creator of rain.[2] Other examples of the same double abstinence are: in Peru preceding the Acatay mita festival, the object of which is to ripen the fruit, and which is followed by a sexual orgy;[3] in Nicaragua from the time that the maize is sown until it is reaped.[4] In Behar in India the Nagin women, sacred prostitutes known as "wives of the Snake-God", periodically go about begging and during this time they may not touch salt; half of their proceeds go to the priests and half to buying salt and sweetmeats for the villagers.[5]

Attention may be called to two features of the preceding collection of customs. First that they occur in all parts of the globe, instances having been cited from Europe, Africa, Asia, and America, North, South, and Central. Secondly, that to a great extent they duplicate the customs previously described in connection with salt alone, thus in relation to religion, to the weather, to important undertakings, and to the production of fertility. Where in one country the presence of salt is indispensable, in another one abstinence from salt—and at the same time from sexual intercourse—is equally essential. Both cases agree in regarding salt as an important agent in these respects; whether this is for good

[1] Lumholtz, *Unknown Mexico*, 1903, Vol. II, p. 126.
[2] Frazer, op. cit., Part I, *The Magic Art*, 1911, Vol. I, p. 266.
[3] Frazer, op. cit., Vol. II, p. 98.
[4] Frazer, op. cit., p. 105.
[5] Crooke, *Popular Religion and Folk-Lore of Northern India*, 1896, Vol. II. p. 138.

or for evil is of secondary interest, the main point being its significance. If, as is here suggested, the idea of salt is generally connected in the unconscious mind with that of semen, it is throughout intelligible that abstinence from sexual relations should tend to be accompanied by abstinence from salt as well (radiation of the affect); it is in perfect accord with all we know of primitive, symbolic thinking. The unconscious logic of the argument seems to be that abstinence from sexuality is incomplete unless all forms of semen, even symbolic forms, are abstained from.

This bipolar attitude of regarding salt as either exceedingly beneficial or exceedingly harmful reminds one of two current controversies—namely, whether alcohol and sexual intercourse respectively are beneficial or harmful to health. Indeed, as with these, there have been at various times propagandist movements started in which salt has been denounced as the cause of numerous bodily evils.[1] In 1851 there was published a volume by a Dr. Arthur Howard entitled: *Salt, the Forbidden Fruit or Food* "The Whole Mystery now Revealed. Its Hurtful Effects on Man (chiefly Woman) and on Animals, showing itself to be the Chief Cause of Diseases of the Body and Mind of Man and of Animals, as taught by the ancient Egyptian priests and Wise Men and by Scripture, in accordance with the Author's Experience of many years." It was described by the *Lancet* as "worthy of immortality". As may be imagined from the title, the author treats of salt as a most obnoxious substance, abstinence from which is essential to the maintenance of health. It is possible even that unconscious associations of the kind under consideration may not have been altogether without influence in relation to more recent medical views. It had long been noticed that urine contained solid constituents which were either evident as such or could be recovered from their soluble state by means

[1] Lawrence, op. cit., pp. 189-92.

of evaporation; these were regarded on the one hand as comprising the essence of the fluid, being thus identified with semen, and on the other as salts, which indeed they mostly are.[1] The sufferings due to the excessive accumulation of these salts, in the form of calculi, attracted a great deal of attention and play a very important part in early surgical writings. When the chemical constituents of urine came to be carefully studied by exact methods there arose a tendency, which reached its acme in the late 'eighties, to attribute a considerable number of disorders to the presence in the system of an excessive amount of these constituents. Thus, to mention only a few examples, gout was thought to be simply a question of poisoning by uric acid, uræmia to be poisoning with urea, diabetic coma (exhaustion following on the continued loss of a vital substance) poisoning by acetone (an occasional urinary constituent), rheumatism poisoning by lactic acid (milk, a sexual secretion, is almost constantly identified with semen in the unconscious), and so on. It is interesting that the two diseases in regard to which this idea was most firmly fixed— namely, gout and rheumatism—are joint diseases, and hence lend themselves to the series of unconscious associations "lameness—incapacity—impotence". Of late years the tendency has taken at the same time simpler and more complex directions. On the one hand there is a return to salt itself, and a "salt-free diet" is vaunted as the sovereign agent for the prevention of arterial disease and old age (impotency), for the cure of epilepsy, and so on. It will also be remembered how, when Brown-Séquard's attempt to recapture youthful vigour by means of the injection of canine semen shocked the medical profession in London, efforts were made to substitute the more respectable, because unconscious, symbol of this—common salt. On the

---

[1] The unconscious association between semen and urine on the one hand and salt and water on the other will be dealt with at length later in this essay.

other hand there is a restless search for more complex organic poisons, usually in the intestinal contents, which are now being as extensively exploited as the urine was forty years ago. The belief in the prime importance of organic poisons is even generally extended to psychosexual maladies, such as hysteria, "neurasthenia", and dementia præcox. It may be questioned whether the important advance in knowledge represented by the toxic theory of disease would not have met with more resistance than it did had it not appealed to a fundamental complex in the human mind, in which, among others, the ideas of poison and semen are closely associated.

A few derivative symbolisms concerning salt may next be considered, which receive an added significance in the light of the hypothesis put forward above. The power of salt is enhanced when it is placed on an object resembling the male organ. Cattle are thus protected by making them step over a bar of iron, or a hatchet, which has been sprinkled with salt;[1] the Esthonians cut a cross[2] under the door through which the cattle have to pass, and fill the furrows of it with salt to prevent evil spirits from harming them.[3]

According to Clement of Alexandria, in the rites that celebrate the voluptuousness of the sea as a token of Aphrodite's birth there a lump of salt and a phallus was handed to the youths who are being initiated into the lore of adultery. In their turn they present her with a coin, as if they were her lovers and she their paid mistress.[4] A similar meaning must originally have attached to the Ancient Greek custom of tossing to the spectators of a

[1] Wuttke, op. cit., S. 440.

[2] The phallic significance of the cross symbolism has been pointed out by many investigators. *See*, for instance, Inman, *Ancient Pagan and Modern Christian Symbolism*, 1874.

[3] Frazer, op. cit., p. 331.

[4] J. C. Lawson, *Modern Greek Religion and Ancient Greek Folklore*, 1910, p. 581.

comedy barley cakes in the shape of phalli, mixed with salt.[1]

In Bohemia when a girl goes out for a walk her mother sprinkles salt on the ground so that she may not "lose her way";[2] this over-solicitous precaution becomes more intelligible when we read Wuttke's[3] explanation that the object of it is to prevent the girl from falling in love. A belief at first sight quite foolish and meaningless is that a boy can be cured of home-sickness by placing salt in the hem of his trousers (!) and making him look up the chimney.[4] We now know, however, that excessive homesickness is due to over-attachment, rooted in unconscious incestuous wishes, to some member of the family, usually the mother, which has the effect of "fixing" his powers of love and rendering it incapable of being transferred in the normal way to a stranger. To look up the chimney symbolizes the daring to face another dark, inaccessible and dangerous passage (the very word "chimney" is derived from the Greek κάμινος= oven, a common unconscious equivalent for the mother's lap or womb). The belief, therefore, which means that if someone can succeed in "making a man of him" he will be freed from his homesickness, is not so unintelligible as it appears, and is merely the clothing in symbolic language of a fundamental fact in human nature. One may learn from it how invaluable a knowledge of unconscious symbolism is for the understanding of superstition, and how impossible it is to comprehend it without this knowledge.

The *Salt-cellar*, the receptacle of the salt, has been held in as much superstitious reverence as its contents.[5] The symbolism of it is usually a feminine one,[6] as indeed is

[1] F. H. Cornford, *The Origin of Attic Comedy*, 1914, p. 102.
[2] Lawrence, op. cit., p. 182.
[3] Wuttke, op. cit., S. 367.
[4] Lawrence, op. cit., p. 181.
[5] Schleiden op. cit., S. 74; Lawrence, op. cit., pp. 196-205.
[6] Though the late Dr. Putnam related to me the case of a man in whose dreams a salt-cellar appeared as a symbol of the scrotum.

indicated by the Spanish compliment of calling a sweetheart
"salt-cellar of my love".[1] Salt-cellars, often of great mag-
nificence, were, and still are, favourite wedding-presents.
In Rome they constituted a special heirloom, the paternum
salinum, which was handed down from generation to
generation with especial care. In general it is just as evident
that an excessive amount of affect, of extraneous origin, has
been invested in the idea of a salt-cellar as it is in salt itself.
In classical times the salt-cellar partook of the nature of a
holy vessel, associated with the temple in general, and more
particularly with the altar.[2] To those who are familiar with
the female symbolism of the altar[3] this will be quite comprehensible. The etymology of the word "salt-cellar" is of
considerable interest in the present connection. The second
part "cellar" is derived from the French salière (salt-cellar),
so that the whole is a redundancy, meaning salt-salt-
receptacle. We see here an instructive example of linguistic
assimilation, for a "cellar" (a dark chamber under the
house) has the same feminine symbolic meaning as salière
itself. The sound resemblance of the words salière and cellar
naturally made the assimilation easier, but the instinctive
intuition of the people was probably the underlying factor
in bringing it about.

The offering of salt as a special mark of favour, and as a
sign of hospitality, has been mentioned above; we have now
to note the reverse of this. In England[4] and France[5] it was
considered unlucky to be helped to salt at table; this superstition still obtains in Anglican circles and finds popular
expression in the saying "Help me to salt, help me to
sorrow". In Russia the quarrel that would otherwise follow

[1] Andrée, Globus, 1867, Band XI, S. 140.
[2] Schleiden, op. cit., S. 74.
[3] G. W. Cox, The Mythology of the Aryan Nations, 1870, Vol. II, pp. 113-21;
Inman, op. cit., p. 74.
[4] Brand, op. cit., Vol. III, p. 162.
[5] Brand, ibid., p. 163.

can be averted if one smiles amicably when proffering the salt.[1] A clue to the original meaning of the superstition is found in the attitude formerly obtaining in Italy,[2] where a courtesy of this kind was thought to be a mark of undue familiarity; when salt was offered by one man to the wife of another it was a sufficient cause for jealousy and even quarrel. This is perfectly intelligible in the light of the hypothesis advanced above, but is hardly otherwise to be explained.

In the North of England to give salt to someone is considered dangerous, for it puts the giver into the power of the recipient;[3] the same belief also used to be held in Russia.[4] In other places the act gives one possession or power over the recipient, and with salt one can acquire either men or knowledge;[5] this idea is probably allied to those of loyalty and of the magical properties of salt (see above). Light is thus thrown on the quaint saying: "To catch a bird you must put salt on his tail." This is commonly accounted for with the obvious remark that to catch a bird one must get near enough to it to be able to touch it, but this does not explain why it should be just salt that has to be applied, nor why it should be just to the tail. Realization of the belief in the magical power of salt makes the saying rather more intelligible, but the explanation thus afforded is still only a general one; constructions of the phantasy, including superstitious beliefs and sayings, are determined not only generally, but precisely and in their finest details. Additional help is furnished by an old legend narrated by Lawrence,[6] in which a young man playfully

[1] Revue des Traditions populaires, 1886, t. I; Sikes, op. cit., p. 329.
[2] Boyle, A Theological and Philosophical Treatise of the Nature and Goodness of Salt, 1612.
[3] Henderson, Notes on the Folk-Lore of the Northern Counties of England, 1879, p. 217.
[4] Schleiden, op. cit., S. 71.
[5] Oxford Dictionary, loc. cit.
[6] Lawrence, op. cit., p. 179.

threw some salt on to the back of a woman who was sitting
next to him at table; she happened to be a witch, and was
so weighted down by the salt that she was unable to move
until it was brushed away. We have here, therefore, again
the idea of salt brought into relation with that of weight
which prevents movement. Now witches were conceived to
be incorporeal beings, and in fact one of the chief ways of
finding out whether a given woman was a witch was by
weighing her;[1] the difference in weight made by a pinch of
salt was therefore quite considerable, or could metaphorically be imagined to be so. This attribute of witches was
closely related to their power of flying by night, and therefore with bird mythology altogether. The bird has always
been a common phallic symbol[2]—sometimes quite consciously so, as with the winged phallus charms of the
Roman ladies—and the tail is a still more familiar one in
common speech; further the act of flying from the ground
is frequently associated in the unconscious with the phenomenon of erection.[3] The significance of salt (=semen) in
this connection is obvious; favouring and hindering are
treated as synonymous terms here as elsewhere in superstition, just as in the unconscious mind, the main point
being the significance.

Finally may be mentioned the belief that to see salt in
a dream indicates illness.[4] When one recalls the frequency
with which the ideas of nocturnal emission and of illness or
loss of strength are associated, it is not difficult to divine
the source of this particular belief.

---

[1] Bekker, *Die Bezauberte Welt*, 1692, Theil I, S. 209.
[2] Abraham, *Traum und Mythus*, 1909, S. 30, 63, etc.
[3] Federn, Cited by Freud, *Die Traumdeutung*, Dritte Aufl., 1911, S. 204.
[4] Schleiden, op. cit., S. 80.

III

In the preceding section of this essay we dealt chiefly with the *adult* roots of salt symbolism and superstitions, and we have now to turn our attention to the deeper *infantile* roots. The reason why the word "deeper" is used here will presently become evident; it has to do with the ontogenetic, as well as phylogenetic, antiquity of symbolism in general.

Before passing to the next stage of the investigation, therefore, it will be necessary briefly to refer to some aspects of infantile mental life that without being realized play an important part in adult life—namely, certain views developed by young children concerning the begetting of children.[1] These are forgotten long before puberty, so that the adult is quite unaware of their existence and is extremely surprised to hear of their great frequency in childhood life. They survive nevertheless in the unconscious mind, and exert a considerable influence on later interests and views.

Early realizing, in spite of the untruths told him by the parents, that a baby is born of the mother and grows inside her, the child sets to work to solve the problem as best he can, the full answer being concealed from him. Knowing nothing of other organs he conceives of the "inside", particularly the abdomen, as simply a receptacle for food, a view amply confirmed by his experience of indigestion and other sensations. The baby, therefore, must have been formed out of food, an inference that is largely correct. Further, there being no other mode of exit possible—at least so far as he is aware—the baby must have then reached the exterior in the same way as digested food

[1] *See* Freud, *Sammlung kleiner Schriften zur Neurosenlehre*, Zweite Folge, 1911, S. 159-64, "Über infantile Sexualtheorien".

(cloaca theory), as it actually does in all animals except mammalia. There is thus established in the child's mind a close connection between the ideas of food, fæces, and babies, one that explains among many other things many an hysterical symptom in later life.

The child next comes to the notion that, since food alone does not in his personal experience have this result, a mixing of two substances must be necessary. On the basis of his excremental interests he observes that there are three possible materials available, for it is only exceptionally that he thinks the fertilizing material is of non-human origin. The phantasy may combine these three materials—solid, liquid, and gaseous—in different ways, the commonest of which, in my experience and in that of other observers, are in order: liquid—solid, liquid—liquid, solid—solid, and gaseous—solid. A knowledge of these facts is indispensable for the full understanding of salt symbolism. As the objection may be raised that they are artefacts of the psychoanalytic method of investigation, it will be well to refer to a little of the mass of purely anthropological evidence that proves the universal occurrence of similar beliefs in what corresponds with the childhood of the race.[1]

The belief that fertilization, and even delivery, can take place through some other orifice than the vagina has been held in the most diverse countries of the world and is still quite prevalent. Any orifice or indentation may be implicated, the nostril, eye, ear, navel, and so on. An interesting historical example was the medieval belief that the Virgin Mary conceived through the ear, one widely held in the Roman Catholic Church.[2] The mouth, however, was the

[1] Since this essay was written a highly interesting paper of Otto Rank's has appeared ("Völkerpsychologische Parallelen zu den infantilen Sexualtheorien", *Zentralblatt für Psychoanalyse*, Jahrg. II, Heft 8) in which a large quantity of additional data is given that both confirms and amplifies the conclusions here enunciated.

[2] *See* Ch. XIII of these Essays, which is devoted to an examination of this belief.

orifice most frequently thought of in this connection, as is apparent from the very numerous legends and beliefs in which eating or drinking bring about pregnancy. The peasantry in England still believe that peahens are impregnated in this way[1] and similar views are entertained in other countries in respect of different animals; we noted above that according to which female mice are impregnated by eating salt.

The belief that women can conceive as the result of eating various articles of diet has existed in most parts of the world;[2] usually the particular food is one to which some sexual symbolism is attached, such as rice, fish, coconuts, and so on. In the more civilized countries this has been reduced to the belief that partaking of such substances will cure barrenness in women or promote their fecundity; Hartland[3] relates a huge number of practices of this kind carried out, mostly at the present day, for the purpose of securing conception.

A digression must here be made on a matter of some importance to the present theme—namely, the association between food as taken into the body and food as it is given out, two ideas which are by no means so remote from each other in the primitive mind, including that of the child, as they usually are in that of the civilized adult. In the first place many savage tribes have the custom of devouring ordure of all kinds, including their own, and indeed seem to partake of it with special relish;[4] a contemptuous reference to it may be found in 2 Kings xviii. 27. In more civilized countries this has long been replaced by sausages[5] (a word, by the way, of the same etymological derivation as

---

[1] Hartland, *Primitive Paternity*, 1909, Vol. I, p. 151.
[2] Hartland, op. cit., pp. 4-16. Numerous examples.
[3] Hartland, op. cit., pp. 32-41, 47, 48, 54-72.
[4] Bourke, *Scatalogic Rites of All Nations*, 1891, pp. 33-7.
[5] In England in the present generation the belief was acted on that a stolen sausage had the power of curing barrenness (Hartland, op. cit., p. 56).

salt), and other products of abdominal organs.[1] The ordure of sacred men has in many countries, e.g., Tibet, a high religious significance, being used to anoint kings, to guard against evil demons, and so on.[2] That it is not very rare for insane patients to eat their own excrement is of course well-known;[3] in such cases the long-buried infantile association may come to open expression in the patient's remark, pointing to the excrement, that he has just produced a baby. Cases of stercophagy are occasionally met with apart from any psychosis, as I know from personal experience of several instances. An association is often formed between the ideas of excrement and corpses, probably through the common notion of decomposition of something that was once a living human body, or part of one. Both ideas are connected with that of fecundity. Hartland[4] refers to "numerous stories wherein portions of dead bodies, given to maidens and other women, render them pregnant." One of the most widely-spread practices in India and elsewhere for remedying sterility is to perform various symbolic acts in relation to dead bodies: thus, to creep under the coffin, to wash in the blood of decapitated criminals, to bathe over a dead body or underneath a person who has been hanged, and so on.[5] The Hungarians hold that a dead man's bone shaved into drink and given to a woman will promote conception, or if given to a man will enhance his potency.[6]

---

[1] The wife of the Elector of Hanover, in a letter to her niece, the sister-in-law of Louis XIV, writes as follows:

Hanovre, 31 Octobre, 1694.

Si la viande fait la merde, il est vrai de dire que la merde fait la viande. Est-ce que dans les tables les plus délicates, la merde n'y est pas servie en ragoûts? Les boudins, les andouilles, les saucisses, ne sont-ce pas de ragoûts dans des sacs à merde?

[2] Bourke, op. cit., pp. 42-53.

[3] According to Obersteiner (*Psychiatrisches Centralblatt*, 1871, Band III, S. 95) this is true of one per cent of such patients, more often with men.

[4] Hartland, op. cit., p. 77.

[5] Hartland, op. cit., pp. 74-6.

[6] Von Wlislocki, *Aus dem Volksleben der Magyaren*, 1893, S. 77.

It is clear that other factors also enter into these last-mentioned beliefs, notably forms of ancestor-worship, but we are concerned here only with the one element of the association between putrefaction and fecundity, one which has of course an extensive real justification in agriculture (manure and fertility). The bone, being a rigid hollow tube containing a vital marrow,[1] is a very frequent phallic symbol in anthropological data and in the unconscious mind generally: the following Egyptian myth also illustrates its power of impregnation.[2] A bone thrown on a dung-heap (!) grew up into so fine a tree (another familiar symbol) that no one had ever seen its like. The daughter of the man who had thrown the bone was desirous of seeing this wonderful tree; when she witnessed its beauty she was so entranced that she embraced it and kissing it took a leaf into her mouth. As she chewed it she found the taste sweet and agreeable and swallowed the leaf; at the same instant she conceived by the will of God.

Mainly derived from the same source are the beliefs and customs relating to the endless magical properties attaching to dead bodies, and notably to their most putrefactive elements (saliva, excretions, etc.).[3] It would be out of place to follow this subject further here, but mention may be made of a West German belief to the effect that unless the person who has clothed the dead body rubs his hands *with salt* his limbs will go to sleep.[4] This is evidently akin to sympathetic magic, the meaning being that close contact with the corpse may transfer his state of deadness to the person; the deeper meaning is that salt (=semen) will protect the member(s) from the risk of death, i.e., impotency.

A more constant unconscious association is that between

---

[1] Cp. the curse, "May his bones lose their sap".
[2] Oestrup, *Contes de Damas*, 1897, p. 26.
[3] Hartland, *The Legend of Perseus*, 1895, Vol. II, pp. 162-74, 313-32, etc.
[4] Wuttke, op. cit., S. 463.

the ideas of *gold* and fæces,[1] one of far-reaching significance in mythology as well as in the reactions of every-day life. Gold as fertilizing principle usually in conjunction with a second sexual symbol is a favourite theme in mythology; perhaps the best known instance is that of Danæ being impregnated by a shower of golden rain. Apples, fish, and other objects, made of or resembling gold, are also familiar instances of the same type of story. This association explains the extensive connection noted earlier between salt and money or wealth (both being symbols of fertilizing excrement), of which a few other examples may be given. In Pomerania at the close of a wedding breakfast a servant carries round a plate containing salt, upon which the guests put money;[2] the combination of the two substances plainly symbolizes fertility. Seligmann[3] refers to a German custom of carrying salt and money together in the pocket as a protection against impotence, so that here we have our surmise directly confirmed as to the meaning of the combination. A more complex variant is found in the Chemnitz saying: "If one washes one's money in clear water and puts it with salt and bread, the dragon and evil people cannot get it."[4]

Pregnancy has been brought about just as frequently by drinking as it has by eating: all manner of fluids have been efficacious in this respect, the sacred soma-juice milk, the sap of grass, leaves and plants, the juice of roots, fruit and flowers, and so on.[5] The idea of a *liquid* stimulus to conception thus stands in contrast with that of a solid one. The practice of drinking various fluids for the purpose of aiding conception is even more widely spread, and exists through-

[1] Freud, op. cit., S. 136, 137; Ferenczi, *Contributions to Psycho-Analysis*, 1916, Ch. XIII, "The Ontogenesis of the Interest in Money"; Ernest Jones, *Papers on Psycho-Analysis*, 1918, pp. 676-8.

[2] Schleiden, op. cit., S. 71.

[3] Seligmann, op. cit., S. 38.

[4] Grimm, op. cit., Nachtrag, S. 434.

[5] Hartland, *Primitive Paternity*, 1909, Vol. I. Numerous instances.

out Europe at the present day. In every country women wishing to have children drink water from various holy springs or wells, the most potent of which is perhaps that at Lourdes.[1] Apart from this numerous allied practices exist, of which the following selection may be given.[2] In Thuringia and Transylvania women who wished to be healed of unfruitfulness drank consecrated (salt) water from the baptismal font; in Rügen such water was efficacious if poured before the door of a childless couple. In Hungary a barren woman drinks from a spring that she has never before seen. A Malagasy woman who has not been blessed with issue is made to go on swallowing water until her stomach is so full that it will not hold another drop. Masur women in West Prussia make use of the water that drips from a stallion's mouth after he has drunk.

As might be expected, more personal fluids are extensively used for the same purpose, this being the primary sense of the proceeding. In Bombay a woman cuts off the end of the robe of another woman who has borne children, steeps it, and drinks the infusion. Other women in India drink the water squeezed from the loin-cloth of a sanyásí or devotee. Saliva has been very extensively employed in this connection, it being almost universally treated as a seminal equivalent (hence the expression "he is the very spit of his father"). Saliva in fact forms throughout in folklore and superstition a regular duplicate of salt, bearing the same relation to hospitality, friendship, compacts, baptism, magical powers and charms, religious significance, and the rest;[3] the theme cannot be further pursued here and obviously needs separate exposition. Other fluids that may be mentioned are: the milk of another woman, blood from the navel of a new-born child, water in which the navel has

[1] Hartland, op. cit., pp. 64-7.
[2] Hartland, op. cit., pp. 67-71.
[3] Hartland, *Perseus*, op. cit., pp. 258-75.

63

been soaked, the lochial discharge of a woman at her first child-bed, water in which the placenta has been soaked, water from the first bath of a woman after delivery. The original sense of all these beliefs and customs is revealed by consideration of the numerous myths and legends, which recur in every part of the world without exception, describing how pregnancy followed the imbibing of semen, deliberate or accidental.

A great part of our mental life, however, is the echo of childhood thoughts, and the child knows nothing about semen. To him the corresponding potent fluid is *urine*, a topic which must next concern us. The prediction was ventured above that the various ideas noted in regard to salt and water would be found to mirror earlier corresponding ones relating to semen and urine. Confining ourselves for the present to the subject of salt water and urine, we find that the resemblances between the ideas relating to them are very striking. They may be considered by following the order in which the properties of salt were enumerated at the outset.

The significance of salt for friendship, loyalty, hospitality, and the ratifying of pacts, was dwelt on above: the same customs and ideas can be duplicated in respect of urine. Until about three centuries ago it was the vogue in Europe to pledge a friend's health in urine,[1] exactly as we now do in wine, and in the same circumstances; by this, perpetual friendship and loyalty, or even love attachment, might be ensured. The same custom still obtains in Siberia, where it also signifies a pact of peace.[2] At a Moorish wedding the bride's urine is thrown in the face of any unmarried man or stranger on whom it is wished to bestow a distinguished favour,[3] just as in other countries salt is presented with the

[1] Bourke, op. cit., p. 129. Numerous references. ("Cobblers' punch" means urine with a cinder in it.)
[2] Melville, *In the Lena Delta*, 1885, p. 318.
[3] Mungo Park: *Travels into the Interior of Africa* 1813, pp. 109, 135.

same intention. In parts of Russia it was customary for the bride to wash her feet and then use the water for sprinkling the bridal bed and the assembled guests; it is probable, as Bourke suggests,[1] that the water thus used represents a survival of a former practice in which the aspersion was with the urine of the bride. The old English custom of the bride selling alcoholic liquor—the so-called Bride-Ale—on the wedding-day[2] is also likely to be ultimately derived from the same primitive source. The Jews still retain the following allied custom at their weddings: A goblet of wine is handed to the bridegroom by the best man, and after the bridegroom has sipped from it he passes it to the principal bridesmaid; she hands it to the bride, who also drinks from it. The following custom, related by Dulaure,[3] seems to be a question both of hospitality and a test of friendship: "The Tchuktchees offer their women to travellers; but the latter, to become worthy of the offer, have to submit to a disgusting test. The daughter or wife who has to pass the night with her new guest presents him with a cupful of her urine; with this he has to rinse out his mouth. If he is brave enough to do so, he is regarded as a sincere friend; if not, he is treated as an enemy of the family." It may be doubted whether the construction Dulaure places on this is objectively arrived at; at all events it is not likely to be the original explanation.

The magical powers of salt are fully equalled by those of urine. In connection with evil spirits and witches it played a triple part. In the first place it was used actually to bewitch people for evil purposes.[4] It is interesting to note that this might occur even unintentionally. In Africa, for instance, it is believed that "to add one's urine, even unintentionally, to the food of another bewitches that other, and does him

[1] Bourke, op. cit., p. 232.
[2] Brand, op. cit., Vol. II, p. 143 et seq.
[3] Dulaure, *Les Divinités Génératrices*, 1825, p. 400.
[4] Frommann, *Tractatus de Fascinatione*, 1674, p. 683.

grievous harm";[1] this may be compared with the belief, mentioned above, that to give salt to someone puts him in one's power. Secondly, like salt, it was used for the detection of witchcraft and of witches.[2] Thirdly it was one of the most potent charms against evil spirits and witches, and was used as such throughout the Middle Ages.[3] In Ireland[4] urine, especially when combined with dung, was invaluable in frustrating the mischief of fairies. It is still used against witches by the Eskimos in disorders of childbirth.[5] The Shamans of Alaska do the same to keep off evil spirits.[6] Osthanes, the magician, prescribed the dipping of our feet, in the morning, in human urine, as a preventative against evil charms.[7] It is still a practice in France to wash in urine so as to guard against the devil and other maleficent influences.[8]

In regard to disease there was still more extensive application made of urine than of salt, both for diagnostic and for therapeutic purposes. As is well-known, urinoscopy was in the Middle Ages one of the principal means of recognizing different diseases, and it was used for this purpose not only in Europe but in Arabia, Tibet, and other parts of the world;[9] for instance, in the index to the works of Avicenna there are no fewer than two hundred and seventy-five references to the appearance and other physical properties of urine in disease. As in the case of salt, this divination was connected with ideas of urine, rain, and weather prophesying in general. The use of urine in the treatment of disease has been so remarkably comprehensive

[1] Bourke, op. cit., p. 376.
[2] Bourke, op. cit., p. 397. Several references.
[3] Frommann, op. cit., pp. 961, 962; Brand, op. cit., Vol. III, p. 13.
[4] Mooney, *"The Medical Mythology of Ireland,"* Trans. of the American Philosophical Society, 1887.
[5] Bourke, op. cit., p. 378.
[6] Boas, *Journal of American Folk-Lore,* Vol. I, p. 218.
[7] Quoted from Brand, op. cit., p. 286.
[8] Luzel, "Le Nirang des Parsis en Basse Bretagne", *Mélusine,* Mai 1888; Réclus: *Les Primitifs,* 1885, p. 98.
[9] Bourke, op. cit., pp. 272-4, 385, 386.

that it is impossible even to touch on the subject here; Bourke has collected a vast amount of information dealing with it.[1] It may be added that sometimes we find salt combined with urine for medical purposes, e.g., to get rid of a fever.[2]

The importance of salt for fecundity is, if anything exceeded by that of urine.[3] It formed the essential constituent of many love-philtres and magical procedures having as their object the winning of affection.[4] Pliny describes the aphrodisiac properties of the urine voided by a bull immediately after copulation; it may either be drunk or used to moisten earth which is then rubbed into the groin. Characteristically enough, urine can also be used as an anti-aphrodisiac or as a charm against love-philtres.[5] At Hottentot weddings the priest urinates over the bride and bridegroom, and the latter, receiving the stream with eagerness, makes furrows with his nails so that the urine may penetrate the farther.[6]

The practice described by Pliny, referred to above, has also been recommended as a remedy for the cure of impotence. The sovereign cure for this, however, consisted in urinating through the wedding-ring, i.e., into an exquisite female symbol. This practice is mentioned by most of the older writers,[7] and has persisted among the German peasantry until the present generation.[8] Pliny[9] states that the urine of eunuchs was considered to be highly beneficial

[1] Bourke, op. cit., pp. 277-369, 375, 384.
[2] Wuttke, op. cit., p. 354.
[3] See Walter Gallichan, Golden Urine: The Elixir of Life.
[4] Bourke, op. cit., pp. 216, 217, 223.
[5] Bourke, op. cit., pp. 224-7.
[6] Cook, in Hawkesworth's Voyages, 1773, Vol. III, p. 387; Kolbein, in Knox's Voyages, 1777, Vol. II, pp. 399, 400; Thurnberg, in Pinkerton's Voyages, 1814, Vol. XVI, pp. 89, 141.
[7] Reginald Scot, op. cit., p. 64; Frommann, op. cit., p. 997; Brand, op. cit., Vol. III, p. 305.
[8] Birlinger and Buck, Sagen, Märchen und Volksaberglauben aus Schwaben, 1861, S. 486.
[9] XXVIII. 18.

as a promoter of fruitfulness in women. In Algiers a woman seeks to cure barrenness by drinking sheep's urine.[1] Schurig[2] describes as a method of inducing conception the use of a bath of urine poured over old iron, with which may be compared the magical properties mentioned above as being ascribed to the combination of salt and iron. Finally two Asiatic legends narrated by Bab[3] may be referred to, in which the symbolical equivalence of urine and semen appears in the most unmistakable manner. In the first one, from Siam, a man urinated daily on to a certain apple-tree, with the result that it bore especially large fruit. A princess ate one of the apples and thereupon became pregnant. In the other, from Cambodia, a hermit had the habit of urinating on to a hollowed-out stone. A girl who had got lost in the woods (her mother had evidently omitted to strew salt as she left the house) drank the liquid out of the stone, and likewise became pregnant.

The use of salt at initiation ceremonies can also be paralleled with that of urine. A young Parsee undergoes a kind of confirmation during which he is made to drink a small quantity of the urine of a bull.[4] At the Hottentot initiation ceremony one of the medicine-men urinates over the youth, who proudly rubs the fluid into his skin.[5] Corresponding with the Christian and Jewish displacement of their initiation ceremonies (baptism, circumcision) from the time of puberty to that of infancy we find a similar displacement in respect of urine ceremonies. The Californian Indians give their children a draught of urine as soon as they are born,[6] and this custom is also in vogue amongst Americans in the country districts;[7] these are of course not

[1] Ploss, *Das Weib in der Natur- und Völkerkunde*, 1891, Bd. I, S. 443.
[2] Schurig, *Chylologia*, 1725, Vol. II, p. 712.
[3] Bab, *Zeitschrift für Ethnologie*, 1906, Band XXXVIII, S. 281.
[4] Monier Williams, *Modern India*, 1878, p. 178.
[5] Kolbein, op. cit., pp. 202-4; Thurnberg, loc. cit.
[6] Bancroft, op. cit., p. 413.
[7] Trumbull, Quoted by Bourke, op. cit., p. 240.

pure examples of initiation. The Injit child selected to be trained as an Angekok was bathed in urine soon after birth as a religious ceremony.[1] When Parsee children are invested with the Sudra and Koshti—the badges of the Zoroastrian faith—they are sprinkled with the urine of a sacred cow and they also have to drink some of it.[2]

The interest aroused by the taste of salt may be compared with that taken in the peculiar taste of urine, a matter that played a considerable part in medical urinoscopy. All bodily fluids, including tears, semen, sweat, blood, etc., owe of course most of their taste to the presence of salt in them. The natives of Northern Siberia habitually drink each other's urine.[3] The African Shillooks regularly wash out their milk vessels with urine "probably", so Schweinfurth[4] thinks, "to compensate for a lack of salt"; this is also done by the natives of Eastern Siberia.[5] The Obbe[6] and other[7] natives of Central Africa never drink milk unless it is mixed with urine, the reason given being that otherwise the cow would lose her milk; we have here a counterpart of the custom of mixing salt with the milk so as to ensure a plentiful supply. "Chinook olives" are acorns that have been steeped for five months in human urine.[8] Of interest is the relation of urine to the manufacture of intoxicating drinks, it being thus an equivalent to alcohol, as we have noted above. When the supply of alcohol runs short in Siberia the natives eke it out by making a mixture of equal parts of urine and alcohol.[9] In Queensland there is an edible nut of a particular species of pine, which is prepared for

[1] Réclus, op. cit., p. 84.
[2] Max Müller, *Chips from a German Workshop*, 1869, p. 164.
[3] Melville, Quoted by Bourke, op. cit., p. 38.
[4] Schweinfurth, *The Heart of Africa*, 1872, Vol. I, p. 16.
[5] Melville, Quoted by Bourke, op. cit., p. 200.
[6] Baker, *The Albert Nyanza*, 1869, p. 240.
[7] Long, *Central Africa*, 1877, p. 70.
[8] Kane, *An Artist's Wanderings in North America*, 1859, p. 187.
[9] Melville, Quoted by Bourke, op. cit., p. 39.

consumption in the following way: clay pans are formed in the soil, into which the men urinate; the nuts are then steeped in this, when a fermentation takes place. The eating of the nuts causes a temporary madness, and even delirium tremens.[1]

We have next to note the analogies between the significance of salt and that of urine in regard to religious performances. In both cases the substance might be either swallowed or applied to the surface of the body, and concerning the latter practice it is expedient to make a few preliminary remarks. The religious practice of sprinkling or baptizing with a holy fluid (salt and water in the Roman Catholic Church, plain water in the Protestant Church) has evidently two principal meanings. In the first place it symbolizes purification, particularly from sin. Probably the simplest and most accurate expression for the psychological meaning of baptism, as perhaps for that of any religious rite, is "purification through re-birth". The earthly incestuous libido, which is now known to be the deepest source of the sense of sin in general,[2] is overcome and purified in a homœopathic manner by passing through a symbolic act of heavenly incest. Purification by fire is a distorted form of the more original purification by water. It will be noticed that in baptism the liquid symbolises both the father's urine (or semen) and the mother's uterine waters, satisfying thus both the male and the female components of the libido. The oldest association between the ideas of liquid and purification is of course the child's experience of urine washing away fæces, thus cleansing dirt (the deepest source for the objectionableness of sexuality).[3]

In the second place baptism imbues the participant with the mystic properties conveyed by, or belonging to, the holy

[1] Mann, Quoted by Bourke, op. cit., p. 38.
[2] Freud, *Totem und Tabu*, 1913, S. 144, 145.
[3] Freud, *Jahrbuch der Psychoanalyse*, Band IV, S. 49, 50.

fluid. This meaning, which was probably the original one of the two, is well illustrated in the Hottentot rite described above, where the participant scratches his skin so as to absorb as much as possible of the precious fluid. At all events we find that the acts of ablution[1] and of swallowing are throughout treated as though they were identical. Where one is performed in one country the other is in another country in exactly corresponding circumstances, and in numberless instances the two are regarded as equivalent. For example, the practice of imbibing water, particularly holy water, for the cure of barrenness, as described above, is throughout paralleled by the equally common one of bathing in water for the same purpose, and often at the same place; Hartland[2] has collected an enormous number of instances of this from every part of the world and shows that it is to-day as frequent as ever.

All the evidence, from comparative religions, from history, anthropology and folk-lore, converges to the *conclusion, not only that Christian and other rites of baptism symbolize the bestowment of a vital fluid (semen or urine) on the initiate, but that the holy water there used is a lineal descendant of urine, the use of which it gradually displaced.* Strange as this conclusion may seem it is definitely supported by the following facts selected from a vast number of similar ones.

To begin with, it is known that salt and water has historically replaced urine in various non-religious or semi-religious usages. Bourke[3] writes: "We shall have occasion to show that salt and water, holy water, and other liquids superseded human urine in several localities, Scotland

---

[1] It should not be forgotten that the original form of Christian baptism was complete immersion; the relatively modern custom of christening, or sprinkling, is a later replacement of this, and is still repudiated by, for instance, the Baptist sect.

[2] Hartland, *Paternity*, op. cit., pp. 77-89.

[3] Bourke, op. cit., p. 211.

included." The following is an example of this. One of the superstitious uses of urine was to wash the breasts of a woman after delivery, no doubt with the aim of securing a good supply of milk. Jouan[1] reports from personal experience that this was still customary in France so late as in 1847. In Scotland the custom widely prevailed of washing the breasts with salt and water in the same circumstances and for the same object.[2] Again, whenever the supply of salt falls short in a given country, particularly in an uncivilized one, the natives are apt to resort to urine as a substitute. Gomara[3] states that human urine served as salt to the Indians of Bogota. The Latookas of the White Nile make salt from the ashes of goat's dung,[4] which again illustrates the conception of salt as the essence of excrement, particularly urine. Pallas[5] says that the Buriats of Sibera, in collecting salts from the shores of certain lakes, are careful as to the taste of the same: "They employ only those which have a taste of urine and of alkali"; Bourke,[6] referring to this, adds: "This shows that they must once have used urine for salt, as so many other tribes have done." The Siberians gave human urine to their reindeer in place of salt,[7] presumably to improve their yield of milk. They also used urine to obtain water from snow by melting it, just as we use salt to prevent the formation of ice on our doorsteps. The Dinkas of Central Africa use the urine of cows for washing and as a substitute for salt, but here other motives also enter in, for with them cattle are sacred animals.[8] Urine has been used for a very great number of industrial purposes, in many of which it has since been

---

[1] Jouan, Quoted by Bourke, loc. cit.
[2] Black, *Folk-Medicine*, 1883, p. 23; Napier, op. cit., pp. 36-37.
[3] Gomara, *Historia de las Indias*, p. 202.
[4] Baker, op. cit., p. 224.
[5] Pallas, *Voyages*, 1793, Vol. IV, p. 246.
[6] Bourke, op. cit., p. 193.
[7] Cochrane, *Pedestrian Journey through Siberian Tartary*, 1824, p. 235.
[8] Schweinfurth, op. cit., p. 58.

superseded by salt;[1] it is not necessary to enumerate them here.

One of the earliest uses of salt was for cleansing purposes. In Ancient Rome salt and water was used instead of toilet paper, every latrine containing a bucket of it.[2] The use of urine as a fluid for washing the body has been reported from the most diverse parts of the world: thus, in Alaska,[3] in Iceland,[4] in Ounalashka (in Russia),[5] amongst the Californian Pericuis,[6] the Siberian Tchuktchees,[7] and the Vancouver Indians.[8] The custom persisted in Spain until quite recent times, and even in the present generation it was to be traced among the Spanish settlers in Florida.[9] Petroff[10] states that the peasants of Portugal still wash their clothes in urine, and German, Irish and Scandinavian immigrants in the United States persist in adding human urine to the water to be used in cleansing blankets.[11] The use of urine as a mouth-wash is also very prevalent. Baker[12] writes: "The Obbo natives wash out their mouths with their own urine. This habit may have originated in the total absence of salt in their country." The Basques and some Hindus do the same, and the custom used to obtain in England and Germany; in Spain and Portugal it persisted until the end of the eighteenth century.[13]

We may now return to the religious aspects of the

[1] Bourke, op. cit., pp. 177-200.
[2] Bourke, op. cit., p. 135.
[3] Coxe, *Russian Discoveries*, 1803, p. 225, quoting Krenitzin.
[4] Hakluyt, *Voyages*, 1599, Vol. I, p. 664.
[5] Solovoof, *Voyages*, 1764, p. 226.
[6] Clavigero, *Historia de Baja California*, 1852, p. 28; Bancroft, op. cit., p. 559.
[7] Lisiansky, *Voyage round the World*, 1811, p. 214; Melville, *In the Lena Delta*, loc. cit.; Gilder, quoted by Bourke, op. cit., pp. 202, 203.
[8] Swan, "The Indians of Cape Flattery," *Smithsonian Contributions to Knowledge*, No. 220, p. 19.
[9] Bourke, op. cit., pp. 203, 205. Many references.
[10] Petroff, *Trans. of the American Anthropological Society*, 1882, Vol. I.
[11] McGillicuddy, Quoted by Bourke, op. cit., p. 205.
[12] Baker, op. cit., p. 240.
[13] Bourke, op. cit., pp. 203-5.

subject. The Romans held a feast to the mother of all the Gods, Berecinthia, at which the matrons took their idol and sprinkled it with their urine.[1] Berecinthia was one of the names under which Cybele or Rhea, the primal earth Goddess, was worshipped by the Romans and by many nations of the East. Juvenal (Sixth Satire) describes how in the rites of the Bona Dea her image used to be sprinkled with copious irrigations of urine. In the early days of Christianity the Manichæan sect used to bathe in urine.[2] It is related of an Irish king, Aedh, that he obtained some urine of the chief priest, bathed his face in it, drank some with gusto, and said that he prized it more highly than the Eucharist itself.[3]

In modern religions of civilized peoples, however, human urine is never used, having been replaced by water, salt and water, or cow's urine. The sacred drink *hum* of the Parsees has the "urine of a young, pure cow" as one of the ingredients.[4] In the Bareshnun ceremony the Parsee priest has to undergo certain ablutions wherein he applies to his body cow's urine,[5] and to rub the *nirang* (cow's urine) over his face and hands is the second thing every Parsee does after rising in the morning.[6] The latter ceremony is by no means a simple one; for instance, he is not allowed to touch anything directly with his hands until the sacred *nirang* has first been washed off with water. In India the urine of a cow is a holy water of the very highest religious significance. It is used in ceremonies of purification, during which it is drunk.[7] Dubois[8] says that a Hindu penitent "must drink the *panchakaryam*—a word which literally signifies the five things, namely, milk, butter, curd, dung, and urine, all

---

[1] Torquemada, Quoted by Bourke, op. cit., p. 394.
[2] Picart, *Coûtumes et Cérémonies Religieuses*, 1729, p. 18.
[3] *Mélusine*, Mai 5, 1888.
[4] Max Müller, *Biographies of Words*, 1888, p. 237.
[5] Kingsley, Quoted by Bourke, op. cit., p. 211.
[6] Max Müller, *Chips*, etc., op. cit., p. 163.
[7] De Gubernatis, *Zoological Mythology*, Engl. Transl., 1872, Vol. I, p. 95.
[8] Abbé Dubois, *The People of India*, 1817, p. 29.

mixed together," and he adds: "The urine of a cow is held to be the most efficacious of any for purifying all imaginable uncleanness. I have often seen the superstitious Hindu accompanying these animals when in the pasture, and watching the moment for receiving the urine as it fell, in vessels which he had brought for the purpose, to carry it home in a fresh state; or, catching it in the hollow of his hand, to bedew his face and all his body. When so used it removes all external impurity, and when taken internally, which is very common, it cleanses all within." Moor[1] similarly writes: "The greatest . . . of all purifiers is the urine of a cow. Images are sprinkled with it. No man of any pretensions to piety or cleanliness would pass a cow in the act of staling without receiving the holy stream in his hand and sipping a few drops." Hindu merchants at Bokhara mix with their food, that it may do them good, the urine of a sacred cow kept in that place.[2] At the Poojah sacrifice the Brahmans prepare the room by sprinkling the floor with cow's urine.[3] In one of the Hindu fasts the devotee adopts as his food the excreta of cows, the urine being allowed as a beverage for the fourth day.[4] The antiquity of urine rites in India is shown by the fact that they are frequently referred to in the oldest of their canonical books. The Brahminical authors of the Maha-Bharata describe how, at the coronation of a Maharajah, Krishna brings the urine of the sacred cow and pours it over the King's head.[5] In the Shapast la Shayast much stress is laid on bull's urine as a purifier.[6] These rites exist not only in India proper, but also on the slopes of the Himalayas,[7]

---

[1] Moor, *The Hindu Pantheon*, 1810, p. 143.

[2] Erman, *Siberia*, 1848, Vol. I, p. 384.

[3] Maurice, *Indian Antiquities*, 1800, Vol. I, p. 77.

[4] Maurice, op. cit., Vol. V, p. 222.

[5] Wheeler, *History of India*, 1867, Vol. I, p. 371.

[6] *Sacred Books of the East*, Vol. V, Part I.

[7] Short, "Notes on the Hill Tribes of the Neilgherries," *Trans. of the Ethnological Society*, 1868, p. 268.

and from India they were introduced into Persia; the Kharda Avesta has preserved the formula to be recited by a devotee while he holds in his hand the urine of a cow, preparatory to washing his face with it.[1]

We need not discuss the various cloud, moon, and other supposed symbolisms of the rites in question, for it is no longer tenable that these are anything more than secondary developments of more primitive interests. After dealing with the subject of animal sacrifice, and showing that this is a later development of the original human sacrifice, a conclusion amply confirmed by the work done since his time, Bourke[2] pertinently asks: "If the cow have displaced a human victim, may it not be within the limits of probability that the ordure and urine of the sacred bovine are substitutes, not only for the complete carcass, but that they symbolize a former use of human excreta?" This question we can to-day with a high degree of probability answer in the affirmative, for both anthropological and psycho-analytical research agree in the conclusion that excessive, e.g., religious, interest in any animal is only a substitute for a corresponding interest in some human being. There can be no doubt that the cow, for instance, is a typical mother-symbol, just as the Lamb of God in Christian mythology is a symbol of Christ, i.e., of the son.

From this point of view the devil's custom of using his urine to baptize, and bless, his worshippers at the witches' Sabbath[3] must be regarded, not—as the medieval theologians indignantly thought—as constituting a wanton caricature of the Christian rites, but as a reversion to the most primitive form of these. Caricature, like wit, is often really a reversion to the unconscious source of the caricatured idea. An example of it may be quoted from another

[1] De Gubernatis, op. cit., pp. 99-100.
[2] Bourke, op. cit., p. 125.
[3] Thiers, *Traite des Superstitions*, 1741, Vol. II, p. 367; Picart, op. cit., Vol. VIII, p. 69.

field, one which also depends on the symbolic equivalent of urine and holy water: In a caricature by Isaac Cruikshank, dated 17th March, 1797, of Napoleon giving audience to the Pope, a French grenadier is represented urinating into a chamber-pot which is labelled Holy Water.[1]

The almost universal custom of rubbing a new-born child with salt, or bathing it in salt and water, has been noted above. In some parts of the world the original fluid, urine, which has been so widely displaced for this purpose by salt, is still in use, or was in historical times.[2] Soranus discusses at length the Roman custom of bathing infants with the urine of a boy who has not reached puberty (thus a peculiarly innocent and pure fluid). The Hottentots use fresh cow's urine for this purpose, while the Indians in Alaska employ horse urine.

The association between urine rites and religious dancing is especially close in many parts of the world. Bourke[3] gives a detailed account of the "urine dance" of the Zunis in New Mexico, and draws an instructive analogy between it and the famous Feast of Fools in medieval Europe.[4] In a painstaking analysis of the circumstances in which dancers in Alaska bathe in urine he has further established the religious significance of this custom there also.[5] The same association exists as well in various other parts of the world, in Africa, Siberia, North America, etc.[6] The ideas that are connected together in these ceremonies are: alcoholic or other intoxication, religious ecstasies, urine rites (drinking and bathing), and sexual excitement. In this connection I venture to throw out the suggestion that perhaps philological research might establish an etymological rela-

[1] Broadley, *Napoleon in Caricature*, 1911, p. 94.
[2] Numerous instances are related by Ploss, *Das Kind in Brauch und Sitte der Völker*, Zweite Aufl., 1911.
[3] Bourke, op. cit., pp. 4-10.
[4] Bourke, op. cit., pp. 11-23.
[5] Bourke, op. cit., pp. 206-8.
[6] Bourke, op. cit., pp. 208-10.

tionship between the Latin word sal and the verbs saltare and salire (= to leap or dance).[1] From saltus (= leap) comes the English saltier (St. Andrew's cross), the substantive salt (meaning sexual desire, especially of animals), and the adjective salt (= lecherous);[2] further words from the same source are assault (adsaltare), assail (adsalire) sally, exult and salient, all of which stand in a psychological relationship to the present subject. The idea of dancing is of course, now as formerly,[3] closely connected with eroticism, and often also with religion.[4]

* * *

Something will now be said about the symbolic significance attaching to the mingling of two liquids, which is ultimately derived from the infantile idea, mentioned above, that the sexual act consists in the combining of the urine of two people. In various customs and beliefs urine has, quite comprehensibly, been replaced by other bodily fluids, particularly the vital ones such as blood. Salt and water has also played an important part in this way.

The interchange of blood as a means of binding two people together with lasting ties is a very general rite. Hartland[5] says of it: "The Blood-Covenant, as it is called, is a simple ceremony. It is sufficient that an incision be made in the neophyte's arm and the flowing blood sucked from it by one of the clansmen, upon whom the operation is repeated in turn by the neophyte. . . . Sometimes the blood is dropped into a cup and diluted with water or wine.

[1] Since writing the above I find that Schleiden (op. cit., S. 17) expresses a similar thought, suggesting that sal and salire are both derived from the Sanscrit 'sar', a root which will be considered later in this essay.

[2] Cp. Shakespeare's "salt as wolves in pride" (Othello, Act III, Sc. 3).

[3] Brill, "The Psychopathology of the New Dances," New York Medical Journal, April 25, 1914.

[4] Bourke, op. cit., p. 24.

[5] Hartland, Perseus, op. cit., pp. 237, 238. See in general pp. 236-58, also Strack, Das Blut im Glauben und Aberglauben der Menschheit, 1900.

Sometimes food eaten together is impregnated with the blood.[1] Sometimes it is enough to rub the bleeding wounds together, so that the blood of both parties is mixed and smeared upon them both. Among the Kayans of Borneo the drops are allowed to fall upon a cigarette, which is then lighted and smoked alternately by both parties. But, whatever may be the exact form adopted, the essence of the rite is the same, and its range is world-wide. It is mentioned by classical writers as practised by the Arabs, the Lydians, and Iberians of Asia Minor, and apparently the Medes. Many passages of the Bible, many of the Egyptian *Book of the Dead*, are inexplicable apart from it. Ancient Arab historians are full of allusions to it. Odin and Liki entered into the bond, which means for us that it was customary among the Norsemen—as we know, in fact, from other sources. It is recorded by Giraldus of the Irish of his day. It is described in the *Gesta Romanorum*. It is related of the Huns or Magyars, and of the medieval Rumanians. Joinville ascribes it to one of the tribes of the Caucasus; and the Rabbi Petachia of Ratisbon, who travelled in Ukrainia in the twelfth century, found it there. In modern times every African traveller mentions it; and most of them have had to undergo the ceremony. In the neighbouring island of Madagascar it is well known. All over the Eastern Archipelago, in Australia, in the Malay peninsula, among the Karens, the Siamese, the Dards on the northern border of our Indian empire, and many of the aboriginal tribes of Bengal, the wild tribes of China, the Syrians of Lebanon and the Bedouins, and among the autochthonous peoples of North and South America, the rite is, or has been quite recently, in use. Nor has it ceased to be practised in Europe by the Gipsies, the Southern Slavs and the Italians of the Abruzzi. The band of the Mala Vita in Southern Italy, only broken

[1] The resemblance of these two last-mentioned customs to the Eucharist of the Christian Churches is unmistakable.

up a year or two ago, was a blood-brotherhood formed in this way. Most savage peoples require their youths at the age of puberty to submit to a ceremony which admits them into the brotherhood of the grown men, and into all the rights and privileges of the tribe. Of this ceremony the blood-covenant is usually an essential part, as it is also, either actually or by symbol, in the initiation-rite not only of the Mala Vita, but of almost all secret societies, both civilized and uncivilized."

The giving of blood, therefore, exactly like that of salt, symbolizes friendship, loyalty, compact, and initiation into manhood. More than this, in many countries it is closely connected with marriage, and may actually constitute the marriage ceremony. The marriage rite of the Dusuns, in Banguey, consists in transferring a drop of blood from a small incision made in the calf of a man's leg to a similar cut in the woman's leg.[1] The marriage of the Wukas, a tribe of New Guinea, is performed by mutual cuts made by the husband and wife in each other's forehead.[2] Among the Birhors of India the wedding ceremony consists entirely in drawing blood from the little fingers of the bride and bridegroom, and smearing it on each other;[3] a similar, though more complicated, ceremony is performed by the Káyasth, or writer caste of Behar.

Among several races of India, in the wedding ceremony known as *sindur dan*, the substance used is red lead, which the bridegroom smears on the bride's forehead with his little finger or a knife; Hartland[4] has shown that this is a later development of the more primitive custom, the red lead simply replacing the blood. In some instances the two are combined: in the Kewat caste the *sindur dan* rite is first carried out, and then blood is drawn from the little finger

[1] Hartland, op. cit., p. 339. The original references may be found there.
[2] Hartland, loc. cit.
[3] Hartland, op. cit., p. 336.
[4] Hartland, op. cit., pp. 334-6.

of the bridegroom's right hand and of the bride's left; the blood is mingled in a dish of boiled rice and milk, and each person eats the food containing the other's blood.[1] Similarly in the Rajput ritual the family priest fills the bridegroom's hand with *sindur* and marks the bride's forehead with it; on the next day each of them is made to chew betel with which a drop of blood from the other's little finger has been mixed.[2] Among the Kharwár, and also the Kurmi, the bridegroom smears the bride with a mixture of his own blood and of paint.[3] Blood rites of the same kind were also performed at Finnish and Norwegian marriages.[4]

More or less elaborate symbolisms of the primitive rite are frequent enough. An Australian bridegroom spits on his bride, and then streaks her with red powder down to the navel.[5] A Carib will sometimes betroth himself to an unborn babe, conditionally on its being a girl, by making a red mark over the mother's womb.[6] In the East Indies, in Borneo, and in parts of Southern India, fowl's blood is used instead of human blood.[7] Blood, like urine, has also been extensively used in Europe as a love charm or philtre,[8] of which custom one example will suffice: lovers who wished to heighten the affections of their mistresses used to transfuse their own blood into the loved one's veins.[9] An example of condensed symbolism is afforded by a Mexican saga, according to which a dead man's bone (i.e., the phallus of an ancestor, or father) when sprinkled with blood produced the father and mother of the present race of mankind.[10]

---

[1] Hartland, op. cit., p. 337.
[2] Hartland, loc. cit.
[3] Hartland, loc. cit.
[4] Hartland, op. cit., p. 341.
[5] Hartland, op. cit., p. 342.
[6] Hartland, loc. cit.
[7] Hartland, op. cit., p. 343.
[8] Numerous examples are given by Hartland, op. cit., pp. 124, 125.
[9] Flemming, *De Remediis ex Corpore Humano desuntis*, 1738, p. 15.
[10] Southey's *Commonplace Book*, Edited by Warter, 1850, Vol. IV, p. 142.

We see from the facts just quoted that blood, like urine, has all over the world been treated as an equivalent of salt, as a vital or holy material. The thesis that external application is symbolically the same as drinking is confirmed in this case as well. Customs and beliefs very similar to those just mentioned could be collected in respect of various other bodily fluids, of which only one or two instances will be given. The sweat of the Finnish deity Wainemoinen was a balm for all diseases, and the same was true of the Egyptian God Ra.[1] The Scandinavian Frost-Giants were born of the sweat of the Giant Ymir.[2] It is probable that the salt taste of sweat has always struck the observation of mankind. This is certainly so with tears, where literary allusions to their saltness abound: thus in *King John* (Act V, Sc. 7):

Prince Henry: O, that there were some virtue in my tears,
That might relieve you!
King John: The salt in them is hot.

* * *

The interest in the combination of salt and water has naturally been extended to the sea, which has always played an important part in the birth fancies of mankind. The association is evident in the use of the Greek word ἄλς (Latin *sale*) to express both "salt" and "sea". The contrast between fire and water has often been seized upon to represent the contrast between male and female elements respectively. The relation between salt and fire is much more extensive than we have here described; most of the customs and beliefs mentioned above could be paralleled by similar ones in which it is necessary to throw salt into the fire in order to produce the desired effect.[3] In mythology the

[1] Lenormant, *Chaldean Magic: Its Origin and Development*, Engl. Transl., 1877, p. 247.
[2] Hartland, Paternity, op. cit., p. 2.
[3] The etymological aspects of this relationship will be discussed later.

combination of fire and water (male and female elements) is symbolized with especial frequency by alcohol, which presumably was the essential constituent of the various sacred drinks of which we read; with singular appropriateness the North American Indians refer to alcoholic beverages as "fire-water".

The association between the ideas fire—salt—sea are well shown in the following myths. From the mythical lore of Finland we learn that Ukko, the mighty God of the sky, struck fire in the heavens; a spark descended from this was received by the waves and became salt.[1] This example is especially instructive for more than one reason. In the first place we here have salt directly derived from fire, thus confirming our previous surmise of the symbolic equivalency of the two. In the next place, as Abraham[2] has clearly demonstrated, heavenly fire descending upon earth, e.g., lightning, is mythologically only another variant of the various divine foods (soma, ambrosia, nectar) that symbolize the male fertilizing fluid; this is in obvious accord with the view here maintained of the seminal symbolism of salt.

In another myth we have the Prometheus-like bringer of salt regarded as a Messiah. Lawrence[3] writes: "The Chinese worship an idol called Phelo, in honour of a mythological personage of that name, whom they believe to have been the discoverer of salt and the originator of its use. His ungrateful countrymen, however, were tardy in their recognition of Phelo's merits, and that worthy thereupon left his native land and did not return. Then the Chinese declared him to be a deity, and in the month of June each year they hold a festival in his honour, during which he is everywhere sought, but in vain; he will not appear until he

---

[1] Quoted from Lawrence, op. cit., p. 154.
[2] Abraham, op. cit., S. 49, 62, etc.
[3] Lawrence, op. cit., pp. 154, 155.

comes to announce the end of the world." The Prometheus theme of a God bringing an all-precious substance as a gift to mankind[1] is here worked into a form that closely resembles the Jewish conception of a Messiah that has to be sought and the Christian one of a prophet who was not received when he delivered his message, but who will return to announce the end of the world.

Tacitus[2] refers to the belief that salt is the product of the strife between fire and water, a belief evidently mirroring the infantile sadistic conception of coitus, but one that happens to have an objective basis in regard to the evaporating action of the sun's heat. On a lowlier plane we may refer to the connection between fire and water as shown by some practices carried out for the purpose of obtaining children. A Transylvanian Gipsy woman is said to drink water into which her husband has cast hot coals, or, better still, has spit, saying as she does so: "Where I am flame, be thou the coals! Where I am rain be thou the water!"[3] A South Slavonic woman holds a wooden bowl of water near the fire on the hearth. Her husband then strikes two firebrands together until the sparks fly. Some of them fall into the bowl, and she then drinks the water.[4] Of the many instances of association between the ideas of fire and urine one only need be mentioned: At the yearly ceremony held by the Eskimos for the purpose of driving out an evil spirit called Tuna, one of the performers brings a vessel of urine and flings it on the fire.[5] The ideas, therefore, of fire-salt, fire-water, and fire-urine are thus seen to be closely related in the primitive mind, a fact which stands in full harmony with the clinical psycho-analytic finding that the ideas of

[1] *See* Abraham, op. cit., for a full analysis of the Prometheus myth.
[2] Cited by Schleiden, op. cit., S. 11.
[3] Ploss, Das Weib, loc. cit.
[4] Krauss, *Sitte und Brauch der Südslaven*, 1885, S. 531.
[5] *Report of the International Polar Expedition to Point Barrow*, Washington, 1885, p. 42.

fire, water, urine, and semen are interchangeable equivalents in the unconscious, fire being a typical symbol for urine.

Leaving now the subject of fire we have to note a few more beliefs concerning salt and water, particularly in a female sense (receptive urine). In the cosmogenical myths of the islanders of Kadiack it is related that the first woman "by making water, produced the seas".[1] In South Africa it is also believed that the sea was created by a woman,[2] doubtless in the same way. In the creation myth of the Australians, on the other hand, it is a God, Bundjil, who creates the sea by urinating over the earth for many days.[3] Among the Mexican Nahuas, again, the sea is of female origin: there the women and girls employed in the preparation of salt dance at a yearly festival held in honour of the Goddess of Salt, Huixocihuatl, whose brothers the raingods, as the result of a quarrel, drove her into the sea, where she invented the art of making the precious substance.[4] In European mythology the sea is conceived of as either male or female, though much more often as the latter. It stands in especially close association with the various love Goddesses, Aphrodite, Astarte, and the rest. Jennings writes:[5] "Blue is the colour of the 'Virgin Maria'. Maria, Mary, *mare*, *mar*, *mara*, means the 'bitterness', or the 'saltness' of the sea. Blue is expressive of the Hellenic, Isidian, Ionian, Yonian (Yoni—Indian), Watery, Female, and Moonlike Principle in the universal theogony. It runs through all the mythologies." As is well known, Friday is holy to this Goddess in most religions, and is named after her in all European languages. On Friday, the day of the Virgin Mary, salted meat must not be eaten by strict

[1] Lisiansky, op. cit., p. 197.
[2] Lang, *Myth, Ritual, and Religion*, 1887, Vol. I, p. 91.
[3] Smyth, *The Aborigines of Australia*, 1878, Vol. I, p. 429.
[4] Bancroft, op. cit., Vol. II, p. 353.
[5] Hargrave Jennings, *The Rosicrucians*, 1887, Vol. I, p. 57.

Catholics (compare this with the ascetic abstinence from salt noted above), and, further, the staple food is, appropriately enough, fish. There exists in the South of England a spell for turning the heart of a recalcitrant lover, which consists in throwing a little salt into the fire on three successive Friday nights; on the third one the lover is expected to return.[1] That the spell has to be carried out just on Friday illustrates very well how detailed is the determination of superstitions, and how careful one should be before concluding that any minor feature of one is devoid of meaning.

As might have been expected, bathing in the sea has been recommended for most of the purposes for which the combination of salt and water has been used. The following instances are characteristic. In Sardinia to drink from, or especially to bathe in, the sea is held to be a cure for childlessness.[2] Among the negroes in Guinea when a woman is pregnant for the first time she has to go through an elaborate ceremony of being purified in the sea.[3] Probably the original sense was to ensure an easy and successful labour.

The whole subject of the relation between salt and water may be concluded by referring to two practices that have nothing to do with the sea. A method of curing disease in Germany is to throw a handful of salt into water while these words are being repeated: "I strew this seed (!) in the name of God; when this seed grows I shall see my fever again."[4] A superstition in Bohemia says that when milk is being carried over water one should throw some salt into the water, otherwise the cow will be harmed.[5] It was remarked above that milk has the same symbolic significance as salt and here we see the two substances treated interchangeably.

[1] Henderson, loc. cit.
[2] *Rivista delle Tradizioni Populari Italiane*, 1894, Vol. II. p. 423.
[3] Bosman, In Pinkerton, op. cit., Vol. XVI, p. 423.
[4] Wuttke, op. cit., S. 335.
[5] Wuttke, op. cit., S. 447.

In this connection it is of interest that Browning, in his "Pietro of Abano", changes the usual belief that sorcerers cannot tolerate salt by describing how a magician dare not drink milk; the poet's insight reveals the meaning of this:

All's but daily dry bread: what makes moist the ration?
Love, the milk that sweetens man his meal—alas, you lack:

In several of the varieties of the Cinderella theme (e.g., in No. 179 of Grimm's fairy tales) salt is equally plainly taken to be equivalent of love: the third daughter, on being asked by her father to describe her love for him, likens it to salt.

* * *

We have next to consider the female, recipient substance conceived of as a solid: namely, beliefs developed from the liquid-solid and solid-solid hypotheses of childhood that were mentioned above. The substance most frequently used in this respect is *bread*, which, from its consistence and food-value, readily lends itself to symbolic purposes. Many of the superstitious beliefs in which it is concerned have already been referred to. Its fertilizing powers may be illustrated by the Indian practice, performed for the cure of barrenness, of "eating a loaf of bread cooked on the still burning pyre of a man who was never married, and who was the only or eldest son in his family, and so received the fullest possible measure of vitality".[1] The association between bread and excrement is even more plainly shown in the following Slavonic beliefs. The spirits of fruitfulness were supposed to dwell in the dung-heaps, and offerings used to be made to them there. In later times witches were believed to hold their revels there, and it was not safe for a peasant to relieve himself on the spot without having in his mouth a piece of bread as a charm.[2] In England the

[1] *Census of India*, 1901, XVII, p. 164.
[2] Krauss, *Slavische Volksforschungen*, 1908, S. 71.

people used to throw wheat on the bride's head as she returned from the church,[1] evidently a precursor of the more modern fertility (seminal) symbol of rice.

The wide-spread use of the combination of salt and bread for all the purposes for which salt alone is used (confirming oaths, warding off evil, etc.) has been previously described. The sexual significance of the combination comes to open expression in the following instances. In Waldenburg the bride secretly places salt and bread in her shoe so that she may be blessed with children;[2] the fecundity significance of the shoe, which is a typical yoni symbol (hence the throwing of it at weddings), has been fully described by Aigremont.[3] In the Potsdam Kreis betrothed couples place salt and bread in their shoes,[4] with of course the same meaning. In Russia salt and bread are the first articles to be carried into the dwelling of a newly married pair.[5] Among the Southern Slavs the combination in question is used as a love charm,[6] while in the more pious canton of Berne it has the function of fortifying against temptation the person who carries it.[7] Going back to Ancient Rome we find that Ceres, the grain Goddess, and Neptune, the sea God, were worshipped together in the same temple;[8] the wife of Neptune, however, was called Salacia[9] (compare our word "salacious" = libidinous).

Other substances than salt were used together with bread at times, with a similar significance. Perhaps the commonest of these was *cheese*. The combination is very potent against

[1] Moffet, *Health's Improvement*, 1655, p. 218.
[2] Aigremont, *Fuss- und Schuh-Symbolik und Erotik*, 1909, S. 55; Wuttke, op. cit., S. 370.
[3] Aigremont, op. cit., S. 42-64.
[4] Seligmann, op. cit., S. 38.
[5] Lawrence, op. cit., p. 185.
[6] Krauss, op. cit., S. 169.
[7] Lawrence, op. cit., p. 182.
[8] Frazer, op. cit., Second Edition, 1907, Part IV, "Adonis, Attis, Osiris," p. 412.
[9] Plutarch, op. cit.

the evil eye, especially when carried round the neck;[1] it
was also used to protect children from witches and malignant spirits.[2] In an old Welsh legend bread and cheese is
used as a love charm to seduce the Lady of the Lake.[3] In
this combination cheese is evidently the active element,
while in others it is treated as the passive, recipient one.
This is so in the various customs relating to what is called,
from its association with child-birth, the "Groaning Cheese"
or "Groaning Cake"; pieces of this, tossed in the midwife's
smock, or placed under the pillow at night, cause young
women to dream of their lovers.[4] The same is true of the
custom, which still occasionally obtains in Europe, of using
urine in the manufacture of cheese.[5] Urine is also used in
some countries in bread-making, and there is reason to
think that this was so even in Europe prior to the introduction of barm and yeast;[6] in 1886 a baker in Paris
"regressed" so far as to be detected in using water-closet
refuse in the preparation of bread, which was said to
deteriorate in quality as soon as the practice was put an end
to.[7] The theme of moisture and dryness of bread plays a
central part in an interesting Welsh legend:[8] A young man
who had fallen desperately in love with a Lake Maiden
sought, on his mother's advice, to woo her with the offer of
some bread—a naïve proposal which would be simply
foolish if taken literally, but which when read symbolically
is seen to be full of meaning. The maiden rejected the offer
on the ground that the bread was too hard-baked. He
returned, again on his mother's advice, with some unbaked

[1] Seligmann, op. cit., S. 38, 94.
[2] Brand, op. cit., Vol. II, p. 79.
[3] Rhys, *Celtic Folklore*, 1901, Vol. I, Ch. I, "Undine's Cymric Sisters,"
pp. 3, 17, 18.
[4] Brand, op. cit., p. 71.
[5] Bourke, op. cit., pp. 181-2.
[6] Bourke, op. cit., p. 39.
[7] Bourke, op. cit., p. 32.
[8] Rhys, op. cit., pp. 4-6, 27, 28.

dough, but was once more unsuccessful for the opposite reason to the previous one. On the third attempt, having achieved the proper consistence, he was successful. In another version of the same group of legends the suitor was enabled to capture the maiden through the magic power he had attained to by eating a piece of moist bread that she had allowed to float ashore.[1] In the Bible (Ezekiel iv. 15) it is stated that the Lord commanded the Jews to prepare their bread with cow's dung instead of with human ordure.

Finally in this connection may be mentioned the combination of *sweat* and bread. This was believed to have powerful aphrodisiac properties, doubtless an extension of the exciting effect that the odour of sweat has on many people, and at the time of the witches women were accused of rubbing dough on their bodies and giving it to men to eat in whom they wished to arouse satanic love.[2] We probably have here, as Aubrey suggested,[3] the explanation of the ancient game of cockle-bread,[4] in which the players, young women, go through the pretence of moulding bread with their back. It is a Negro, as well as a Belgian, superstition that if you give a dog some bread soaked in your sweat he will follow you to the ends of the earth: he is yours.[5] We have here a repetition of the loyalty idea so characteristic of salt, the bond, however, being cemented here by the combination of the male and female elements in place of the male alone.

Nor is bread the only recipient substance in such customs. Of the many other combinations may be mentioned: milk and resin,[6] curds and beans[7]—both of these combinations

[1] Rhys, op. cit., p. 17.
[2] Paton, *Folk-Lore*, Vol. V, p. 277.
[3] Aubrey, *Remaines of Gentilisme and Judaisme* (1686), 1881 Edition, p. 43.
[4] See Brand, op. cit., p. 413.
[5] Hartland, Perseus, op. cit., p. 124.
[6] *North Indian Notes and Queries*, Vol. III, p. 96.
[7] *Sacred Books of the East*, XXIX, p. 180.

are cures for sterility—salt and meal[1]—a charm to enable
girls to see their future lover in a dream—sweat and cake[2]
—used throughout Northern and Central Europe as a love
charm—blood and cake[3]—used in Transylvania for the
same purpose—and blood mixed with the excrement of a
dead person[4]—a cure for impotence. The reverse of the
same idea is presented in the superstition that if one eats an
egg without salt one will get a fever,[5] significance being
evidently attached to the combination. The erotic meaning
of this is indicated by association in the saying that "to kiss
a man without a moustache is like eating an egg without
salt". There is of course an extensive nativity symbolism
attaching to eggs, especially in religion. In Bavaria and elsewhere an egg will guard against the evil eye.[6] A Devonshire
cure for ague was to bury an egg in earth at the dead of night.[7]

The act of partaking of the same food has constantly
been used to symbolize a more intimate union, representing
the solid-solid infantile hypothesis described above. It is a
Scandinavian saying that if a boy and girl eat of one morsel
they grow fond of each other.[8] In many parts of the East
Indies the betel-nut is employed as a love charm, is given
as a love pledge, and the chewing of one quid by both
parties is the essential part of the wedding ceremony.[9]
Among the Manchus a dumpling is brought into the bed-
chamber, when the bride and bridegroom each partake of a
piece so as to ensure numerous offspring.[10] In Ancient Greece
the bride and bridegroom used to eat of a quince together.[11]

[1] Wuttke, op. cit., S. 244.
[2] Hartland, op. cit., p. 123.
[3] Hartland, op. cit., p. 124.
[4] Von Wlislocki, op. cit., S. 140.
[5] Wuttke, op. cit., S. 311.
[6] Seligmann, op. cit., S. 330.
[7] Brand, op. cit., Vol. III, p. 298.
[8] Thorpe, *Northern Mythology*, 1851, Vol. II, p. 108.
[9] *L'Anthropologie*, Vol. III, p. 194.
[10] *Folk-Lore*, Vol. I, p. 488.
[11] Plutarch, Solon, XX.

With many Hindoo tribes a woman never eats together with a man throughout her whole life, with the sole exception of the wedding-day, when after the *sindur dan* ceremony described above she sits at table together with her husband. Hartland[1] records a very large number of instances, from all parts of the world, in which eating together, particularly from the same dish, constitutes an important or even essential part of the wedding ceremony, and there is no need for us to enumerate any more of these. The best known is the *confarreatio* ceremony of the Romans in which the man and woman ate together of the sacrificial cake, the panis farreus. Our own wedding-cake is a survival of these customs.[2]

The religious significance of the act, as illustrated by wedding ceremonies, is of considerable interest. In Christianity there has been a close association between it and the rite of the Holy Eucharist. In the old Parisian marriage ceremony the priest, after saying mass, blessed a loaf and wine; the loaf was bitten and a little of the wine drunk by each of the spouses, one after the other, and the officiating priest then taking them by the hands led them home. In a Yezidi wedding a loaf of consecrated bread is handed to the husband, and he and his wife eat it between them. The Nestorians require the pair to take the communion. Indeed, until the last revision of the Book of Common Prayer the Church of England commanded that "the newly married persons the same day of their marriage must receive the Holy Communion", a practice that continues to be recommended.[3]

The material of the Eucharist, like all other consecrated substances, has been endowed with various non-religious powers, such as ability to ward off the evil eye, to cure

---

[1] Hartland, op. cit., pp. 343-53; *See* also Rhys, op. cit., Vol. II, pp. 649, 650.
[2] Brand, op. cit., Vol. II, pp. 101, 102; Hartland, op. cit., pp. 351, 352.
[3] The preceding instances are quoted from Hartland, op. cit., p. 347.

sterility,[1] and so on. A curious example, full of symbolism, is the Welsh tradition that "flying snakes"[2] originated in ordinary snakes that had become transformed by drinking the milk of a woman and eating the bread of the Holy Communion.[3] We have traced above the underlying significance of the Catholic salt and water baptism, and also that of the various customs and beliefs relating to bread. It is interesting that in Italy the combination of salt and bread is known as "lumen Christi", and is of course endowed with magical properties.[4]

Consideration of the symbolism dealt with above, particularly the equivalency of salt and wine and the alimentary connotations of bread, makes it plain that the deeper significance of the Eucharist and Holy Communion is throughout a sexual one. This sexual meaning forced itself into open expression with some of the Christian sects. Thus, according to St. Augustine, the Manichæans prepared the sacred host by incorporating the Eucharistic bread with human semen, and their descendants, the Albigenses and Catharistes, preserved this custom.[5] Here, as elsewhere, heresy, by unveiling the symbolism of a given aspect of religious dogma or ritual, has uncomfortably compromised the religion it caricatures, just as the perversions of a brother often disclose the meaning of his neurotic sister's symptoms which are merely disguised manifestations of the same tendencies.

It need hardly be said that demonstration of the sexual origin and meaning of the materials used in a given religious ritual is far from explaining even the unconscious basis of that ritual. To do so with the Eucharist, for example, it would be necessary to discuss a number of other matters not

---

[1] Hartland, Paternity, op. cit., p. 7.
[2] The armorial emblem of Wales is a dragon.
[3] Owen, *Welsh Folk-Lore*, 1887, p. 349.
[4] Seligmann, op. cit., S. 38.
[5] See Bourke, op. cit., p. 220, where full references are given.

directly connected with the present inquiry, particularly the incestuous basis of the union implied in the ceremony, its relation to theophagy and anthropophagy, and so on.

*　　*　　*

I wish here to say something about an interesting feature of superstition in general, and of salt symbolism in particular—namely, its *ambivalency*. It has often puzzled observers of superstitions to note that the very same custom or happening is supposed in one place to bring luck, in another ill luck, in the one place to lead to fertility, in another sterility, and so on. The explanation is to be found in the ambivalent attitude of consciousness to the content of the unconscious, the source of all superstitions. If the affect, which is always positive, that accompanies the unconscious idea finds a passage-way into consciousness, as happens, for instance, in the process known as sublimation, then the attitude towards the conscious representative of this idea (i.e., towards the symbol) will be correspondingly positive, and the symbolic idea will be considered the source of all good. If, on the contrary, it is the affect belonging to the "repressing" tendencies that gets attached to the symbolic idea, then the latter will come to be the sign of all that is unlucky or dangerous. The same ambivalency is seen in regard to all products of the unconscious, for instance in totemism—whether of the race or of the individual; the same animal can be loved in infancy and unreasonably feared in later childhood. So, as was remarked earlier in this essay, it is really irrelevant whether a given superstition is met with in a positive or a negative sense, the essential point being the evidence given by both of an excessive significance derived from the unconscious.

This ambivalency can be well demonstrated in salt superstitions. One finds that practically every attribute described above as being attached to the idea of salt may in other places be replaced by its exact opposite. We may illustrate this feature by selecting a few examples of contrasting pairs.

1. *Fruitfulness—Unfruitfulness.*

The remarkably close association between the ideas of salt and fecundity was dwelt on in detail in the earlier part of this essay (pp. 31, 32, 45, 46), and a few examples were also quoted in which the former idea was related to that of barrenness. This latter seems to have been more especially common in Eastern countries, and is repeatedly referred to in the Bible (e.g., Deuteronomy xxix. 23; Job xxxix. 6; Jeremiah xvii. 6; Psalms cvii. 33, 34, etc.); it is also remarked on by Pliny, Virgil, and other classical writers.[1] A real ground for it was no doubt the frequent sight of salty deserts and waste places where an excess of salt had prevented all growth. This real justification for the association between salt and barrenness makes still more striking the far commoner one between it and fertility, and again shows how the latter belief must have been caused by a false association of ideas, as has been maintained above.

The analogy is again evident here between the ideas of salt, of which either the absence or the excess prevents fruitfulness, and sexuality, concerning which the same is widely believed. It is thus appropriate that Lot's wife, as a punishment for regretting the (homosexual) sins of Sodom, should have been turned into a pillar (phallus) of salt.

2. *Creation—Destruction.*

This antithesis is of course closely allied to the last one and might also be expressed as the contrast between immortality and death. It has at all ages been a common custom to add strength to a curse by strewing salt as a

[1] Schleiden, op. cit., S. 94.

symbol of destruction; historical examples are: after the destruction of Sichem by Abimelech, of Carthage by the Romans, of Padua by Attila, and of Milan by Friedrich Barbarossa. The custom seems to have had especial reference to the overpowering of a town (a mother symbol), another hint of the unconscious association between creation and destruction (compare the beliefs in the fructifying and the destroying sun).

3. In the same connection may be mentioned the antithesis between *the use of salt and the abstention from salt.* This has been discussed above in relation to religious observances and the question of sexual abstinence (pp. 47–9).

4. *Value—Worthlessness.*

The extraordinarily high sense of value often attached to the idea of salt, and also the close relation between it and that of money or wealth, has been described above (pp. 27, 28, 62), and we have now to note the opposite of this. Schleiden,[1] after quoting passages from Homer and Theocritus to the same effect, says: "A grain or two of salt thus became an expression for the most worthless thing that one could name. We still say, when we want to denote anything trifling: 'With that one couldn't even earn the salt for one's bread'." The same attitude of depreciation is shown in the joke of the traveller who after partaking of an extremely poor meal at an inn called the landlord to him and said: "There was one thing in this meal that I have not seen surpassed in all my travels." On the expectant landlord inquiring what it was, the traveller crushingly answered: "The salt."

5. *Health—Unhealthiness.*

We have noted above (pp. 31, 50, 51) the discussion

[1] Schleiden, op. cit., S. 101.

whether the partaking of salt is especially a health-bringing procedure or the exact opposite.

6. *Purity—Impurity*.

Salt has always served as an emblem of immaculateness and purity. Pythagoras says in this connection: "It was begotten of the purest parents, of the sun and the sea" (another example, by the way, of the signification of fire and water that was pointed out above). The important part salt has played, e.g., in religion, in regard to purification need not again be insisted on. The extraordinarily close association between the ideas of salt and of the excretions, i.e., dirty processes, on the other hand, has been pointed out in detail above, and we shall presently have to note the same thing in connection with the etymological history of the word. There is thus here the sharpest contrast between two opposite conceptions.

7. *Friendliness—Unfriendliness*.

Whereas the offering of salt is generally a sign of friendly intentions, we have also noted examples of the exact opposite (pp. 24, 25, 54, 55).

We have already discussed the significance of this striking ambivalency. It is a characteristic of all ideas that have deep unconscious roots, and may roughly be said to corres-. pond with the antithesis of "the repressing" and "the repressed" as well as that between love and hate. The qbverse of this statement is also true, that an idea which shows pronounced ambivalency in its affective values must have important associations in the unconscious. From the fact alone, therefore, that the idea of salt shows such marked ambivalency it could have been surmised that it has been invested with extrinsic significance of unconscious origin. One also gets here a further clue as

97

to the meaning of ambivalency: it is evidently related to the contrast between on the one hand the over-valuing of sexuality in general, and the excremental aspects of sexuality in particular, in the unconscious and in infantile life, and on the other hand the under-valuing of these in consciousness and in adult life. An individual analysis, however, of the infantile origin of all the separate attributes belonging to the salt idea, e.g., the relation of purification to fertilization, though of considerable importance, cannot be undertaken here, for it would lead us too far from the main theme of the work.

*   *   *

We may now pass to another aspect of the subject, the *etymological* one. It is becoming more and more realized by psycho-analysts that symbolisms gradually formed through "repression" during the progress of civilization leave traces of their original meaning as word-deposits. It is even probable that the correctness of the interpretation of a given symbol, such as the one attempted in this essay, could be accurately tested by being submitted to a sufficiently exhaustive comparison with the etymological and semantic history of the words denoting the ideas in question. From this point of view it becomes desirable, therefore, to say a little about the history of the word "salt", though a lack of expert knowledge will necessarily render the present consideration of it very incomplete.

It seems to be definitely established that the names for salt in nearly all European languages find their earliest expression in an old Celtic word which meant "water" or "bog". Schleiden[1] writes as follows: "The Celts brought with them from their original Indo-Germanic sources some form of the root 'sar', which in Sanscrit meant in the first place 'to walk', 'to go', 'to flow', etc., and then in a derived

[1] Schleiden, op. cit., S. 15, 16.

form as 'sara' also 'river', 'water', 'sea', 'pond'. No such word meaning salt is to be found in the Vedas, in the Avesta, nor in any of the cuneiform writings, but in Armenian it occurs as 'agh' (*gh* is a common substitute for *l*), thus constituting a bond between 'sara' (= water) and the Greek ἅλς[1] (= sea-water and salt). . . . Many words that are either truly Celtic or else have passed through the Celtic language still recall the original meaning of this root word as 'sea', 'lake', 'pond', 'pool', 'puddle'. In Old Irish 'sál' means moor or swamp; 'salach' is Old Irish, 'halou' Old Welsh for dirty;[2] the Old High German, Middle High German, and Anglo-Saxon 'sol' means a puddle or pool; the sporting words in German 'suhl' (= slough) and 'suhlen' (= to wallow), which are used in regard to wild swine; the Low German 'solig', meaning dirty, the French 'sale' (= unclean, impure). . . . The word has always retained a specially close association with the idea of water.[3] In Greek the word 'hals' with an altered gender, feminine, practically means the sea, just as 'sal' did with the Latin poets. Also the rivers which contained salt water or which passed by sources of salt are called by names that in all probability are all related to 'salt'." (Schleiden then gives a long list of such rivers and places.)

Hehn[4] suggests that σάλος (= salum), meaning "bog", "lagoon", "brackish water", belongs to the same series. It originally signified the sea outside the harbour, and thus also the swell of the sea within the harbour; we get here perhaps another hint of the relation between "sal" and "salire" mentioned above.

It has been suggested[5] that this root word "sar" was

---

[1] The initial *s* has been replaced by *h* only in Greek and Welsh.

[2] So the Old Welsh "halog" (=contaminated, impure) and "halou" (=faeces).

[3] In New Persian also "neme" (=salt) originally meant "moist".

[4] Hehn, op. cit., S. 25.

[5] Schleiden, op. cit., S. 17.

applied to salt to indicate the crackling or spurting of salt when thrown into fire or water, and in support of this it may be added that in the only European languages where the word for salt does not proceed from this root (Lithuanian "druska", Albanian "kripe")[1] a word signifying "to strew" is used to denote it. This suggestion is not, however, accepted by any philologist, and it seems certain that the main reason for the use of "sar" was the connotation of the latter as "flowing", "bog", etc., and the resemblance of this to salt-water.

It is thus plain that the original signification of the word was "a dirty fluid". The facts just adduced are certainly striking, and, especially in view of the derivative words that bear the closest relation to the idea of excrement, they may be regarded as an extrinsic confirmation of our conclusion—one which would hardly have been suspected without a detailed investigation—that the idea of salt and water is inherently allied to that of excretion, particularly urine. What was once a conscious association has in the course of centuries become more and more concealed, but though it has disappeared from sight it has in so doing by no means disappeared from existence.

IV

After this somewhat prolonged excursion we may now return to our original starting-point, namely, the superstitious belief that to spill salt at table is unlucky. The belief is practically universal and was as prevalent in Ancient Greece and Rome as in Modern Europe.[2] It has been applied to other precious substances besides salt: for

[1] Hehn, op. cit., S. 29.
[2] Lawrence, op. cit., pp. 167, 168.

instance, in China it is unlucky to spill the contents of an oil-jar.[1] In Germany even to play with salt is unlucky,[2] and for every grain spilt one will have to wait a day (or a week) before heaven's gate.[3]

It has been thought that the superstition in question arose from the over-spilling of the salt by Judas at the Last Supper,[4] a rationalistic explanation on a level with that which traces the superstitions concerning the number thirteen to the presence of thirteen at the same meal. Folk-beliefs of this order have a far wider and older range than purely Christian ones. The evidence adduced above points unequivocally to a quite different explanation, one which may be indicated by comparing the unlucky act in question with that of Onan described in Genesis (xxxviii. 9). In the light of it attention may be directed to the following features of the superstition. Although the spilling of salt is supposed to bring ill-luck in general,[5] its specific effect is to destroy friendship[6] and to lead to quarrelling;[7] moreover it brings ill-luck to the person towards whom the salt falls[8] as much as to the one who has spilt it. It acts, in other words, by disturbing the harmony of two people previously engaged in amicable intercourse. From what has been said above about the unconscious symbolism of eating in company it will be intelligible why the spilling of a vital substance at such a moment should be felt to be, somehow or other, a peculiarly unfortunate event. To the unconscious, from which the affective significance arises, it is equivalent on one plane to ejaculatio præcox, and on a more primitive plane to that form of infantile "accident" which psycho-

---

[1] Marian Cox, *An Introduction to Folk-Lore*, 1904, p. 10.
[2] Wuttke, op. cit., S. 311.
[3] Wuttke, loc. cit.
[4] Lawrence, op. cit., p. 166.
[5] Brand, op. cit., Vol. III, pp. 160, 162.
[6] Lawrence, op. cit., pp. 169-71.
[7] Brand, loc. cit.; Lawrence, op. cit., pp. 166, 167.
[8] Lawrence, op. cit., p. 166; Brand, op. cit., pp. 161, 162.

analysis has shown[1] to be genetically related to this unfortunate disorder. The original meaning of the superstition is hinted at in the Prussian belief[2] that to spill salt at a wedding betokens an unhappy marriage, and in the opinion of the "antiques",[3] who

> "thought love decay'd
> When the negligent maid
> Let the salt-cellar tumble before them".

It is probable that the ill-luck was formerly conceived of as rendering the salt-spiller susceptible to the malevolent influences of evil spirits,[4] and the throwing of salt over the left shoulder, with the idea of averting the ill-luck,[5] has been thought to have the object of hitting the invisible demon in the eye and so disabling him.[6] This apparently wild suggestion has its proper meaning, which we need not go into here, but it is more likely that the true object of the proceeding was to make a propitiatory offering to the demon;[7] it has a suspicious resemblance to the Burmese custom of throwing food over the left shoulder in order to conciliate the chief spirit of evil.[8] The maleficium of evil beings is predominantly concerned with interference with sexual relations and disturbances of the sexual functions; I have elsewhere pointed out in detail that the dread of it comes from the fear of impotence.[9] Counter-charms against maleficium largely consist of symbolic acts which either assert the person's potency or serve to re-establish it;

---

[1] Abraham, "Über Ejaculatio præcox," *Internationale Zeitschrift für Psychoanalyse*, 1916, Bd. IV, S. 171.

[2] Wuttke, op. cit., S. 210.

[3] Brand, op. cit., p. 163.

[4] Lawrence, loc. cit.

[5] Dallyel, op. cit., p. 101.

[6] Lawrence, op. cit., p. 167.

[7] Dalyell, loc. cit.; Lawrence, loc. cit.

[8] Lawrence, loc. cit.

[9] Der Alptraum, loc. cit.

instances of both kinds may be found in connection with the averting of evil due to the spilling of salt. In the latter class may be counted the procedure of throwing some of the spilt salt, over the left shoulder, into the fire,[1] the symbol of virility; this custom is still practised in America.[2] To the former class belong the counter-charms of throwing some of the salt out of the window,[3] and of crawling under the table and coming out on the opposite side:[4] to throw something through an aperture, or to crawl through one, symbolizes in folk-lore, dreams, and mythology, the effecting of the sexual act, a symbolism which has given rise to a large group of beliefs and customs.[5] The explanation of why the salt has to be thrown *backwards*, and why precisely over the *left* shoulder, would open up themes too extensive for us to enter on here; it is one of the many respects in which the analysis offered in this essay remains incomplete.

V

Two alternative hypotheses were set forth above concerning the origin of the excessive significance that has so widely been attached to the idea of salt, and it is maintained that the evidence detailed establishes an enormous balance of probability in favour of the second one. According to this a great part of the significance is derived, not from ideas relating to salt itself, but from ideas with which these have been unconsciously associated. Significance has been unconsciously transferred to the subject of salt from emotional sources of the greatest importance to the per-

[1] Brand, op. cit., p. 161.
[2] Johnson, *What they say in New England*, 1896, p. 92.
[3] Wuttke, op. cit., S. 312.
[4] Lawrence, op. cit., p. 170.
[5] Róheim, "The Significance of Stepping over," *International Journal of Psycho-Analysis*, 1922, Vol. III.

sonality. The natural properties of salt, which in themselves can account for only a part of the feeling with which the salt-idea has been invested, are of such a kind as to render the association of it with another substance, of universal import, an easily-made, if not an inevitable one. The significance naturally appertaining to such an important and remarkable article of diet as salt has thus been strengthened by an accession of psychical significance derived from deeper sources. Freud's view that superstitions always have a hidden logical meaning, that they constitute a betrayal of unconscious mental processes, is thereby fully confirmed in this particular example, as it has been with all the other superstitions I have investigated. This hidden meaning has the characteristic attributes of the unconscious, notably in its ambivalency, its typically sexual nature, and its close relation to infantile mental processes.

The conclusion reached, therefore, is that *salt is a typical symbol for semen*. But semen itself is ontogenetically not a primary concept, being a replacement of an earlier one concerning urine, and we have correspondingly been able to trace the roots of salt symbolism to an older source than the seminal one. There is every reason to think that the primitive mind equates the idea of salt, not only with that of semen, but also with *the essential constituent of urine*. The idea of salt in folk-lore and superstition characteristically represents the male, active, fertilizing principle.

An intuitive appreciation of the truth of this last sentence is afforded by the following panegyric paragraphs taken from the daily press, where they were headed: Man as "Salt of the Earth", Science versus Suffragists.

"Whilst the suffragists are loudly claiming equality with man—if not superiority—it has been left to scientists to establish that man is literally the 'salt of the earth'. Two famous French savants have just announced the result of a long series of investigations, which convinces them beyond all question of doubt that woman is unalterably man's inferior, because of the smaller percentage of chloride of sodium in her blood.

"In other words, the blood of the male is more salt than that of the female, and observations of animal life show that the more salt there is in the blood the higher the intelligence and general development. The indictment does not end there, for these savants declare that their combined physiological and psychological investigations have proved that woman is inferior to man in everything—intelligence, reason, and physical force. The facial angle of the female, they add, more closely resembles that of the higher animals than the male, while woman's senses are less keen than those of man and she feels pain less.

"The scientific explanation is that the blood of the female is poorer in red blood corpuscles, and therefore relatively poorer in brine, which has been found to be the important factor in the development of the individual."

*   *   *

The fact that the customs and beliefs relating to salt are exactly parallel to those relating to sexual secretions and excretions, the complex and far-reaching way in which the salt-idea is interwoven with matters of sex, particularly with potency and fertilization, the universality of the beliefs in question, the faultless illumination that every detail of the customs and beliefs relating to salt receives as soon as their symbolic signification is recognized, and the impossibility of adequately explaining them on any other basis, are considerations that render it exceedingly difficult to contest the hypothesis here sustained; in fact this can hardly be done except by ignoring the facts adduced above. The validity of the hypothesis rests on the grounds that it completely fulfils both canons of scientific reasoning: it enables one to resume disparate phenomena in a simple formula that renders them more comprehensible, and to predict the occurrence of other, previously unknown phenomena in a way that is susceptible of verification.

The only opposing position that can seriously be maintained is that, however important the association in question may have been in the past, it is no longer operative—except possibly among primitive peoples, so that the only agent responsible for the persistence of the superstition in modern times is the force of meaningless tradition. This raises an extremely important general problem—namely, how far ancient symbolisms are still operative in the minds of civilized people. The tendency of the average layman would be to regard such symbolisms as merely relics from a distant past, and to look upon knowledge concerning them as having no direct bearing on matters of present-day life.

The importance they have, however, is far from being a simply antiquarian one.[1] Psycho-analytic investigation has shown not only that symbolism plays a much more extensive part in mental functioning than was previously imagined, but also that there is a pronounced tendency for the same symbolisms to recur quite independently of the influence of other people. This is in entire accord with modern mythological and anthropological research,[2] since it is

---

[1] Roughly speaking it may be said that owing to the action of "repression" the sexual meaning of such symbolisms retreats from view during the development of civilization in much the same way as it does during the development of the individual. In both cases, however, the retreating from view means only a disappearance from consciousness, not from existence.

[2] It will be gathered from the whole tone of the present essay that the author attaches especial importance to the inter-relation of psycho-analytic and anthropological research. The anthropologist's material is rendered much more intelligible by psycho-analysis, and his views can there be submitted to verifiable tests with actual individual minds, while on the other hand through this material the psycho-analytical conclusions receive extensive confirmation, correction, and amplification. The comparative study of both fields is mutually instructive, and much is to be expected in the future from the work of men such as Róheim who are equally trained in both fields.

known that identical symbolisms occur in different parts of the world, and in different ages, in circumstances that preclude the possibility of their having been merely transmitted from one place to another. There appears to be a general tendency of the human mind to symbolize objects and interests of paramount and universal significance in forms that are psychologically the most suitable and available. That these stereotyped forms of symbolism are produced quite spontaneously is a matter capable of direct demonstration. One finds, for instance, a country farmer unconsciously exhibiting in his dreams, in his mental reactions and in his psycho-neurotic symptoms the identical symbolisms that played a part in the religions of Ancient India or Greece, and in a way so foreign to the conscious life of his environment as to exclude with certainty any course in either suggestion or tradition. In my observations of the seminal symbolism of salt, for instance, with actual patients I have come across reactions indicating unconscious attitudes of mind exactly comparable to that implied in many of the antiquated practices detailed earlier in this essay.

The most that these external influences can accomplish is to direct the unconscious process into a given form, but it cannot maintain this direction of interest unless the form of symbolism assumed becomes linked with a spontaneous interest of the individual. Thus, a person brought up in a society that took no interest in a given superstition would be less likely to develop the superstition himself than if brought up in a different society—though he might easily do so, nevertheless, especially if he were of the obsessional type of mind; but—and this is the important point—a person brought up in however superstitious a society would not develop a given superstition unless it was of such a kind as to be capable of being associated to his personal mental complexes. This association is a purely individual one, and without it the superstitious belief fails to appeal; it need hardly be said that the process, particularly in civilized communities, is most often entirely unconscious. To put the matter more concretely: what is meant is that with every person who has made his own a superstitious practice regarding salt, who follows it from an inner motive, from a "superstitious feeling"—even though he might consciously maintain that he did not believe in it—analysis would show that the idea of salt was symbolizing the idea of semen (or urine) in his unconscious mind, that this association was a personal one of his own.

The reason why certain superstitions are so widely prevalent is because the ideas are such as to render easily possible the forging of associations between them and personal ideas of general interest and significance. The conditions, however, have their definite limitations: the forging of the associations must not be either too easy or too difficult. From this point of view one may venture to suggest that the general decline of superstition among educated classes is not entirely due—as is commonly thought—to the more enlightened intelligence of such classes, but is also in part due to their greater cultural inhibition of symbolical thinking in general, and of sexual symbolism in particular.

A superstition such as that of salt-spilling is usually dismissed either as being too trivial to warrant the dignity of an explanation, or else with one that is obviously superficial and inadequate. Even in the opinions on the subject enunciated in psychological text-books the writer often gives the impression of having dispensed with an investigation sufficiently detailed to establish their validity. On the other hand, attentive consideration of any given superstition reveals how much we have to learn about the subject, and demonstrates that it is often, as in the present instance, connected with aspects of the human mind that are of fundamental importance. A psychology of religion, for example, is impossible without an understanding of superstition. Here, as elsewhere, Freud has shown that a by-way in psychology may lead to country that yields an unexpectedly rich harvest.

III

BELIEFS CONCERNING THE NIGHTMARE[1]

THERE is perhaps no sharp line to be drawn between the nightmare and other intense anxiety dreams, but the typical one is characterized not only by the overwhelming awfulness of the terror but also by a sense of oppression on the chest as of a heavy body lying there, with a consequent dread of suffocation. Intense apprehension and helpless paralysis may persist for hours after waking. The usual somatic accompaniments of morbid anxiety are also present, such as cold sweat, polyuria, and so on. Altogether it is one of the most distressing experiences that can be endured.

The beliefs, medical, theological and popular, concerning the meaning of nightmares are of peculiar historical interest, and it is only recently that a theory has been evolved which can discriminate between the admixture of truth and error in each of them.[2] The problem is evidently related to that of "morbid anxiety" in general, i.e., anxiety disproportionate to actual stimuli. In the past twenty or thirty years the extensive investigations of Freud and his co-workers have made important contributions to the pathology of morbid anxiety. They have revealed that the disproportion in question is only apparent. The anxiety is disproportionate only to the stimuli coming from the outer world, the only ones generally recognized, but not disproportionate to certain instinctual stimuli proceeding from within the organism. These are capable of evoking anxiety only when

---

[1] Read before the Royal Society of Medicine (Section of the History of Medicine), 6th April, 1932.

[2] I have dealt with this extensively in a book, *On the Nightmare*, 1931.

they are in a state of repression and so belong to the system of the unconscious. They are always sexual in nature, often with marked algolagnic components.

In early days all illness and suffering was believed to arise from malignity, proceeding either from an enemy or a hostile spirit. The development of scientific medicine meant the de-moralizing of pathology. In this laudable endeavour medicine has, however, made the old mistake of emptying the baby with the bath, for there remains an important group, nowadays recognized as neurotic suffering, where moral factors play an essential part. Repression of certain instinctual impulses is usually effected by agencies that may broadly be called moral, although they are much cruder than what perhaps should properly be so termed. Few problems illustrate this better than the pathology of the nightmare.

The popular view, dating from prehistoric times and accepted by the Christian Church, has till relatively lately been that both erotic dreams and nightmares represented sexual assaults on the part of some lewd demon, male or female according to the sex of the victim (Incubi or Succubi respectively). This view was supported by the interesting clinical observation that no sharp line of distinction can be drawn at any point in the following series: entirely agreeable erotic dreams with seminal emission (not common in this pure form)—pleasant erotic dreams with emission accompanied by a varying amount of anxiety and distress (the more usual kind)—unpleasant erotic dreams with emission accompanied or preceded by considerable anxiety —anxiety dreams with emission where it is not easy to trace any erotic element in the dream—nightmares with emission —nightmares without emission. As one proceeds along this series the erotic element, so evident at first, becomes increasingly, and finally altogether, extinguished from consciousness by the emotions of anxiety and distress, the explanation being that the (moral) repression of that element is increasingly great. The person at the beginning of the series may enjoy the embrace of the welcome demon; later on the situation becomes one of rape and finally of physical assault.

A permanent feature of this popular belief, and probably the point of it, was the disavowal of personal responsibility for any of these experiences. Had the lewd demon not put in an appearance nothing would have happened; it was entirely his doing. During the witchcraft epidemic in the closing centuries of the Middle Ages, when the Church had assimilated these experiences to matters of heresy and devil-lore, ecclesiastics began to get suspicious of this plea of innocence. Some of their investigations resembled a modern judicial inquiry into a charge of rape, and the subjects were closely examined to determine whether they had willingly submitted to the demon or had been tormented by him entirely against their will. The series described above shows that this was a very nice question, hence the difficulty in answering it.

The alternative to this spirit origin of dreams was that they originated in the body, a view which shared with its opposite the advantage of disclaiming any personal responsibility for whatever happened in them. It is older than is generally thought. The suggestion, for instance, that nightmares are provoked by gastric disturbances—now the commonly accepted opinion—may be found in the works of Galen, and it was also supported by Paulus Aegineta. This medical, somatic ætiology prevailed over the popular demon view by the sixteenth century in the case of erotic dreams, full seminal vesicles taking the place of the demon, but with nightmares it did not succeed until the eighteenth century. The delay with the latter was doubtless due to the lingering belief in witchcraft, with which, as was mentioned above, the whole subject had become interwoven.

With Freud's work on dream life at the turn of the present century an entirely different light was thrown on the whole matter. Without settling the vexed ethical question of moral responsibility for the ideas and actions occurring in dreams, his conclusion that they are the disguised expression of repressed (i.e., unconscious) wishes brings them back into the sphere of personal mental life from which both the theologians and the physicians had conspired to divorce them. The psycho-analytical conclusion about nightmares is that the causative sexual wish—so evident in most erotic dreams—is subject to an exceptional degree of repression, the reason for this being that they always originate in an incestuous wish. The attacking animal, demon, or vague pressure really represents the parent. It is probable that the extreme classical form of nightmare occurs only in persons with a considerable masochistic element in their constitution.

For the history of medicine the feature of special interest is the unwitting co-operation of the physicians with the theologians, although on apparently opposite lines, in the aim of directing thought away from the personal mental origin of these phenomena and thus ensuring that the repressed (incestuous) source of them should not be discovered. The physicians were right in maintaining that these experiences arose from within, but wrong in thinking that "within" could mean only the body. The theologians were right in maintaining the spiritual origin of the experiences and their purposive, intentional nature, but wrong in ascribing it to outside entities instead of those within the personality.

IV

PSYCHO-ANALYSIS AND ANTHROPOLOGY[1]

WHEN a worker in one field presents to those in another field some of his conclusions in the hope that they may be of interest and use when applied to other data, it behoves him to do so in a duly tentative and modest spirit. This attitude is particularly called for when his sphere of activity possesses such peculiar characteristics as does that of psycho-analysis, where he knows that he can count only on incredulity and opposition from those not familiar with the subject. The instinctive resentment, however politely disguised, which is felt towards an intruder who ventures to make suggestions concerning the work of a strange group can only be intensified when these suggestions are as unwelcome and unflattering as so many psycho-analytical ones are. The present occasion possesses, however, one feature which may prove to be of historical interest; it is, I believe, the first time that the doctrines of psycho-analysis have been propounded before an anthropological audience.

Three considerations encouraged me to accept our President's invitation to say something about the work on which we are engaged, and to point out the bearing which I conceive it to have on anthropological studies. In the first place, a psychologist has after all a certain claim to be represented in such studies, inasmuch as the mental data there investigated form a part of his own province. Indeed, in appraising the interpretation of mental data, and in coming to some judgement on their meaning and significance,

[1] Read before the Royal Anthropological Institute, 19th February, 1924. Published in the *Journal* of the Institute, Vol. LIV.

the psychologist should really have as much to say as the collector of the data; that he has had so little say in the past has depended more on the backwardness of his own science than on the logic of the situation. The earlier authorities on anthropology, such as the founders of this Institute, had two deficiencies so apparently overwhelming that the distance to which they were able to proceed in spite of them must compel our deep respect. For they had not observed themselves the mental phenomena which they studied, nor were they trained in the psychological interpretation of such phenomena. Anthropologists have freely recognized this state of affairs, and the members of the younger generation have taken practical steps to remedy at least the first of the two deficiencies just mentioned. As a result the field-worker to-day has an unquestioned advantage over those to whom in overweening pride he sometimes refers as "arm-chair anthropologists". He also starts fair with the psychologist, each possessing one advantage and one defect. In these circumstances the two can only profitably approach each other in a spirit of mutual benevolence and co-operate together in their work until they are both superseded by a race of anthropologists who are experienced in field-work and also trained in the methods of modern psychology. The first member of this race, however, has yet to make his appearance.[1]

In the second place, the similarity of the data investigated by anthropologists and by psycho-analysts is often so striking and unexpected as positively to call out for explanation, so that it becomes one's duty at least to draw the attention of anthropologists to the fact. In our laborious investigations of the hidden recesses of the mind we come across some group of ideas, some implicit belief, some mode of mental functioning which is altogether alien to our experience of the conscious mind as we know it, and for which

[1] Since this was written he has appeared, in the person of Dr. Geza Róheim.

no counterpart is to be found in our experience of life. The findings are so unequivocal that we have to accept them empirically even when we may not be able to relate them to any previous knowledge. Further, certain features accompanying them lead us to infer that they represent a more archaic layer of the mind than those we are accustomed to, one which has been passed and covered over by the latter in the course of development. Then to our amazement we read that identical beliefs or forms of thought have been recorded either in the folk-lore and mythology of bygone days or in savage races of the present time. What are we to think of this? To begin with, it must confirm our conclusion that the findings were not artefacts of our observation, and also that they represent some more primitive stage of mental development. But the obvious question of the relation of the two sets of phenomena to each other at once raises some of the most obscure problems of biological psychology, and opens up the whole subject of culture and inheritance. Of the innumerable examples that could be brought forward I will cite only one, but it should be enough to indicate the sort of thing with which we have to deal. In his investigations of the sources of "dream thoughts", the thoughts that lie behind the "manifest content" of dreams, Freud made the astonishing discovery that they never contain a negative, so that a positive idea and its exact opposite are treated as being identical. To put it plainly, contrasting ideas like "big" and "little", "strong" and "weak", "old" and "young" are treated as if they were interchangeable identities, and it is only from the context that one can discover which of the two is meant in any given case. It would be hard to imagine anything more senseless or more remote from our ordinary mental processes, but repeated confirmations of the finding forced Freud to accept it empirically, although he could give no reason for its existence. It was only many years later that the matter became somewhat more comprehensible to him[1] on coming across a work by a philologist, Abel, dealing with just the same phenomenon in the early stages of the oldest languages, Egyptian, Arabic and Indo-Germanic, and showing that the present differentiation has proceeded from an original identity of opposite ideas. There are interesting traces still left even in modern languages, such as with the German "schau" and the English "show". This example is one of a mode of thought, not content, and alike ones could be quoted relating to definite beliefs or other groups of ideas.

The third of the considerations referred to above is the gradual convergence of anthropological and psycho-analytical points of view. Psycho-analysis, being from the start concerned with obviously human and individual problems, has not had the chequered career that we have seen with anthropological interpretations, nor the same opportunity and temptation to take flight into the abstract and remote. Myths, rituals, and the other data studied by the social anthropologists have in the past been read in terms of very recondite mental pursuits which were imagined to be the chief preoccupation of primitive man. I need hardly mention the engrossing interest in the forms of clouds, the rounds of the moon, the movement of the sun, the constructing of calendars, and purely linguistic exercises which have at times been supposed to prepossess mankind to the exclusion of more mundane matters. Sir James Frazer, it is true, brought man nearer to earth by positing his absorption in the phenomena of agriculture, and other workers have tracked him still nearer home. The news brought to Europe at various times in the last century that man in other continents seemed to manifest an unseemly interest in the organs and functions of sex was quickly re-interpreted in a more becoming way, and the flicker of agitation induced in

[1] Freud, "Über den Gegensinn der Urworte," *Jahrbuch der Psycho-Analyse*, 1910.

this Institute by the phallicists of the seventies, Burton, Fergusson, Furlong, Jennings, King, Sellon, Staniland Wake, and Westropp, was soon quenched by more sedate reflections. But voices continued to be raised in favour of the view that man has always been moved by motives similar to those that occupy our own deepest thoughts, by the topics of birth, love, and death, and the most recent authorities in this country, such as Elliot Smith, Malinowski, Perry, and Rivers, have made considerable contributions to what may be called the humanization of primitive man. This theme will take up the greater part of my paper this evening, so that I can leave it for a moment at this point.

I have now to return from these reflections on anthropology to consider more closely the subject of psychoanalysis, but before I can indicate any of the bearings it may have on anthropological studies it will obviously be desirable to say something about psycho-analysis itself.[1] The name is properly applied to the special method devised by Freud for investigating the deeper regions of the mind, and to the findings thus made. The subject-matter of psycho-analysis is quite exceptionally complex, and thus the task of presenting any adequate account of it in the ten minutes or so at my disposal for the purpose is clearly an impossible one. In addition, there is an even greater difficulty in the way than this merely quantitative consideration. The most significant discovery made by psychoanalysis is that there exists in the human mind a region, known as the "unconscious", which is split off from consciousness. Much of it, indeed the most important part, is in what is technically called a state of "repression"; that is, as

---

[1] The literature in English most apposite in the present connection is as follows: Abraham, *Dreams and Myths*; Ferenczi, *Contributions to Psycho-Analysis*; Freud, *Introductory Lectures on Psycho-Analysis*, and *Totem and Taboo*; Ernest Jones, *Papers on Psycho-Analysis*, and (more advanced) *Essays in Applied Psycho-Analysis*; Rank, *The Myth of the Birth of the Hero*; Rank and Sachs, *The Significance of Psycho-Analysis for the Mental Sciences*.

regards both content and form it is incompatible with the conscious mind, its constituents are powerfully inhibited from entering the latter, and its very existence is vehemently denied by the conscious ego. Any attempt at introducing them into consciousness evokes an instinctive resistance which manifests itself as incredulity, violent opposition, or strong antipathy. Those who follow the easy path of yielding to this instinctive resistance spare themselves a great deal of trouble, but they thereby forfeit the right to express any opinion about psycho-analysis, for this subject may well be defined as the study of the unconscious mind.

This is not the place to enter into the perfectly arid discussion of whether processes of which we are not conscious can properly be called "mental", one which in my opinion is nothing but a quarrel about words,[1] and I will therefore ask you to allow me to describe what I have to say in the only possible terminology, namely, psychological. The main point is this: Our investigations (inaugurated by Freud) show that various processes, which can only be described in mental terms, go on in the personality without the conscious self having the very faintest idea of their existence. We call them "unconscious" because man is totally unconscious of their existence, and I wish to lay stress on the completeness of his ignorance; the subject not only has no suspicion of them, but if they were mentioned to him he would regard them as exceedingly remote and alien to himself, and would greet with incredulity or horror the possibility of their being actually vivid constituents of his own personality. In fact, I know of no way of anyone's appreciating the reality and significance of these unconscious processes except by experiencing the analytic bringing to awareness of ideas whose existence he had never before recognized. This state

---

[1] *See* Freud, *Das Unbewusste*, Sammlung Kleiner Schriften, 4e Folge, 1918, S. 294-301.

of affairs raises two obvious questions: Can any generalizations be made about the nature and meaning of these
unconscious processes, and if so what reason is there for
thinking that such generalizations have a wide validity outside the small group of individuals actually investigated by
these methods?

The answer to the first question is in the affirmative, and
I propose presently to relate a selection of the generalizations that have been made. As to the second question, the
following are some of the reasons for believing that these
generalizations possess a wide validity outside the sphere—
that of neurotic disorder—in connection with which they
were originally made. Though the actual number of individuals thoroughly investigated by means of psycho-
analysis is relatively small, only a few thousand, yet
certain features warrant the expectation that they do not
differ from the rest of mankind in fundamental structure.
In the first place, the investigations have been made, with
a general uniformity of result, in many countries of every
continent, among widely differing races, and by very
different types of observer. The main selecting element has
been the presence of neurotic disorder in the majority,
though by no means all, of the persons investigated, but in
estimating this fact certain popular misconceptions have to
be borne in mind. Modern clinical psychology has shown
that neurotic disorder is not a disease or defect in the
ordinary sense, but on the contrary simply one particular
mode of expression of certain social difficulties and conflicts
arising within the emotional and instinctual life; they are
merely one way among several of responding to human
conflicts and impulses of a kind that are common to all
people. The reactions are not even very peculiar, being
merely magnifications of the normal and not qualitatively
different; apart from the fact that most people exhibit
some form of neurosis, more or less pronounced, these

PSYCHO-ANALYSIS AND ANTHROPOLOGY

neurotic reactions fade imperceptibly into what are called character-formations and idiosyncrasies. No person is entirely neurotic, so that we have the opportunity of examining in the same person both normal and neurotic reactions to the same conflicts and impulses. Further, the control experiment has been performed a good number of times of carrying out a psycho-analysis on so-called normal people, and the fundamental conclusions are just the same. Then, again, once one is familiar with the manifestations of unconscious activity, one observes other indications of similar processes in the most various spheres of everyday life. Let me take the simplest example. A psychologist may discover, perhaps to his great astonishment, that the dreams of his patients show that they, without ever having been consciously aware of the fact, have associated, for instance, the ideas of penis and banana so closely that the idea of the latter can in certain contexts be treated as quite equivalent to the latter. He is thus no longer surprised when he observes that, again given a certain context, a whole music-hall audience can consciously recognize an allusion to the first idea when the second alone is mentioned. Slang, anecdotes, folk-lore and superstition are fields in which one meets with special frequency associations and beliefs the existence of which may have to be laboriously excavated from a part of the mind where they are in a state of repression. The final answer to the question raised above, however, lies in the nature of the findings themselves. These are of such a fundamental character that, roughly speaking, *they can only be true of mankind in general or else not true at all.* If a similar question had been put to Harvey: "You have demonstrated the circulation of the blood by a detailed examination of five thousand animals, but how do you know that they are not all exceptions in this respect?" I imagine he would have answered such a question only by shrugging his shoulders.

Something must now be said about the nature of the unconscious mind. It possesses quite peculiar features in both its form and its content, though these need not, of course, be present with every single unconscious process. Common to all features is some indication of their belonging to a primitive mental level, and here comes in the importance of these studies for anthropology, for we have in them one of the possibilities of ascertaining at first hand what primitive mental levels really are. The term "primitive level" is used here in two senses: first, as indicating an earlier and more lowly stage in mental evolution, one out of which further, more elaborate and more highly differentiated forms of thought demonstrably develop; and, secondly, in direct reference to individual growth. For we find that the features in question, both those of form and of content, approximate in kind far more nearly to those of infantile mental life than to those characteristic of adult life; in fact, we are frequently in a position to trace the gradual development of the former into the latter. This evolution has been an imperfect one in the case of the neuroses, so that we often connect neurotic reactions with what are called "fixations" or excessive attachment to primitive, i.e., infantile, modes of mental functioning. Put in a more figurative way, we may say that the neurotic reactions are like residues or deposits from earlier times, and the interesting question arises how far this may be true phylogenetically as well as ontogenetically.

It was pointed out above that the unconscious mind is unconscious, i.e., unknown to consciousness, mainly because of its being in a state of repression, that is, of being incompatible with the conscious ego and intolerable to it. To describe it in more dynamic terms: the relationship between the two mental systems is the expression of serious intrapsychical conflicts. Now the importance of the unconscious in actual life is not merely that it is a system of the mind which can function in an autonomous way, but that *all* mental functioning originates in it; all our thoughts, interests, and conscious impulses leading to conduct have their source in the unconscious. The conscious mind contributes nothing beyond criticism, control and direction; the part it plays is essentially obstructive. Unconscious processes can come to external expression only under one of two conditions; either they undergo a transformation of such a kind as to render them acceptable to the conscious ego, into which they are then assimilated; or their true nature is disguised in certain characteristic ways, such as, for instance, when unavowed personal feelings find a vent in excessive acerbity under the guise of scientific criticism. Neurotic symptoms, incidentally, belong entirely to the second class; the dynamic impulses giving rise to them are primitive, i.e., untransformed, and merely disguised.

Out of a large number of features characteristic of the unconscious I now propose to call your attention to two or three of a general, formal nature and two or three relating to its content. The first one can perhaps best be described as an attitude of excessive belief in the value and significance of psychical processes in general. Psychical causation is felt to be more real than physical causation, the latter being merely the agent of the former. This registers itself most clearly in what is called belief in the "omnipotence of thoughts", or, more accurately, of wishes. In the unconscious, little distinction is drawn between intention and the carrying out of the act; intent and performance are treated as identical. If the intention is pleasurable, the pleasure is already tasted; for the wish passes immediately into fulfilment, as to some extent it can in conscious phantasy. Similarly, if the intention is dangerous or reprehensible, the punishment is already felt. Perhaps the most striking example of this mode of thought is that of those death wishes that are in a state of repression because of their being directed against a loved object. On the occasions when the imaginary fulfilment of this wish coincides with a real fulfilment brought about by some accident in the outer world, the person feels unconsciously just as responsible for the death, and just as guilty, as though he had actually committed murder. The effect in consciousness then is a greatly exaggerated sense of self-reproach for various minor sins of omission and commission relating to the deceased person. I have several times known this state of affairs to be followed by ghostly visitations accompanied by acute dread of the ghost's hostility, this evidently being an idea of retribution for the supposed murder.

These repressed but all-powerful wishes are dealt with in many different ways, of which one only will be mentioned here. On the basis of a preliminary identification, usually with a person, but occasionally with an animal or inanimate object, the wishes are "projected" outwards and then are *consciously* believed to belong only to the other person. The most glaring example of this is, of course, in the delusions of the insane, where the irrational beliefs held about other people can often be traced to unconscious beliefs held by the subject about these same people.

One result of this unconscious over-estimation of the power of thought is a tendency to ascribe external happenings to spiritual forces and to depreciate the significance of physical factors, just as a truly religious man must logically ascribe everything immediately to God's will and has only a limited interest in the rest of the causative chain. Its consummation is a perfectly animistic state of mind, of which we see plain traces in our children when they get angry with the table for being so wicked as to injure them.

Now I feel confident that what I have just been relating will sound a good deal less novel to anthropologists familiar with savage races than it does to the average European. Case after case could be quoted from the literature where savages have held one another just as responsible for their intentions as for their deeds, and on reading the descriptions given I for one cannot avoid the impression that they must at times possess a high capacity for divining the unconscious thoughts of their neighbours. Their judgements are therefore often psychologically accurate, even when objectively unjust. The extraordinarily objective significance they often attach to dream processes is a part of the same phenomenon and, as Freud has shown,[1] it really underlies the whole of the practice of magic. It seems clear that savages live to a much greater extent than we do in a mystical or supernatural world. They constantly manifest beliefs in various occult forces, influences and activities that are imperceptible to sense, but which are nevertheless obviously and unquestionably real to them; this is not a matter of inference and explanation so much as direct intuition. It is practically certain that many of these supposed purposive agents in the outer world are projections from the unconscious mind. The remarkable extent to which savages seem to be preoccupied with thoughts about wizardry, witchcraft, and evil spirits of all kinds inevitably makes a psychoanalyst suspect that their unconscious minds must contain specially intense wishes of a hostile nature, which have been extensively projected into the outer world.

A word on the vexed question of symbolism in its relation to the unconscious.[2] It can often be observed that in certain circumstances various ideas or objects may be treated identically in consciousness, the points of distinction between them being ignored for the time being, and just the same is true of the unconscious. But a further process has to take place before we can speak of true symbolism. That is the repression of one member of the equation, and the sub-

[1] Freud, *Totem und Tabu*, 1913, Ch. III.
[2] *See* my essay on the "Theory of Symbolism", reprinted in *Papers on Psycho-Analysis*, Fifth Edition, 1949.

stitutive use of the other member to "symbolize", i.e., carry
the significance of, the first. One half of this equation is
practically always more important psychically than the
other, the important one being the repressed and symbolized
part. From the nature of things, therefore, symbolism is a
unilateral process only; A can symbolize B, but B cannot
symbolize A. Almost all unconscious symbolism is confined to
the themes of birth, love and death, and to thoughts about the
body and the nearest relatives—from which we infer that
these must comprise the fundamental interests of mankind.

The two groups of ideas I shall select from the content of
the unconscious are those relating to incest and death
respectively. Perhaps the most vital discovery made by
psycho-analysis, and certainly the source of most of the
hostility it has met, was that every young child passes
through a phase of incestuous attachment, mostly to the
parent of the opposite sex, and that the ideas relating to
this constitute throughout life a nuclear content of the
unconscious. To the individual's reaction to this "complex"
they would ascribe a very great part of his character-
formation, especially on the moral and social side, and very
many of his conscious reactions to life—his interest, conduct, and so on. To put the matter in its crudest terms so
that there may be no misapprehension, we believe that
every man cherishes in his unconscious the wish for sexual
intimacy with his mother and the desire to remove by
death any disturbing rival, particularly his father; the converse applies equally to the woman, the term "Œdipus
complex" being used in both cases. Such a statement,
abhorrent as it must sound, is nevertheless the core of
psycho-analysis and inseparable from it. For the evidence
in support of this apparently grotesque hypothesis I can
only refer you to the extensive psycho-analytical literature
dealing with it, nor could I have any hope of demonstrating
its truth and convincing you of it in the few minutes at my

disposal. My reason for mentioning it here at all is to point out that, if it is true, it is bound to throw a flood of light on some of the most obscure problems in anthropology. To take but one of them: the almost universal horror of incest, and the extraordinarily complicated and fierce laws that have been devised in the most varied parts of the world with the object of preventing it. It is well-known that previous explanations of this have proved most unsatisfactory, and no one has answered Frazer's[1] convincing argument that laws of this order are made only for crimes towards which a strong and widespread temptation exists. The argument ends in a *non possumus*; incest could not be forbidden so stringently unless there were a general inclination towards it; but the laws do exist and there is no inclination. Psycho-analysis, on the other hand, points out that the strong and universal inclination towards incest, which is logically implied in the argument, *does* really exist, only that for the most part it is repressed in the unconscious; it is an inclination of which we are mostly quite unaware, but it is none the less real and important. Time forbids me to enter on the endless ramifications that lead from this idea, but anthropologists know how numerous and important are the problems that relate, directly or indirectly, to incest. I can do no more than mention one or two; the endless initiation rites and ceremonies of both savage and civilized races,[2] the numerous myths and cosmogonies where the content is either openly or symbolically incestuous, and the vast problems of totemism itself.[3]

The second group of ideas in the unconscious of which I wish to say something, namely, those relating to death, will be discussed presently in connection with some current anthropological views. After this absurdly imperfect sketch

[1] Frazer, *Totemism and Exogamy*, Vol. IV, p. 97.
[2] *See* Reik, *Problems of Religious Psychology*, Ch. III.
[3] *See* Freud, op. cit., Ch. IV, and a forthcoming work on the subject by Róheim.

of the psycho-analytical theory we must turn to the bearing of it on anthropological problems, and here too I can offer only the briefest of outlines.

It is an easily made observation that the ire of anthropologists is almost as readily aroused by the assertion that savages cannot be compared with children as by the opposite one that they can be so compared. Similarly, one invites contradiction by maintaining either that a vast gulf exists between savages and ourselves, or that there is no appreciable difference between us. I trust, therefore, that I shall be striking a peaceful note when I suggest that there is truth in all of the four statements though a more profound truth than is sometimes recognized. The reason why this diplomatic attitude is possible is because the psycho-analytical view of both children and civilized adults differs in some important respects from the usual one. We find, on the one hand, that the two modes of thought that for present purposes may be called infantile and adult respectively—corresponding roughly with unconscious and conscious thinking—differ from each other very profoundly indeed, far more so than might ordinarily be imagined; but on the other hand that children and adults manifest the two modes of thought in no very dissimilar measure. Thus there is more of the infant in the adult than is commonly recognized, and also more of the adult in the child. Or, to put it in another way, there are enormous differences, but these are not so much between child and adult as between two modes of thinking which are present in both. Stated in terms of values, this results in a greater respect for the mind of the child and a less respect for that of the adult.

Now I surmise that very much the same may prove to be true as regards the relationship between savage and civilized peoples. If so, this would mean two things. First, that much of the supposed deficiency of primitive peoples in such functions as concentration, reason, powers of discrimination and logic, and so on, is not due to the lack of these qualities so much as to a different orientation of emotional interest from our own, as Hocart[1] has brilliantly demonstrated in his study of the Fijian language; recognition of this would lead to a greater approximation of the savage mind to our own. Secondly, however, the difference between primitive emotional thinking and logical reason uninfluenced by subjective factors must be regarded as very great, and it is quite possible that there is a quantitative difference between savages and civilized peoples in this respect, just as there is after all between children and adults. In other words, it is possible that the conscious thinking of savages is more directly and extensively influenced by unconscious factors than is that of civilized peoples, just as is so with the child. In making this suggestion I wish to guard myself against the charge of underestimating the complexity of the relationship in question. Naturally there is no thought of mental evolution having progressed in a uniform and orderly manner, without any retrogressions and other complications, nor do I imagine that there is anything more than the very grossest correspondence between this evolution and the ethnological grading that may be effected in regard to the present races of mankind.

I come next to the convergence of psycho-analytical and modern anthropological views to which reference was made earlier in this paper. The most important point of correspondence is the tendency in both cases to interpret data in terms of purely human and self-centred motives of a kind which critics might dub materialistic. Few anthropologists to-day would expect savages to be primarily concerned either with ethical abstractions or with lofty philosophical speculations about the universe. Those who used to imagine this did not recognize the more lowly nature and origin of

[1] Hocart, "The Psychological Interpretation of Language," *Brit. Journal of Psychology*, 1913, Vol. V.

their own interests. The primitive interests of mankind lie nearer home, in his own breast, and that must be as true of the savage as psycho-analysis has shown it to be of ourselves. Man is primarily concerned with his immediate personal interests; to these everything else is really secondary. The world is originally viewed from within out, and our inmost thoughts and interests are projected on to it as on a vast screen. Elliot Smith, for instance, declares the *leit motif* of man's civilization to be his desire for continuous self-preservation, in both this life and the next, and he holds that from the search for the various objects which were supposed to ensure this resulted much of man's cultural endeavour. This view will be considered more closely in a moment, and I only wish to remark here on its agreement with the psycho-analytical theory in attaching importance to the more human, personal, and indeed egocentric motives as being the fundamental ones. His tremendous generalization, further, that "all the beliefs of primitive man concerning the nature of life can ultimately be referred back to the story of his own origin, his birth or creation,"[1] is one that would meet with extensive support from the side of psycho-analysis and is quite on the lines of a recent important study by Otto Rank.[2]

Another field in which the convergence of conclusions is very striking in many ways is that of symbolism, and I venture to think that the correspondence would be even closer were it not for the confusion that exists about what actually constitutes symbolism. For us the expression denotes the process whereby one idea is used (mostly unwittingly) as a substitute for an unconscious idea. The number of unconscious ideas is relatively small, far smaller than that of the symbolizing ideas. From the interpretation side the two questions are: when is a given idea being used

---

[1] Elliot Smith, *The Evolution of the Dragon*, 1919, p. 45.
[2] Otto Rank, *Das Trauma der Geburt*, 1924.

symbolically? a matter that cannot be gone into here; and which unconscious idea or ideas is it symbolizing? It should be remembered that none of the psycho-analytical conclusions about symbols and the interpretation of them were derived from familiarity with anthropological data, but from laborious studies carried out on individuals. The circumstance makes the correspondence with anthropological data especially interesting. I can give here only a few examples of this, and for the sake of uniformity will choose them from the writings of two members of the same school, Elliot Smith and W. J. Perry. Psycho-analysts have long remarked that objects possessing a fancied resemblance to the female pudenda, as cowry shells are supposed to, can function as symbols of the latter. Elliot Smith[1] quotes two eighteenth-century writers, Rumphius and Adanson, who pointed out this attribute of cowries, and comes to the conclusion that the whole of the complex shell-cult was based on this circumstance. The cowry, being thus a symbol of the female pudenda, became endowed with various life-giving powers. But Elliot Smith has made two further steps in this connection, both on purely psycho-analytic lines. A common mode of unconscious representation is by the mechanism known as *pars pro toto*, when a part is used to represent the whole, as with an allusion. A much more curious one is the exact opposite of this, when the whole is used to represent a part, such as when a little man appears in a dream as a symbol of the male organ itself, or a woman as a symbol of the female organ. Now, Elliot Smith, after pointing[2] out how the cowry "came to be identified with, or regarded as, the mother and creator of the human family", then becoming personified in the figure of the Great Mother Goddess, states it as a fact that this "Great Mother was

[1] Elliot Smith, Introduction to Wilfred Jackson's *Shells as Evidence of the Migrations of Early Culture*, 1917, p. 111.
[2] Elliot Smith, *The Evolution of the Dragon*, p. 26.

nothing more than the cowry shell".[1] We should describe this same fact by saying that the Goddess was here functioning as a symbol of the womb, or, put in another way, that the only interest in the Great Mother *in this particular context* resided in her genital organ. Thirdly, in just the same sense as I insisted above that unconscious association was really actual identification, he writes:[2] "The cowry was not merely an amulet to increase fertility: it was itself the actual parent of mankind, the creator of all living things." The identification of the Mother Pot with the Great Mother, or rather with her womb, is a similar example of what we mean by true symbolism, and Elliot Smith points out some of its extraordinary ramifications: "At first, it was merely a jug of water or a basket of figs, but elsewhere it became a witch's cauldron, the magic cup, the Holy Grail, the font in which a child is reborn into the faith, the vessel of water here being interpreted in the earliest sense as the uterus or the organ of birth."[3] Yet another familiar group of symbols in psycho-analytical work is a portal, door, or gateway as unconscious representatives of the vaginal opening, and here also Elliot Smith[4] is in full accord with us. One of the most recent discoveries in our field is that the spider or octopus may function as a symbol for the Mother,[5] but I find that Elliot Smith had already independently pointed this out, though the way he suggests the symbolism arose[6] (cowry—Red Sea "spider shell"—octopus) is assuredly not the only one possible, unless we are to suppose that our patients have all inherited memories of their ancestors' sojourn by the Red Sea.

An unexpected psycho-analytic finding was that animals,

[1] Idem, op. cit., p. 216.
[2] Idem, op. cit., p. 151.
[3] Idem, op. cit., p. 181.
[4] Idem, op. cit., p. 188.
[5] Abraham, "The Spider as a Dream Symbol," *Internat. Journ. of Psycho-Analysis*, 1923, Vol. IV, p. 313.
[6] Elliot Smith, op. cit., p. 169.

in dreams or neurotic symptoms, most often symbolize one or other parents or else children, and that the thoughts to do with them were often connected with ideas about birth. Perry[1] tells us that in Egypt "the cow was regarded as a form of the Great Mother, because she feeds children with her milk"; and, of course, endless similar examples could be quoted from mythology and folk-lore. This one discovery opens up a large chapter in anthropology, particularly in relation to totemism, as Freud[2] has shown in detail.

Another remarkable discovery of psycho-analysis was that every individual passes in early life through a phase of bisexuality, and that the unconscious always retains important traces of this stage in development. This means that, although the masculine and feminine principles can be fairly clearly differentiated, neither of them is anything like so definitely confined to the appropriate sex as is commonly thought. The unconscious not only interchanges the two sexes with an astonishing freedom, but other curious traces are left of the primitive attitude towards sex.[3] Ample evidences of the same free interchange are to be found in anthropological data. A characteristic bisexual symbol may be mentioned in this connection, that of water. We find that water plays a very extensive part in dream symbolism, and other products of the unconscious, in connection with ideas of birth,[4] and that it plays the same part here as the amniotic fluid does in reality. From Elliot Smith[5] we hear that in Ancient Egypt "a bowl of water became the symbol of the fruitfulness of woman.[6] Such symbolism implied that

---

[1] Perry, *The Origin of Magic and Religion*, 1923, p. 19.

[2] Freud, ibid.

[3] This word is used here in a narrower sense than "sexuality".

[4] The late Dr. Rivers (*Folk-Lore*, 1922, Vol. XXXIII, p. 20 *et seq.*) showed considerable misconception of the psycho-analytic views on this point in his unsuccessful attempt to controvert them.

[5] Elliot Smith, op. cit., p. 152.

[6] In my opinion, it would be more accurate to say here that it was a symbol of the pregnant womb and was only a metaphor for the idea of fruitfulness.

woman, or her uterus, was a receptacle into which the seminal fluid was poured and from which a new being emerged in a flood of amniotic fluid", and he adds elsewhere[1] that water became an essential part of any act of ritual (i.e., symbolic) rebirth. He points out further[2] the womb origin of the Mother Pot conception, and that a bowl of water was the hieroglyphic sign for the female principle in the words for vulva and woman. On the other hand, we find in psycho-analysis that water, rain, etc., are also common unconscious symbols for the male fertilizing fluid, whether this is regarded as semen or, in infantile language, as urine. Perry[3] tells us that Osiris differed from the Mother Goddesses in one important particular, namely, that he presided over irrigation, and Elliot Smith[4] says that it is not surprising in consequence that Osiris "should have had phallic attributes, and in himself have personified the virile powers of fertilization"; he also comments[5] on the equivalency of the ideas of spilling water on or irrigating the earth and the act of coition. As is well known, ideas concerning water constituted one of the respects in which the attributes of the Egyptian Gods and Goddesses respectively became extraordinarily confounded one with the other, and I would suggest that this process was greatly facilitated by the existence of a primitive stage of bisexuality.

An interesting relic of this stage is derived from the primitive belief that women, particularly the Mother, are similar anatomically to men, and that there is no noteworthy difference between the clitoris and the penis. This idea plays a huge part in the psychology of neurotic disorder in both sexes, and is one of the sources of the dread of the "terrible Mother", which may of course exist side by side

[1] Idem, op. cit., p. 33.
[2] Idem, op. cit., pp. 178, 182, 183.
[3] Perry, op. cit., p. 28.
[4] Elliot Smith, op. cit., p. 30.
[5] Idem, op. cit., pp. 28, 29.

with profound affection. This plays also an extensive part in mythology, as witness the many portals with phallic emblems, the male attributes ascribed to Mother Goddesses in Egypt and elsewhere (uræus, vulture, papyrus, etc.) and, as Freud has shown,[1] it is the ultimate basis of the widespread taboo of virginity.

I come finally to the famous "self-preservation" theory of the modern British school of ethnology, and will begin by quoting a discerning passage from Elliot Smith,[2] who I understand is the author of the theory: "The interpretation of ancient texts and the study of the beliefs of less cultured modern peoples indicate that our expressions: 'to give birth', 'to give life', 'to maintain life', 'to ward off death', 'to insure good luck', 'to prolong life', 'to give life to the dead', 'to animate a corpse or a representation of the dead', 'to give fertility', 'to impregnate', 'to create', represent a series of specializations of meaning which were not clearly differentiated the one from the other in early times or among relatively primitive modern people." Now I would submit that this vagueness and imperfect differentiation relate rather to the conscious apprehension and expression of these peoples than to the facts themselves on which the ideas were based, so that it may not be a hopeless task for us to attempt to distinguish the relative strength of the actual motivating forces. If we were to ask the authors and supporters of the self-preservation theory to effect this differentiation, I am inclined to think that their answer could be summed up in the statement that the strongest motive in the group they are considering, or possibly even in all mankind, was the wish to overcome death. This includes both the desire to ward off death (i.e., to prolong life, to maintain life, etc.) and the desire to perpetuate life beyond the grave,

---

[1] Freud, *Das Tabu der Virginität*, Sammlung kleiner Schriften, 4e Folge, 1918.

[2] Elliot Smith, op. cit., p. 25.

which, as we know, was effected by a ritual of rebirth (the central idea of mummification). We have thus to inquire into the primordial conception of death and life after death, and here also I will take a passage from Elliot Smith[1] as a text. "From statements in the earliest literature that have come down to us from antiquity, no less than from the views that still prevail among the relatively more primitive peoples of the present day, it is clear that originally man did not consciously formulate a belief in immortality. It was rather the result of a defect of thinking, or as the modern psychologist would express it, an instinctive repression of the unpleasant idea that death would come to him personally, that primitive man refused to contemplate or to entertain the possibility of life coming to an end. So intense was his instinctive love of life and dread of such physical damage as would destroy his body that man unconsciously avoided thinking of the chance of his own death: hence his belief in the continuance of life cannot be regarded as the outcome of an active process of constructive thought. . . . It would, of course, be absurd to pretend that any people could fail to recognize the reality of death in the great majority of cases. The mere fact of burial is an indication of this. But the point of difference between the views of these early men and ourselves was the tacit assumption on the part of the former that in spite of the obvious changes in his body (which made inhumation or some other procedure necessary) the deceased was still continuing an existence not unlike that which he enjoyed previously, only somewhat duller, less eventful and more precarious. He still needed food and drink as he did before, and all the paraphernalia of his mortal life, but he was dependent upon his relatives for the maintenance of his existence."

There are two chapters in this matter of preserving life after death, according to whether it is a question of our own

[1] Idem, op. cit., pp. 145, 146.

136

life or someone else's. The latter part of the problem appears to have been unduly subordinated by the British school of ethnology, and for that reason I will omit discussion of it here. But I would express my belief that it is highly important, and that a clue to its meaning is given by the fact that the significance attached to the second person's survival is much greater when he is a king, chief, elder or other great person[1] (i.e., a father substitute).[2] We will, however, confine ourselves to the problem of what may be called self-survival, which is an integral part of the self-preservation theory.

To those who have followed the argument of this paper so far it may be of interest to hear what ideas concerning death are to be found in the unconscious. In one sense it may be said that there are none, for the unconscious conceives of this idea in quite a different way from the conscious mind. The nearest approach it makes to the latter is when it is a matter of other people's death. This it regards, as does the child, simply in the light of a removal or absence, more or less prolonged, the question of eternity hardly entering in. One's own death, on the other hand, in the sense of the extermination of life, is absolutely inconceivable to the unconscious, and, indeed, the idea is hard fully to realize in consciousness. In the context where one would expect it to occur one of two other ideas appears in its stead. In the first place, the idea of dying—really of being killed—may be taken in the sense of being severely injured in a vital part, i.e., castrated, and this idea of being castrated (in either sex) is always regarded as the punishment for incestuous wishes. The second, and deeper, way in which the unconscious regards death is as a reversal of the birth act,

---

[1] See Freud, *Totem und Tabu*, Ch. II.

[2] This is an illustration of the quite one-sided nature of the argument in the latter part of this paper, for it deals only with the individual's relation to the Mother and omits consideration of the almost equally important relation to the Father.

leading to a return to the pre-natal existence within the maternal womb. It is plain that this must have relation to the innumerable rituals or rebirth symbolism, both in heathen religions and in Christianity, as the sovereign measure for conquering death and securing immortality; endless myths and folk beliefs, which I have no time to quote here, bear witness to this primitive conception of death as a return to the womb, to the conviction that life can only return to the bourne whence it set forth. Both the ideas mentioned, therefore, are related to the act of entering once more through the maternal portal, whether partly, as in coitus,[1] or wholly, as at birth. It is noteworthy, further, that these two acts are regarded as equivalents by the unconscious, another example of the extraordinary extent to which it differs from our conscious thinking.

If our findings are correct, and no one qualified by personal investigation has any doubt on the matter, then we should be in a position to supplement the self-preservation theory in a number of important respects, of which I shall briefly indicate three. The first has to do with the maternal symbols used in the ritual of rebirth. I imagine that Elliot Smith and his colleagues would be inclined to regard these somewhat as follows. Believing that the womb was either the creator or, at all events, the source of life, the ancients effected an abstraction of the idea and used various tokens possessing some resemblance to the female pudenda as representatives of this abstract idea. They would present these to the dead body as much as to say: "This is the sort of thing that will enable you to achieve re-birth and continued existence." To us, on the contrary, the symbolism is much more literal and concrete. The metaphorical and abstract side of it is purely secondary and conscious, and the

[1] In the woman this idea is replaced by that of incorporating the father in the act of sexual union, so that she becomes permanently pregnant, this being equated to being in the mother's womb by the familiar mechanism of reversal.

138

real meaning is much more definite. The cowry, to take this example, is not merely an emblem of creativeness in general, or of wombs or Mother Goddesses in general, but is a symbol of the actual womb of the mother of the individual dead person, and the sense of the ritual is as follows: "As you know in your deepest heart, the only hope of attaining immortality is to penetrate into the Valley of the Shadow of Death, to pass once more through the portals of your mother's womb, to undergo a second birth that will annul the effects of the first[1] and will thus enable you to re-enter Paradise: here is her womb."

[1] Re-birth is really de-birth. The symbolism is an example of the mechanism of reversal, and really means passing into the womb instead of out of it; it thus annuls the original birth.

Recently this symbolism of the return to Mother Earth was portrayed by Thomas Hardy with a quite final precision and delicacy in his poem on the death of Sir Frederick Treves, and I cannot refrain from quoting it here, with his permission.

IN THE EVENING
(Dorchester Cemetery)

In the evening, shortly after he was dead,
    He lay amid the dust and hoar
Of ages, and to a spirit attending said,
      "This chalky bed?—
    I seem to have been here before?"

"Oh yes. You *have* been here. You knew the place,"
    The sprite replied, "long ere your call;
And if you cared to do so you might trace
      In this white space
    Your quality, your substance, and your all."

Thereat he said: "Why was I called away?
    I felt no trouble or discontent.
Why did I not prolong my ancient stay
      Herein for aye?"
    The sprite looked vague. "None knows! You went.

"True, Time has not as yet revealed to you
    Your need to go. But, some men tell,
A marvellous deftness called you forth—to do
      Much that was due.
    Good. You have returned. And all is well."

In the second place, we can throw further light on the fact that for the re-animation of the Egyptian corpse various male symbols, both phallic and seminal (the serpent-shaped wand, the adze of the Anubis who invented mummification, libations, saliva, red ochre and other blood equivalents), are necessary in addition to the female ones discussed above. It may be correlated with the astonishing fact mentioned previously, that in the unconscious the two ideas of sexual union (particularly incest) and of re-birth (i.e., return to the mother's womb) are regarded as equivalents; the distinction is hardly drawn between the whole person entering the mother's body or only that part of him known in legal phraseology as his "person", i.e., penis. In this way it comes about that (re-)birth and coitus are equivalent ideas when the object is the mother, and it is thus comprehensible that rituals symbolizing either of these acts have the power of restoring life. This is also the reason why bisexual symbols, notably water, play such a prominent part in these rituals, for they are connected with the ideas of both coitus and birth. Here, as so often, we may fall back on Elliot Smith[1] in support of our conclusions: "The study of folk-lore and early beliefs makes it abundantly clear that in the distant past which I am now discussing no clear distinction was made between fertilization and vitalization, between bringing new life into being and re-animating the body which had once been alive. The process of fertilization of the female and animating a corpse or a statue were regarded as belonging to the same category of biological processes. The sculptor who carved the portrait-

Compare also Wordsworth's "Ode on the Intimations of Immortality", which expresses a similar idea; and the well-known passage from Shelley's "Adonais":

> "Life, like a dome of many-coloured glass,
> Stains the white radiance of Eternity,
> Until Death tramples it to fragments.—Die,
> If thou wouldst be with that which thou dost seek!"

[1] Elliot Smith, op. cit., p. 25.

statues for the Egyptian's tomb was called *sa'nkh*, 'he who causes to live', and 'the word 'to fashion' (*ms*) a statue is to all appearances identical with *ms*, 'to give birth'.''

This brings us to the elixir of life, in connection with which I shall quote the following text:[1] "In delving into the remotely distant history of our species we cannot fail to be impressed with the persistence with which, throughout the whole of his career, man (of the species *sapiens*) has been seeking for an elixir of life, to give added 'vitality' to the dead (whose existence was not consciously regarded as ended), to prolong the days of active life to the living, to restore youth, and to protect his own life from all assaults, not merely of time, but also of circumstance. In other words, the elixir he sought was something that would bring 'good luck' in all the events of his life and its continuation. Most of the amulets, even of modern times, the lucky trinkets, the averters of the 'Evil Eye', the practices and devices for securing good luck in love and sport, in curing bodily ills or mental distress, in attaining material prosperity, or a continuation of existence after death, are survivals of this ancient and persistent striving after those objects which our earliest forefathers called collectively the 'givers of life'.''
Essentially, therefore, the elixir procures two desiderata; immortality in the next life and the restoration of youth in this, and I shall point out presently the intimate association between the two. Long before the era of Steinach, psychoanalysts had recognized this concern about 'youth' to be a euphemism for concern about virile powers, and Abraham[2] and Rank[3] have shown that the various magical fluids possessing the virtue of restoring it are all seminal symbols; such are the divine mead, soma, ambrosia, nectar and so on. Now a very remarkable clinical observation bears on this

[1] Ibid, p. 145.
[2] Abraham, op. cit.
[3] Rank, "Völkerpsychologische Parallelen zu den infantilen Sexualtheorien,'' reprinted in his *Psychoanalytische Beiträge zur Mythenforschung,* 1919.

double function of elixir, its powers of restoring youth on the one hand and of securing immortality on the other. When a patient consults us with the complaints that he has an undue dread of death (thanatophobia) or of the next world, that life feels to him so short and that youth is rapidly passing away, i.e., the two complaints which the elixir of life is designed to cure, then we know something about his inner mind with absolute certainty, for the analysis of such symptoms always leads to the same conclusion. He is suffering from a (conscious or unconscious) dread of impotency, and this dread always comes from the fear of being castrated as a punishment for his incestuous wishes. Since we have reason to think that these wishes are the main source of fear and guilt in general, and that the dread and horror of them was even stronger in primitive man, it is little wonder that the search for magic objects whose phallic or seminal attributes would counteract such terrors has played a tremendous part in the history of our race.

The third, and perhaps the most important, supplement to the self-preservation theory I would propose is that a more equal balance should be restored between the ideas of life and death. This theory would seem to be based on a somewhat morbid over-estimation of the part played by the fear of death, important as this undoubtedly is. The motives we have been considering apply just as much to the positive side of life as to this negative side. The desire for unbounded virility probably plays a greater part than the desire for indefinite existence, for the latter is often taken for granted by the primitive mind, and always by the unconscious mind,[1] whereas experience is constantly placing limits on both the capacity and the exercise of the sexual functions. Clinically both dreads, of impotency and of death, always indicate the action of castration fears in

[1] Eternity is really a negative concept and simply means the timelessness so characteristic of unconscious thinking, and therefore of pre-natal existence.

relation to incestuous wishes, while the man who is not troubled by either is the man who has overcome his dread of incest.[1]

The two means of re-union with the mother, part or whole (penis or body), are each accompanied by corresponding horrors; the first by impotence, i.e., castration, and the second by having to experience once more the terrible passage of the womb canal in the transit through death to paradise. What is astounding is that the two desires are equated in the unconscious mind, as are the two horrors. Yet these two desires—or shall we decide to call them one, as the unconscious does?—are the supreme driving force of our life, and their fulfilment its final goal.

The nearest approach to the gratification of this primordial desire is achieved in a happy sexual union with a loved object, and this explains the value of this act as an affirmation of life and a denial of the horrors of castration and death. Yet this only avails in so far as the primal wish— to re-enter the womb as a whole—is exchanged for the incomplete form of union represented by coitus, and in so far as the primal love-object (the mother) can be exchanged for a permissible and accessible one. It would seem that neither of these exchanges is ever completely accomplished —at least in the unconscious—so that man is condemned to an imperfect satisfaction of his deepest desires. Hence his restless and insatiable strivings for some other substitute for his heart's desire. Hence the astonishing wanderings and explorations of the Ancient Egyptians related to us by modern ethnologists. Surely somewhere there is to be found a wonderful Isle of the Blest,[2] with beautiful maidens,

[1] *E.g.*, by transforming the desire, transferring it to another woman than his mother and satisfactorily gratifying it with her.

[2] For the peculiar womb symbolism of this, see the chapter on "The Island of Ireland" in Vol. I, Chap. VIII. I hope to deal in a future paper with the interesting "El Dorado" theme, which Perry (*Folk-Lore*, 1921, Vol. XXXII, p. 150) has shown to be so interwoven with it.

golden fruit, and a fountain of "youth". But there are limits to man's powers of searching in the outer world, and every few hours even he has to have recourse, in the state of sleep, to what psycho-analysis teaches us is an imaginary re-establishment of pre-natal existence.[1] And when faced by the grim fact of death, though he may shrink in fear from the thought of the painful re-birth it unconsciously symbolizes, nevertheless the deepest part of his being cannot refuse the wild hope that once this final struggle is over he may, in spite of all his disappointments, enter at last into the longed-for haven (or heaven) of peace and partake yet again of the lost bliss of Nirvana.

[1] Incidentally, here is the solution of the problem raised by Perry (*The Origin*, etc., op. cit., p. 46) of whether the crouching position in which bodies were placed in caves is to be related to the attitude during sleep or during intra-uterine life. The answer is, to both, for the two are psychologically the same.

MOTHER-RIGHT AND THE SEXUAL IGNORANCE OF SAVAGES[1]

Introduction — Explanations of Mother-right — A Psycho-Analytical Theory of Mother-right — The Relation of Mother-right to Father-right.

I. INTRODUCTION

EVER since the appearance, in 1861, of Bachofen's famous work *Das Mutterrecht*, which was based largely on the study of classical literature, steadily increasing attention has been paid to the views of early man there revealed, until at the present day they constitute one of the central themes of anthropological interest. It may be said that subsequent research, although it has had to modify extensively some of his conclusions, has nevertheless amply confirmed many of them, and has shown that they hold good over a far larger field than he was able to investigate.

For reasons that will presently be indicated, however, the subject is apt to arouse intense emotional reactions, so that bias in the conclusions reached, and probably also in the observations made, is only too common. There are certainly fanciful elements in some of the pictures drawn of what is alleged to have been the primordial "matriarchal" state. A highly coloured description of it, for instance, will be found in Vaerting's *The Dominant Sex*, where we are introduced to an extreme inversion of the relation between the sexes. According to the account given there, not only do the children belong solely to the mother, the father being quite unrelated to them either in blood or in kinship,

---

[1] Read before the British Psycho-Analytical Society, 19th Nov., 1924. Published in the *International Journal of Psycho-Analysis*, Vol. VI.

but property belongs only to the women and is inherited only through them. The woman is the active wooer, has as many husbands or lovers as she pleases and as long as she pleases; she can at any time divorce her husband, but he cannot divorce her; he comes to her abode to live there as a guest; in fact he exists only for the sexual pleasure he gives her, and the work he can do at her bidding, being in all other respects merely tolerated very like a drone in a bee-hive. The woman has a correspondingly dominating position in society, in counsel and in government. The description reads like a feminist's wish-fulfilment dream, a vision of a paradise out of which she has been driven by the protesting male, but to which she hopes one day to return.

Very little knowledge of sex psychology or of mam-malian biology is needed to cast doubt on the authenticity of the account just mentioned, and the cold facts of an-thropology only go to attenuate its ardour. Scepticism is at once aroused by the assumption that in savage times men were more docile than now, and that the growth of civiliza-tion has been accompanied by a great increase in fierceness towards his womankind on the side of the brutal male. On the contrary, if one examines the institutions of existing savages, and still more if one submits these to an analytic scrutiny, one cannot resist the conclusion that these people have, in order to make social life possible at all, to maintain much more elaborate and formidable devices than we do in order to help them in securing some degree of control over their cruel and sadistic impulses, including those specific-ally directed against their womenfolk; we may refer, for instance, to Reik's study of the pseudo-maternal couvade,[1] as well as to the general experience of explorers. One may appropriately quote here the following passage from Frazer's *Golden Bough*:[2] "In order to dissipate misappre-

---

[1] Reik, *Probleme der Religionspsychologie*, 1909, Chap. II.
[2] Frazer, *Adonis, Attis, Osiris*, Vol. II, pp. 208-9.

hensions which appear to be rife on this subject, it may be well to remind or inform the reader that the ancient and widespread custom of tracing descent and inheriting property through the mother alone does not by any means imply that the government of the tribes which observe the custom is in the hands of women; in short, it should always be borne in mind that mother-kin does not mean mother-rule. On the contrary, the practice of mother-kin prevails most extensively amongst the lowest savages, with whom woman, instead of being the ruler of man, is always his drudge and often little better than his slave. Indeed, so far is the system from implying any social superiority of women that it probably took its rise from what we should regard as their deepest degradation, to wit, from a state of society in which the relations of the sexes were so loose and vague that children could not be fathered on any particular man. When we pass from the purely savage state to that higher plane of culture in which the accumulation of property, and especially of landed property, had become a powerful instrument of social and political influence, we naturally find that wherever the ancient preference for the female line of descent has been retained, it tends to increase the importance and enhance the dignity of woman; and her aggrandizement is most marked in princely families, where she either herself holds royal authority as well as private property, or at least transmits them both to her consort or her children. But this social advance of women has never been carried so far as to place men as a whole in a position of political subordination to them. Even where the system of mother-kin in regard to descent and property has prevailed most fully, the actual government has generally, if not invariably, remained in the hands of men. Exceptions have no doubt occurred; women have occasionally arisen who by sheer force of character have swayed for a time the destinies of their people. But such exceptions are rare and their effects transitory; they do not affect the truth of the general rule that human society has been governed in the past and, human nature remaining the same, is likely to be governed in the future, mainly by masculine force and masculine intelligence."

There are few themes, if any, that arouse more emotional prejudice than the comparison of male and female, particularly if it includes the question of the respective parts played in life by the father and the mother. Without the insight gained into the characteristic complexes of men and women by means of psycho-analysis, it would be well-nigh hopeless to expect a really serious approach to impartiality, and even with the knowledge now at our service one cannot walk too warily in this delicate path.

The second difficulty is of a more material kind. It is the enormous complexity and almost endless variation in the phenomena themselves. A slight impression of this may be given by the following considerations. Anthropologists are agreed that the central and perhaps the only essential one of many phenomena grouped under the name of mother-right (*Mutterrecht*) is "mother-kinship", i.e., the custom of reckoning descent through the female only; there is matrilineal descent, as it is called, and no patrilineal, or agnatic, descent.[1] This central feature is normally accompanied by a number of other characteristic ones, the chief of which will

[1] Rivers (Hastings' *Encyclopedia of Religion and Ethics*: art. Mother-Right) would use the term mother-kinship in a different and narrower sense, distinguishing it from matrilineal descent. For him "kinship" is much the same as our "relationship" when used in a genealogical sense, though perhaps the actual conception of a blood-bond may not be always essential in the savage mind. In this strict sense mother-kinship probably never exists in a pure form, so that we may ignore it for our purpose; that is to say, there are no peoples where no kinship whatever is recognized between the child and the father (and the father's relatives). By descent, whether matrilineal or patrilineal, is meant the origin of the child that determines to which social group (moiety or clan) it shall belong. If this is determined by the status of the mother, we have matrilineal descent—which other writers denote by the term "mother-kinship" —and this is the most essential feature of mother-right.

be mentioned presently, but the actual correlation found to exist among the various features is so extraordinarily irregular as to bewilder anyone who is seeking for any degree of order. The complications begin with what we have called the central feature, for the child does not necessarily belong to his mother's clan even if his descent is reckoned through the female; the totem who happened to impregnate his mother, to whose clan he therefore belongs, may be different from his mother's totem and clan. The descent may, of course, be matrilineal, patrilineal, or both together. The complexity increases as soon as we consider some of the connections between mother-kinship and the accompanying features.

1. *Authority*—The term "matriarchy" should be limited to the cases where there is true mother-rule, i.e., where the mother is the head of the household and disposes of the final authority over the children. This is extraordinarily rare, but when present constitutes the purest form of mother-right. Often the father is the head of the family and exercises the *potestas*—to use the legal term—as of course he mostly does where there is patrilineal descent. The most frequent case, however, and one so typical that its presence, even in an attenuated form, always makes one suspect the existence of mother-right (whether in the past or present), is that in which the *potestas* is wielded by the mother's brother, the child's maternal uncle; this is the so-called avunculate organization. Other varieties are where the *potestas* is shared between the father and maternal uncle, according to the matters over which it is exercised, or where the uncle has authority over the son and the father over the daughter, or where the father has authority up to a given age and the uncle after this.

2. *Inheritance and succession*—With mother-right succession of rank (kingship, chieftainship, etc.) mostly, but not always, passes from a man to his sister's son, not to his

wife's son; in other words, whether the rank can be held by a woman or not, it is often transmitted through the female, instead of as with us, through the male. But again there is no rule about this. In Melanesia, for instance, where matrilineal descent mainly holds, succession is usually patrilineal.

The laws about inheritance (of property) are also extremely variable. The property may, very rarely, be held only by women; most typically it is transmitted to the sister's son, but there are instances of mother-right (as with the Malays of Moerong) where nevertheless the boy inherits from his father.

It should be borne in mind that there is no close correlation between the individual features just enumerated. Out of an endless number one only need be quoted: In Torres Straits the *potestas* is avunculate, but the descent, inheritance and succession are all patrilineal.

3. *Residence*—In the most extreme forms of mother-right the husband only visits his wife or else resides with her and her people (matrilocal marriage), in which case he is usually subject to the head of her household, her brother or uncle. Matrilocal marriage is nearly always accompanied by matrilineal descent, there being only two exceptions known to this rule. Patrilineal descent almost always involves patrilocal marriage, but the converse does not hold, since patrilocal marriage is often found with mother-kinship; Australian marriages, for instance, are mostly patrilocal, whereas mother-kinship is nearly as common with them as father-kinship.

The difficulties in correlating the institution of mother-right with the status of women accompanying it, whether high or low, with the level of civilization in which it is found, and with the knowledge or certainty about paternity possessed by the peoples concerned will be mentioned in discussing the various hypotheses relating to the subject.

II. EXPLANATIONS OF MOTHER-RIGHT

After these introductory remarks we may proceed to consider the main problems relating to mother-right, its general significance and the causes of its genesis and supersession. In doing so it will be seen that we at once impinge on some of the most fundamental problems of anthropology —those relating to the evolution of totemism and religion, of marriage and the family, as well as of other social institutions. To us the conception of a family where the father plays such a subordinate part, being to a great extent replaced by an uncle, certainly seems strange and needful of explanation. Yet many authorities, including McLennan, Spencer, Avebury, Frazer, and Hartland, find this state of affairs a perfectly natural one in an early stage of society, so that for them the greater problem would be to explain how it came to be superseded. They point to the more intimate connection between child and mother and the various uncertainties concerning the relationship of the father. Other authorities, on the other hand, regard the institution of mother-right as a secondary state of affairs to be accounted for by purely temporary circumstances. The causes for it may be either factors connected with the status of women, perhaps the part they are often supposed to have played in regard to agriculture, or more obscure ones of the kind that will be discussed below. The main hypotheses will next be considered in more detail.

The most obvious explanation for the existence of mother-right, one first put forward in 1757 by Schouten and since repeated by many travellers, is that it is due to uncertainty about the individuality of the father. As it has been cynically put, maternity is a question of fact, paternity a question of opinion. The slightest investigation, however, disposes of this view as being quite out of accord with the facts. There is no correlation at all between father-right and conjugal fidelity or between mother-right and infidelity.[1] On the one hand, mother-right obtains, for instance, on the coast of West Africa and in Northern Abyssinia, where wifely fidelity is very strict, adultery exceedingly rare and often punished by death. On the other hand there is the far commoner state of affairs where conjugal morality is loose though father-right prevails. As Hartland puts it in connection with the Kafirs of the Hindu Kush, where the strictest father-right holds, "that Kafir would be of a highly sporting disposition who ventured to stake much on the authenticity of any child of whom he was legally the father."[2] More than this: among many patrilineal peoples the men appear to show the greatest indifference about their actual blood-relationship to their legal son, so long as they have one at all for their ritualistic and economic purposes where a son is desirable, and an adopted son, or their wife's son by some other man, serves these purposes as well as one they have themselves begotten.

Closely akin to this hypothesis are those that postulate a specially close association between mother and child on account of either polygyny (Winterbottom) or polyandry (McLennan). Neither can be substantiated by reference to the actual facts.

A more subtle and interesting view, hinted at by McLennan over half a century ago in his *Primitive Marriage* and developed by Hartland in 1895 in his *Legend of Perseus*, is that mother-right represents a survival from a time when there was ignorance of the facts of procreation. If the father was not thought to play any necessary part in procreation, then it would seem to follow that the child's status could only be determined by the mother's, i.e., that there would be mother-right; and it is the essential presupposition of

---

[1] For a sufficiently full discussion of the point, see Hartland, *Primitive Society*, 1921, pp. 12-17.

[2] Hartland, *Primitive Paternity*, 1909, Vol. I, p. 101.

this hypothesis that mother-right necessarily preceded father-right throughout the world. It is true that mother-right is often found where the paternal role in procreation is fully understood; not only so, but, as Westermarck points out in this connection,[1] there are Australian tribes who have matrilineal descent in spite of their belief that the child is created solely by the father and merely nourished by the mother. Nevertheless there might well be psychological or sociological reasons why a given organization should persist after the originating agent had ceased to operate, so that the considerations just adduced would not necessarily negative the hypothesis in question. We are thus led to investigate, as an essential preliminary in our inquiry, the much discussed topic of the sexual ignorance of the savages.

The surmise expressed by Hartland in 1895 that sexual ignorance[2] may have played an important part in the development of social beliefs and institutions was within a few years brilliantly confirmed by Spencer and Gillen's discovery that there were still tribes in Australia, notably the interesting Aruntas, who were ignorant of the facts of paternal procreation. The findings have been disputed by other field-workers, such as Strehlow and von Leonhardi, and the inferences contravened by Westermarck, Heape, and Carveth Read. The question is not easily answered. Like all inquiries in the sphere of sexuality, the truth is peculiarly difficult to elicit and the fallacies unexpectedly numerous. The only field-worker who seems to have made a special study of these fallacies, and who exhibited remarkable acumen in dealing with them, is Malinowski. The account he gives of the sexual life of the Trobrianders, a Papuan-Melanesian race inhabiting an archipelago off the coast of New Guinea, is certainly the fullest extant, and its

[1] Westermarck, *The History of Human Marriage*, Fifth Edition, 1921, Vol. I, p. 294.
[2] By "sexual ignorance" I mean in this context particularly the ignorance that semen is the fertilizing fluid.

quality is such as to inspire great confidence in the correctness of his observations.[1] After a careful sifting of all the available data he comes to the definite conclusion that these natives have no knowledge whatever of the part played by semen in procreation. They appear to believe that pregnancy results only from a "baloma", a spirit (usually female) of a dead person, inserting a spirit child, "waiwaia", into the womb. They admit, however, that for this to happen it is necessary that the vagina be first opened up and this is, of course, usually done by sexual intercourse. Apparently the Australian Aruntas hold a similar view, that women are prepared in this way for the reception of the "ratapas". In making this belief more comprehensible Malinowski points out that the causal connection between intercourse and pregnancy is far from obvious to a race accustomed to frequent copulation from early childhood; the sexual act may take place hundreds of times before a single conception occurs. He has no doubts about the correctness of his observations and concludes: "My firm conviction is that the ignorance of paternity is an original feature of primitive psychology, and that in all speculations about the origins of Marriage and the Evolution of Sexual Customs, we must bear in mind this fundamental ignorance."[2]

If we accept these observations as correct, particularly Malinowski's careful investigations, as it seems to me we are bound to,[3] then the question would appear to be settled. Nevertheless, the voice of scepticism refuses to be quieted. A number of other considerations strongly hint that even yet we are not at the end of the matter.

[1] Malinowski, "Baloma; the Spirits of the Dead in the Trobriand Islands," *Journal of the Royal Anthropological Institute*, 1916; "The Psychology of Sex and the Foundation of Kinship in Primitive Societies" and "Psycho-Analysis and Anthropology" both in *Psyche*, Vol. IV.

[2] *Psyche*, Vol. IV, p. 128.

[3] I may report, however, that Professor Malinowski expressed his keen regret to me that he had known nothing of psycho-analysis *before* making these investigations.

In the first place we have the indisputable fact that most savages all over the world, including those with mother-right, are fully aware of the part played by the man in procreation. This is proved not only by their own direct statements, but also by numerous practices based on the knowledge.[1] Then even the savages who are apparently ignorant in regard to paternal procreation yield hints that they nevertheless have some inklings of similar knowledge in other fields of thought. Thus the Intichiama ceremonies of the Australian natives definitely imply some knowledge of the processes of fertility in both animals and crops. They appear to make the same reservations about human kind as a child does about its family in this matter: "Other people may make babies that way, but not *my* parents." A very curious feature observed by Malinowski among the Trobrianders, discussion of which will be reserved till later, points in the same direction: a Trobriander is horrified at the idea of physically resembling his mother, brother or sister; i.e., those who are thought to be his only blood-relatives, and is intensely insulted at the mere suggestion; he maintains on the contrary, that he is the physical image of his father.

A psycho-analyst cannot fail to be struck by the unmistakable symbolism these ignorant savages display when propounding their views on procreation, symbolism of so accurate a kind as to indicate at least an unconscious knowledge of the truth. Thus water plays a prominent part in regard to conception. The spirit-children, waiwaias, come from over the sea, often in a basket (like the womb symbol in which Moses arrived), they usually enter the woman's body when she is bathing in the sea, and the thing that has most carefully to be avoided by those who do not wish to conceive is the scum or froth of the sea—an obvious seminal symbol. In Australia impregnation may take place by stones, snakes, or birds, well-known phallic symbols.

[1] *See* Westermarck, op. cit., pp. 287, 288.

The churinga nanja among the Aruntas are stone boulders connected with ancestors from whom the seed-spirit comes; in the Acheringa dream-world there are two ancestors for each child, not one as might be expected, on the hypothesis of parthenogenesis.

Ideas of causality are known to be particularly difficult to unravel with savages, for they are often curiously different from our own. It is not easy to interpret, for instance, a belief that two causes are necessary for conception, an opening-up copulation and the introduction of spirit-children by a baloma. The natives say that the first of these allows the second, which is the essential one, to operate; but it is very well possible that the converse is the real meaning of the belief, i.e., that it is the influence of the baloma (the ancestral spirit) which permits the copulation to take effect. This multiplicity of causes is very common in regard to conception, for there are fewer topics that have more adjuvant agents associated with them, from bathing in holy water to the cure of barrenness by gynæcological curettage. The use of these agents, and the faith in them, may co-exist with every degree of conscious awareness of the true agent in procreation; it would be absurd, for instance, to maintain that the Greeks were ignorant of the facts of procreation simply because their women practised various fertility rites and regarded the resultant offspring as the gift of the gods.

The argument put forward by Hartland and Malinowski to the effect that it must be hard to recognize the connection between frequent acts of copulation and rare ones of conception is not only incompatible with the simple fact that after all most peoples have recognized this connection, but has been penetratingly countered by Carveth Read on psychological grounds. He writes:[1] "We must remember that

---

[1] Carveth Read, "No Paternity," *Journal of the Royal Anthropological Institute*, Vol. XLVIII, p. 146.

the knowledge of animals and a great deal of the knowledge of savages and even of civilized people, is not of the discriminated, relational, propositional texture to which, under the influence of formal logic, we are apt to confine the name." This is exactly in accord with what we find in the analysis of infantile mental life, where instinctive intuition plays a considerable part in divining the main outline at least of sexual knowledge. If a child of two years old can frame an image of genital coitus, and a year or so later connect it with the birth of another child, then the feat should certainly not be beyond the mentality of any adult savage.

III. A PSYCHO-ANALYTICAL THEORY OF MOTHER-RIGHT

The foregoing considerations raise the question of whether the ignorance among these savages is after all so genuine and complete as it would appear. The curious combination of ignorance where one would reasonably expect knowledge and of half-knowledge is a phenomenon with which we are very familiar in other fields of thought.

Writers who are sceptical concerning the thorough-going nature of this ignorance have tended to regard it as something secondary or artificial, and a few have even propounded reasons for its occurrence. Thus Frazer, in speaking of the Australian belief that a "ratapa" enters the womb at the moment of quickening, refers to the "sick fancies of pregnant women". Heape[1] expresses the following views: "All the evidence we can bring to bear on a subject from a comparative point of view indicates that primitive man was not ignorant of this fundamental fact, and such evidence appears to me so strong that I consider it is irre-

[1] Heape, *Sex Antagonism*, 1913, pp. 103, 112.

futable. Moreover, there is evidence that while these Australian savage people now declare their ignorance they still act in a variety of ways as if they knew the true facts. This being so, I maintain that the initial cause of this conceptional idea of totemism is due to a superstition which overrode instinctive knowledge of the facts; in other words, that the idea is not derived from ignorance, but is a manufactured scheme, originating at a period in the history of man which is subsequent to his conception of superstitious fear of personal or individual spirits, and arising out of such superstition." "It is thus I interpret the story of conceptional totemism; an impulse due to the sick fancies of the pregnant woman, due to fear or dread or desire, or all of them, has bred a superstition which necessitated the relinquishment of instinctive knowledge previously acquired, and all but buried it—not quite buried, however, the Intichiuma ceremonies are performed just when there is promise of a good breeding season, and thus necessity demands recognition of the truth; the Tully River[1] blacks grant that the breeding of animals, at any rate, is governed by the laws of Nature, while human beings are only exempt from the force of those laws because they are thereby confirmed in their belief of their superiority over the brute creation." He suggests that the (purely conscious) motives why the natives maintain the beliefs they do is either to facilitate adultery[2] and condonement of it, or else to gratify the mother's hope of benefiting the child by conferring on it the qualities of some totemic spirit. These suggestions, however, evidently do not carry us far.

[1] Heape here quotes Roth, "North Queensland Ethnography," Bull. No. 5, p. 22.

[2] He cites (p. 100) the Baganda custom of punishing adultery only when the banana tree is out of blossom, for otherwise the conception is ascribed to the latter. But as the banana tree blossoms all the year round—compare our saying "when gorse is out of bloom then kissing is out of fashion"—and the banana is an obvious phallic symbol, there would seem to be need for further investigation gathered in respect of this custom.

THE SEXUAL IGNORANCE OF SAVAGES

Carveth Read[1] makes a decided step forward in suggesting that the knowledge really present is only unconscious, having been "repressed"; he speaks of its having been "repressed by the animistic philosophy and expelled from consciousness". Malinowski, however, thinks that such knowledge cannot have been obliterated by any animistic superstructure because in determining "descent" no importance is attached by these savages to blood-relationship.

When the question comes up whether ideas are present in a state of repression, and, if so, what are likely to have been the reasons for the repression, then surely a psychoanalyst has a word to say. At this point, therefore, I propose to put forward an hypothesis along psycho-analytical lines, one which, if correct, would indicate that there is the closest collateral relationship between ignorance about paternal procreation on the one hand and the institution of mother-right on the other. My view is that both these phenomena are brought about by the same motive; in what chronological relation they stand to each other is another question altogether, which will be considered later. The motive, according to this view, in both cases is to *deflect the hostility felt by the growing boy towards his father*.

The following considerations may be adduced in support of this hypothesis. In the first place, it is known that of the two components of the primordial Œdipus complex—love for the mother and hatred for the father—the latter has played by far the more important part in leading to repression of the complex and in giving rise to the various complicated devices whereby this repression is brought about and maintained. The reason for this is evident: the dangerous rivalry between two murderous males with all its consequences. There is much reason to think that the ambivalent conflict between love and hate is sharper among

[1] Carveth Read, op. cit., p. 146.

159

savage people than among ourselves[1] hence it is not surprising that they should possess more elaborate institutions subserving the function of guarding them from their repressed impulses; it is as if they had more reason than we to fear them, or less power of diverting them. As examples of institutions of this kind one may quote totemism and exogamy[2] on the one hand and the innumerable initiation ceremonies on the other.[3] (In accepting the view that the function in question is the essential one of these institutions one does not, of course, ignore the fact that they also subserve numerous other ones.)

It would seem to be the fashion at present among anthropologists to regard kinship and "descent" as not necessarily having any close connection with blood-relationship. I am inclined to think that in so doing they are following a tendentious striving present among savages themselves. For it seems pretty plain that savages try in all sorts of ways to divorce the two matters,[4] although there is much reason to infer that fundamentally they attach an enormous, and even exaggerated, importance to blood-relationship. Not only is the child's social status determined by birth to a much greater extent than with us, but the central importance of birth to the savage mind in connection with the Œdipus complex has been made highly probable by Reik's brilliant work on puberty rites.[5] He showed there that the real significance of these rites is, by means of a complicated castration and birth symbolism, to annul the original birth by the mother and substitute for it an imaginary homosexual birth; the idea evidently being that attachment to the mother is due simply to the fact of being born of her,

[1] One example is illustrated in Reik's interpretation of the postural couvade as a means of coping with the sadism aroused by the sight of the suffering wife.

[2] *See* Freud, *Totem und Tabu,* 1913.

[3] *See* Reik, *Probleme der Religionspsychologie,* 1919, Chap. III.

[4] This is perhaps one reason why mother-right so often persists, even when the facts of paternity are fully recognized.

[5] Ibid.

so that the only way to neutralize the incest tendencies that stand in the way of friendly relationship with other men is to nullify the supposed cause of them (birth) by a symbolic re-birth. If, according to savage theory, the maternal half of the Œdipus complex, the attachment to the mother, depends on the fact of being born by her, it is only reasonable to suppose that the same, *mutatis mutandis*, is equally true of the paternal half, the father-hate. At all events, as we shall see, savages appear to act on this assumption.

In unconsciously explaining incest tendencies as being due to the act of birth, savages would appear to indulge in the same "retrospective phantasying" as our neurotics who so often behave exactly like them in this respect, where we know the motive is to escape the guilt of infantile sexuality by substituting harmless thoughts about birth: contact with the mother's genitals is by birth only, not by coitus. Nevertheless, if Freud's hypothesis is substantiated about the inheritance of impulses dating from the primal horde, the savages and neurotics would prove to have some right on their side, though in a very indirect way. For in that event there would be some causal connection between birth, i.e., heredity, and the Œdipus complex.

Be this as it may, it is clear that any objectionable tendencies the source of which is imputed to the act of birth can most radically be countered by simply denying this act, as is done, for example, in the puberty rites. Now in the analysis of our neurotics we are very familiar with the wish-phantasy in which this happens in regard to the father. Many of them cherish, consciously or unconsciously, the idea that their "father" had nothing to do with their conception or birth, this being entirely a matter between them and their mother. It is well known how extraordinarily widespread this myth of the Virgin Mother has been throughout the world, and there is every reason to think that it has generally the same significance as we find in the analysis of individuals.[1] The general belief evidently fulfils more than one deep-seated tendency; repudiation of the father's part in coitus and procreation, and consequently softening and deflection of the hatred against him, a consummation desired equally by son and father. This is what has happened where the institution of mother-right is combined with denial of paternal procreation. It might be said that just as the postural couvade is designed to protect both wife and child from the father's hostility,[2] so the combination of mother-right and sexual ignorance protects both father and son from their mutual rivalry and hostility.

I should be inclined to bring into connection with this tendentious denial of paternal procreation the curious and unexpected finding recorded by Malinowski[3] that the topic of sexual intercourse between man and wife is regarded by the Trobrianders as highly indecent, although they are unusually free people in regard to sexual matters in general. This seems to represent a higher degree of the common aversion which most people feel in regard to the idea of parental coitus, and serves the same function of keeping at a distance the possibility of an Œdipus jealousy.

But the father is not so easily disposed of, a fact which might be used in support of Freud's suggestion that the inherited idea of the primal father is still actively alive in our unconscious. The father disappears from the scene only to reappear in a disguised form. The idea of the powerful and hated father is sacrificed in favour of an ancestral spirit, who in a supernatural manner impregnates the mother; for both the Australian ratapas and the Trobriand waiwaias emanate from ancestors, and no one who has had the opportunity of analyzing a member of an ancient Eng-

[1] *See* Rank, *Der Mythus von der Geburt des Helden*, 2e Auflage, 1922, and Ernest Jones, Section XIII of the present volume.
[2] Reik, op. cit.
[3] Malinowski, *Psyche*, Vol. V, p. 207.

lish family or an American with a passion for genealogy can
fail to discover that forefathers are psychologically nothing
but fathers at a slight remove. This elevated father is therefore the original powerful father in another guise. The idea
corresponds with the deep belief that after all only the great
father can procreate (or permit it by giving his sanction),
with the added wish on the part of women to conceive of the
father, as the Virgin Mary did.[1]

When put to the test of practice this way of treating the
father does appear to achieve its aim of bringing about a
far more intimate and friendly relationship between father
and child than is usual in patrilineal societies. Among the
Trobrianders, where the father has of course no authority
whatever over his children, the society, being matrilineal
and the *potestas* devolving on the uncle, the father is
described as being a "beloved, benevolent friend",[2] Malinowski writes[3] as follows: "Among the Melanesians, 'fatherhood', as we know, is a purely social relation. Now, part of
this relation consists in his duty towards his wife's children;
he is there 'to receive them into his arms,' a phrase we have
already quoted; he has to carry them about when on the
march the mother is tired, and he has to assist in the nursing
at home. He tends them in their natural needs, and
cleanses them, and there are many stereotyped expressions
in the native language referring to fatherhood and its hard-
ships, and to the duty of filial gratitude towards him. A
typical Trobriand father is a hard-working and conscien-
tious nurse, in which he obeys the call of duty, expressed in
social tradition. The fact is, however, that the father is
always interested in the children, sometimes passionately
so, and performs all his duties eagerly and fondly."

The solution of the father complex, however, was not

[1] A contribution from the woman's side which may be compared with
Frazer's remark (see above) about the sick fancies of pregnant women.
[2] Malinowski, *Psyche*, Vol. IV, p. 298.
[3] Ibid., p. 304.

ESSAYS IN APPLIED PSYCHO-ANALYSIS

always so easy, and with the obsessional ambivalence of savages room had to be found for an object towards whom could be directed the less amiable attitudes of awe, dread, respect and suppressed hostility which are inseparable from the idea of the father imago. It will be remembered that it took Christian theology many centuries before they could afford to dispense with the devil (whom I have shown elsewhere to be a genetic counterpart of God) and allow themselves to face a God who would carry the responsibility for both good and evil. Similarly the savage had to be provided with a figure who would incorporate the disliked and feared attributes of the father imago. In nearly all matrilineal societies, and in some that have partly passed over into the patrilineal form, the maternal uncle plays this part. It is he who wields over the children the direct *potestas*, he who is the main source of authority and discipline, from him that they inherit possessions and acquire various accomplishments, and often it is he who is responsible for their food and keep. Still, in the majority of cases he does not reside with the children, and often not even in the same village, while his relations with their mother are extremely formal and surrounded by taboos. Malinowski[1] contrasts the status of the two men as follows: "To the father, therefore, the children look only for loving care and tender companionship. Their mother's brother represents the principle of discipline, authority and executive power within the family." As might be expected, affection is not the most prominent feature in the relation between boy and uncle, though doubtless there is much companionship during the adolescent stage when the serious duties of life are being inculcated. Malinowski[2] describes this stage: "The father suffers at this time a temporary eclipse. The boy, who as a child was fairly independent and became the member of

[1] Loc. cit.
[2] Op. cit., p. 324.

164

the small, juvenile republic, gains now on the one hand the additional freedom of the *bukumatula*, while on the other he becomes much more restricted by his various duties towards his *kada*, maternal uncle. He has less time and less interest left for the father. Later on, when friction with the maternal uncle makes its appearance, he turns, as a rule, to his father once more and their life friendship then becomes settled."

My suggestion is that the state of affairs just mentioned is an example of the process with which we are familiar in mythological studies under the name of "decomposition", one common enough also in the psychoneuroses. It is one whereby various attributes can become detached from an original figure and incorporated in another one, which then personifies these attributes. In the present case, as in so many others, the process serves the function of unloading affect in a relationship where it might have unpleasant consequences and depositing it at a safer distance. The British Constitution has evolved a similar arrangement; in it the father of the country, the King, can do no wrong and so is immune from criticism, retaining only the affection and respect of his subjects. This was made possible, after the people refused to tolerate the system of absolute monarchy, by providing a counterpart, the Prime Minister, against whom all complaints, resentment and hostility could be directed; the volume of this opposition periodically and inevitably accumulates until he has to make way for a successor. A more subtle example has been analyzed by Freud in his study of the "taboo of virginity".[1] He has shown that the custom of a bride being deflorated by someone other than the husband is to ensure that the resentment which this operation is apt to provoke shall be directed away from her future life-partner and precipitated elsewhere.

[1] Freud, "Taboo of Virginity," 1918, *Collected Papers*, Vol. IV, 1925.

The two men being unconscious equivalents, it is not surprising that in some tribes the same name is applied to both, as, for instance, in Loango, where the uncle is called Tate (= father).[1] A story recalled by Hartland[2] well illustrates the psychological complexity of the relationship. "When a child dies or even meets with an accident with fatal results, the mother's relatives, headed by her brother, turn out in force against the father. He must defend himself until he is wounded. Blood once drawn the combat ceases; but the attacking party plunders his house and appropriates everything on which hands can be laid, finally sitting down to a feast provided by the bereaved father." The father is thus punished because his repressed hostile wishes have come true and the child has met with harm. Now this is in a patrilineal society—of Maoris—and the action taken by the maternal uncle points to an earlier avunculate and doubtless matrilineal social organization. In this transition from one organization one sees how the parts played by father and uncle respectively can change to the exact opposite. Mrs. Seligmann[3] informs me that in some Soudanese tribes a similar change can be observed to be at work, where the father is becoming dreaded and the uncle loved.

In this decomposition of the primal father into a kind and lenient father on the one hand, and a stern and moral uncle on the other, it is not chance that the latter person was chosen to fill this part. I will sketch the order of development here somewhat schematically. If we start with the primal trinity of father, mother, son, then in seeking for a surrogate to whom the jealous hatred felt for the father can become displaced there are two persons who naturally present themselves, the mother's father and her brother. The reason for this goes back to the mother's own incestu-

[1] Hartland, op. cit., p. 281.
[2] Ibid., p. 279.
[3] Personal communication, for which I am much indebted.

166

ous attachments; her father and brothers are also in a sense rivals of her son, though they are at a greater distance from him than his own father. It is therefore not surprising that the Œdipus legend can be paralleled by similar ones relating to the other men. Thus it was foretold of Acriseus that he would be killed by his daughter's son; and, in spite of all his efforts—first by isolating his daughter Danae, and then by attempting to drown her and her son, Perseus, after Zeus had managed to evade the endeavours of her father to keep her a virgin—the prediction is verified; Perseus did kill his grandfather. Similar tales are related of other heroes besides Perseus, such as Cyrus, Gilgam, and Telephos.

We know from psycho-analytic work that the girl's attachment towards her father commonly becomes dis· placed on to her brother, just as the son displaces his mother-attachment on to his sister. The tendency towards filial and parental incest is thus exchanged for that towards brother-sister incest, which even to-day is much less taboo than the former and is often realized in actuality. As is well known, royal marriages between brother and sister were customary in ancient Egypt, and till our times in Hawaii,[1] though forbidden to commoners. It is thus comprehensible enough that jealous rivalry over the woman between nephew and uncle should duplicate that between son and father, or that the former psychological situation can replace the latter. The classical legend displaying this situation is, of course, the Tristan saga, particularly in its earlier versions. Before winning Isolde, Tristan logically kills her maternal uncle, Morolt, (of course on other ostensible grounds), and, after she has espoused his own maternal uncle, Mark, he enters into rivalry with the latter; in the most recent version of the story, Thomas Hardy unveils the mask of benevolence that had been cast over Mark and lays bare the natural enmity between the two men. In the earliest versions of the

[1] Rivers, *Social Organization*, 1924, p. 39.

Lancelot legend in the Arthurian cycle[1] there are plain indications of the same theme. In the first account it was Gawain who loved Guinevere, the wife of Arthur, his maternal uncle. In the later accounts his place is taken by Lancelot (who also usurped his position as the first Grail hero), but that the underlying theme is only disguised is shown by the circumstance that Lancelot's foster-mother was also Arthur's sister. At the end the original theme comes again to the surface, since it is another nephew, Mordred, who abducts Guinevere and kills his maternal uncle, Arthur. The further stage in repression, familiar to us in the Hamlet form of the Œdipus complex,[2] can also be traced in the uncle-nephew relationship, the nephew avenging his uncle's murder; an example of this is the Otuel story in the Charlemagne cycle.[3] The most complete inversion is perhaps that of the Caucasian legend of Chopa,[4] for he avenges his maternal uncle, whom his father had slain, by attacking his own father.

We may now return to the Trobrianders. There, as with most matrilineal societies, there is an extraordinarily severe taboo against sexual relations between brother and sister, one which begins at the earliest age. It could not escape Malinowski's discernment that this taboo must be the expression of repressed incestuous tendencies, though he does not appear to have recognized the connection between this and the presence of an avunculate organization; i.e., that the uncle, being the unconscious lover of the mother, is therefore the imaginary father of her children, and logically wields the *potestas* over them. He sees, however, that the uncle plays the negative part of the father in our civilization, and formulates the following neat statement on the

---

[1] *See* Jessie L. Weston's works, *Arthur and Guinevere, King Arthur and his Knights, The Legend of Sir Gawaine,* and *Lancelot du Lac.*
[2] *See* Ernest Jones, *Hamlet and the Oedipus Complex,* 1949.
[3] Ellis, *Specimens of Early English Matrical Romances,* 1805, pp. 375 ff.
[4] Cited by Hartland, op. cit., p. 271.

whole matter:[1] "Applying to each society a terse, though rather crude formula, there is in our society the repressed desire 'to kill the father and marry the mother', while in the matrilineal complex of Melanesia, the wish is 'to marry the sister and to kill the maternal uncle'." One striking piece of evidence he finds in support of this conclusion in a very typical set of myths among matrilineal peoples—corresponding with the European Œdipus myths—in which incest occurs between brother and sister and hatred between nephew and maternal uncle.[2]

Malinowski's conclusion is doubtless correct on the purely descriptive plane, but he goes on to use it as the basis of an extremely doubtful hypothesis in which he attempts to modify Freud's theory of the nuclear family complex. As is well known, the latter regards the relationship between father, mother, and son as the prototype from which other more complicated relationships are derived. Malinowski, on the contrary, puts forward the idea that the nuclear family complex varies according to the particular family structure existing in any community. According to him, a matrilineal family system arises for unknown social and economic reasons, and then the repressed nuclear complex consists of brother and sister attraction, with nephew and uncle hatred; when this system is replaced by a patrilineal one, the nuclear complex becomes the familiar Œdipus one.

If attention is concentrated on the sociological aspects of the data, this will appear a very ingenious and perhaps even plausible suggestion. I would submit, however, that imperfect attention to the genetic aspects of the problem has led to a lack of what I have elsewhere called a "dimensional perspective", i.e., a sense of value and proportion based on intimate knowledge of the unconscious, and that the opposite of Malinowski's conception is nearer the truth. It

---

[1] Malinowski, *Psyche*, Vol. V, p. 195.
[2] Ibid., p. 216.

would seem more probable, in my opinion, that the matrilineal system with its avunculate complex arose in the way described above as a mode of defence against the primordial Œdipus tendencies than that it arose for unknown sociological reasons with then the avunculate complex as a necessary consequence and the Œdipus complex appearing only when the patrilineal system was subsequently introduced. The forbidden and unconsciously loved sister is only a substitute for the mother, as the uncle plainly is for the father. On Malinowski's hypothesis the Œdipus complex would be a late product; for the psycho-analyst it was the *fons et origo*.

IV. THE RELATION OF MOTHER-RIGHT TO FATHER-RIGHT

In 1861, the year Bachofen's famous work *Das Mutterrecht* appeared, an equally famous work was published by Sir Henry Maine, entitled *Primal Law*. In it he enunciated, largely on the basis of juristic studies in India, the view that the primal state of society must have been a patriarchal one. In the years that have elapsed since that date more historical and ethnological evidence and arguments, expounded especially by McLennan, Lewis Morgan, Lubbock and Hartland, have accumulated in favour of the first of these views, to the effect that the primal system of society (with or without a still earlier state of promiscuity) was a matrilineal one; and perhaps the majority of anthropologists to-day are inclined to support this view. It is at all events certain that mother-right is extremely widespread among savage races, and there is much reason to think that this was still more so five thousand years ago.

A heated controversy has taken place over the question of whether father-right as we know it or mother-right as we find it among the savages was the earlier system of the two. The view here represented is different from either. It is that the question has not been justly put, since the two alternatives mentioned do not exhaust the possibilities. We know from psycho-analytic work that there are often three mental layers where there appear to be only two. A perky conceitedness, for instance, is usually the compensatory reaction to a deep-seated sense of inferiority, but analysis shows that this in its turn is based on repressed narcissism. The first and the third layers are similar in their content, but they are not on that account to be identified. The present problem may well prove to be of a like nature.

Before developing this idea we may briefly review the opinions that have been expressed by other writers. Those who take the primal patriarchal view have to explain why mother-right ever came into existence, whereas for those who take the opposite view the question is rather why the primal mother-right was ever supplanted by father-right. The former tend to regard mother-right as a temporary and necessarily evanescent phase, and the chief explanation offered for its existence seems to be that it was dependent on the development of agriculture where woman's work was found to be of special value; the correlation, however, between agriculture and mother-right is far from close enough to establish the connection.[1] The second set of writers, who often wax enthusiastic over the idyllic situation prevailing under mother-right, tend to regard this as the natural state of affairs and to take the view that women were driven from this paradise by brute force.[2] Hartland, for whom father-right is "a purely artificial system"[3] says: "The conclusion seems irresistible that

[1] *See* Westermarck, op. cit., p. 297.
[2] One cannot refrain from wondering what part the infantile "sadistic conception of coitus" may have played in the idea that men imposed "father-right" on "mother-right" by brute force.
[3] Hartland, op. cit., Vol. II, p. 248.

father-right is traceable not to any change in savage or barbarous theories of blood-relationship, but to social and economic causes."[1] Both he[2] and Rivers[3] who, by the way, expresses no opinion about the relative antiquity of mother-right and father-right, would ascribe great importance in this connection to the violent immigrations of primitive times whereby the will of the conqueror was imposed on the weaker.

The view advanced in this paper is based on the psycho-analytic recognition of the fundamental importance of the nuclear Œdipus complex. It is in accord neither with the idea of primitive promiscuity, nor with that of primal right, nor even with that of patriarchy as we nowadays conceive it in its monogamic form. Far from being led by consideration of the subject, as Malinowski was, to abandon or revise Freud's conception of the "primal horde" (Atkinson's "cyclopeian family"), it seems to me, on the contrary, that this conception furnishes the most satisfactory explanation of the complicated problems which we have been discussing. According to this, the system of mother-right, with its avunculate complex, represents one mode of defence among the many that have been adopted against the tendencies denoted by the term Œdipus complex. We cannot, of course, say whether it represents a necessary stage in the evolution towards the present patriarchal system; I see no reason why it should, and the fact that some of the lowest type of Australian savages, whose primitive instincts are hard enough to curb, find it possible to cope with them by an alternative method—that of taboo and the totemic system—might be quoted in support of the doubt. Nor is there any reason to suppose that the savage ignorance, or rather repression, of the facts of paternal pro-

[1] Ibid., p. 100.
[2] Idem, *Primitive Society*, 1921, p. 161.
[3] Rivers, op. cit., p. 97.

creation is a necessary accompaniment of mother-right, though it is evident that it must be a valuable support to the motives discussed above which led to the instituting of mother-right.

The patriarchal system, as we know it, betokens acknowledging the supremacy of the father and yet the ability to accept this even with affection, without having to have recourse to a system either of mother-right or of complicated taboos. It means the taming of man, the gradual assimilation of the Œdipus complex. At last man could face his real father and live with him. Well might Freud say that the recognition of the father's place in the family signified the most important progress in cultural development.

So far as we can tell, the way in which this has been—at least partly—accomplished has been the replacement of hate by sublimated homosexuality, of murder thoughts by castration thoughts. The necessary price paid has been the diminished sexual potency of civilized man, with all the complicated consequences of this.

VI

A PSYCHO-ANALYTICAL NOTE ON PALÆOLITHIC ART[1]

THE material Dr. Heilbronner adduces in his interesting essay[2] would seem fully to justify his conclusions that "man in the Ice Age attributed an especial significance—at first unconsciously and later consciously—to composite representations of the male and female sexual organs". This finding must forcibly remind psycho-analysts of the familiar observation that the same state of affairs is true also of the unconscious phantasies in early infancy. These are nowadays, following Melanie Klein, often referred to under the designation "combined parental image". Two explanations have been proffered for them. One would account for the phantasies on the basis of congenital homosexuality. The other would regard them as an early expression of the Œdipus conflict and of the mingled love and hate this engenders. Both explanations may, of course, be correct, but some analysts would attach greater weight to the former one, others to the latter. It is at all events highly interesting to learn that similar forces were at work among men of the Old Stone Age to those among our young children of the present day—one more example of the resemblance between primeval mentality in phylogenesis and ontogenesis.

Archæologists are generally of opinion that the motives impelling early man to execute his remarkable drawings in

[1] Published in the *International Journal of Psycho-Analysis*, Vol. XIX, 1938.
[2] P. Heilbronner, "Some Remarks on the treatment of the Sexes in Palæolithic Art," *International Journal of Psycho-Analysis*, 1938, p. 439.

remote and hardly accessible caves were not so much concerned with æsthetic feeling—in spite of the high artistic
skill displayed in some epochs—as with what may broadly
be called magic. This view was especially developed in
respect of animal drawings, it being supposed that the
craftsmen hoped thereby to acquire virtue and luck in their
hunting activities, which afforded at that time a main
source of food. It has also been suggested that an allied
motive was what analysts would call one of restitution, an
expression of guilt at the killing and a consequent desire to
expiate it by re-creating the animal in effigy. Since even
nowadays, when feelings may be supposed to be more sensi-
tive, there is relatively little remorse at killing animals for
food, and nothing in the way of expiatory rites on the part
of those who do so, we may take it for certain that any such
attitude could proceed only from a totemistic mentality, in
which the animals in question represented other human
beings, notably parents or ancestors. This equation
would suggest a possible prevalence of cannibalism at that
epoch.

Returning to the human drawings and statuettes
described by Dr. Heilbronner, we are impelled to inquire
into the significance of the changes he notes between the
Aurignacian and Magdalenian epochs of the Palæolithic
era. It is generally thought that these two epochs have to do
with the same, or a very similar, race, though this is not
quite certain; but it will be remembered that they were
separated from each other by a space of many thousands of
years through the curious intrusion of the Solutrians.
Nevertheless there is an unmistakable continuity between
the two in the custom of cave drawings, as well as certain
pronounced differences in the form these display at the two
epochs.

The salient feature of the earlier Aurignacian drawings
is the remarkable concentration on female sexual charac-

teristics. It is plain that the central concern of the craftsmen was with these. Not only do the number of female
statuettes greatly exceed those of male ones, in the proportion of seventy to five, but not one phallus has been found
to set beside the numerous images of the vulva; even when
a phallus is present in male figures it is small and incon-
spicuous. Moreover, the main features of the female figures
consist of exaggerated breasts, buttocks and abdomen
(almost pregnant in size), whereas no trouble is taken to
depict the face, even when the head is drawn in frontal
view; one is here reminded of the famous "'A was Gesicht"
passage from Schnitzler's *Reigen*. The limbs are similarly
obscured, and the description of them given by Dr. Heilbronner, together with the phallic head, seems to point
plainly to the operation of unconscious castration phantasies. It is as if the draughtsman wished to assert: "This is
emphatically a sexual and fertile woman, and anything
male connected with her must be disregarded or destroyed."

In contrasting this picture with that characteristic of the
Magdalenian epoch there would appear to have been three
important changes. Instead of the female sex predomina-
ting, the male sex is here the more prominent of the two.
Images of the vulva have become rare, those of the phallus
common. The Magdalenians are evidently more preoccupied
with their own sex than were their predecessors.

Then the artistic impulse seems to have nearly disappeared, since the figures are debased and lifeless repetitions
in a flat two-dimensional plane in place of the vivid and
plastic representation of the Aurignacian epoch. May one
not infer from this that the more purely libidinal motive has
been displaced by others of a more conflicting order?

Thirdly, the figures are represented no longer *en face*, but
in profile. One cannot but bring this feature of the drawings
into relation with the fact that palæolithic man invariably
depicted animals in profile, this being the natural posture

he was accustomed to when shooting at them to obtain food.

This last point suggests the action of aggressive or sadistic motives. The attitude of the draughtsman towards the human beings he depicted approximates in the Magdalenian epoch to that towards his prey. This could result from either an increase in cannibalism or a heightened hostility among males.

We do not know enough about the conditions of life in the two epochs to venture a sociological explanation for these differences, but we cannot resist the conclusion that for some reason, climatic or cultural, life was harder for Magdalenian than for Aurignacian man; it may well have been a time when the conscience was undergoing an important development.

VII

FREE WILL AND DETERMINISM[1]

I t is nowhere better known than in Oxford that the problem of free will is one of the most profound and baffling in the whole of philosophy, and that in consequence its literature is replete with subtle and intricate arguments about it. This, however, is a psychological Society, and I propose to deal principally with the psychological aspects of the problem. I hope at least to show that these aspects are more interesting than might be expected.

At the outset one might pose the psychological question of how it comes that this problem has possessed such an extraordinary interest for the thinkers of all ages. As far back as we have historical records, to ancient Babylon, we find the problem keenly discussed and various solutions propounded. In those times, and indeed until a couple of centuries ago, it was generally involved in theological doctrines, but even when it was not—as at times in Rome and of course in more recent days—it was just as hotly debated, with often a display of very considerable acrimony. It cannot be said that the matter has much troubled the common man, who probably takes one solution or another for granted without reflecting on it. But there must be few serious thinkers who have not in some period of their life been perplexed by the antinomy that seems to inhere in every solution. The perplexity may even reach the intensity of the *folie de doute* of those afflicted with an obsessional neurosis, who endlessly oscillate between two opposite con-

[1] Address delivered before the Oxford Psychological Society, 27th October, 1924.

clusions or decisions. But, as in that case also, it is highly unlikely that we have to do with a purely intellectual problem, like one of the teasers of mathematics. The concern alone that is manifested shows that strong emotions are involved in the argumentations. The fact that the concern seems to be restricted to a relatively small group of people does not in itself prove that the emotions are of an unusual kind, remote from the general ones of humanity, since it is known these can be stimulated in many different ways.

A second consideration that calls for psychological inquiry is the ambivalence so often to be noted among those expressing opinions on the matter. Even when a philosopher or theologian avowedly commits himself firmly to one side or the other, freedom of the will or absence of freedom, one may often observe that his conclusion is so phrased as to permit of the opposite opinion having also a place. I read this as signifying an intuition on such a person's part that there are two truths concerned in the answer to the problem, and that even when they appear to be diametrically opposite and therefore mutually exclusive there may perhaps be some plane, as yet undiscovered, on which they are to be reconciled. I intend to support this thesis in what I have to say here.

The problem of free will has constantly been involved in a number of others, among them the most profound that have vexed the mind of man. It may legitimately be asked whether it owes its emotional significance to its connection with those other problems or how much, on the other hand, do they owe some of their importance to that inhering in the matter of freedom of the will. According to Kant the existence of God, the belief in Immortality, and the question of Free Will are bound up together, and metaphysics has for its especial object the solution of these problems. They thus become the three postulates of his "practical reason". The existence of free will is equally bound up with the relation of mind to matter, and especially of mind to brain: i.e., between Idealism and Realism, the subjective versus the objective view of what appears to be external reality. Allied to this is the controversy between vitalism and the physio-chemical view of physiology, and that over the inheritance of acquired characteristics in biology. As to theology the most vital matters are concerned: the problem of evil in the world, the meaning of sin, the various methods of salvation of the soul, whether by grace or by good works, the question of moral responsibility, the basis of ethical behaviour, and the possibility or not of improving one's own character. This list of problems of cardinal import is not exhaustive, but it suffices to show what is at stake when we try to decide on some answer to that of free will.

And yet in spite of all this the sociologist makes the curious observation that in practical daily life it does not seem to make any difference whether a given person, community, or religion adopts one or the other belief, in free will or determinism. The Babylonians, who firmly believed that one's destiny was fixed at birth by the influence of the stars then in conjunction, were not in the least a fatalistic people, as one might have expected, but on the contrary a people full of enterprise and initiative with evident powers of original thought. The Calvinists who hold to pre-destination strive to lead as good a life as other Christians, although theoretically it would appear to be irrelevant to their fate in the next life. The part played in Greek tragedy by Fate, from which there was no escape, does not prevent the struggles and conflicts there depicted from being of just the same order as in a modern drama. The determinist Stoics were as set on following the path of duty and leading a moral life as the libertarian Epicureans. In the history of Christianity we can cite great names on either side. St. Paul, having been a Pharisee and not a Sadducee, adhered to the doctrine of predestination as did St. Augustine and later on both Luther and Calvin. To do otherwise would have seemed to them to derogate from the omnipotence and omniscience of God. Yet on the other side, from St. Thomas Aquinas onwards, more theologians have been believers in freedom of the will, and indeed have based on it the whole conception of salvation. At the anti-Pelagian Synod of Orange, in 529, the Catholic Church effected an interesting compromise to which most other Christian Churches have adhered. Denying predestination as a heresy, they asserted that man's innate freedom of will had been so restricted as a result of Adam's Fall that it needs the direct intervention of God to enable it to function in the desired direction.

It would be hard to maintain that these religious beliefs, vehemently attached to one side or the other, made any perceptible difference to the life of action. Those who held to free will showed no more tendency to licence or lack of responsibility than their opponents, nor did the determinism of the latter degenerate into fatalism and deprive their votaries of initiative. One could scarcely imagine more active, vehement and enterprising persons than Calvin and John Knox, the arch-priests of predestination.

Similarly with the philosopher. No one could say that Spinoza, Leibnitz, David Hume and John Stuart Mill, convinced determinists, led a restricted life or strove less than other people to perfect their character and ethical behaviour.

All this is very odd. Here we have a question on the answer to which the most momentous and vital matters depend, and which one would suppose must affect profoundly the whole outlook of a man. And yet we cannot detect any difference it makes to his life or conduct according as he adheres to one answer or to its very opposite. Surely this remarkable fact calls for much consideration.

Another interesting observation is that man's belief in free will seems to be stronger in proportion to the unimportance of the decision. Everyone is convinced that he is free to choose whether to stand or to sit at a given moment, to cross his right leg over his left or vice versa "as he wishes". With vital decisions, on the other hand, it is characteristic that he feels irresistibly impelled towards one and one only, and that he really has no choice in the matter nor desires to have any. Luther's famous "Hier stehe ich. Ich kann nicht anders" at the turning point of his career is a classical example of this, and if one asked a man why he chose to risk his life at some critical juncture he would mostly reply: "I couldn't help it. I just had to," as would a lover when asked to explain why he fell in love with one particular person.

Kant would seem to have got further than anyone else towards a solution of this great dilemma when he took the view that pure reason dictated a belief in complete determinism whereas what he called practical reason dictated an equally convinced belief in freedom of the will. His division between the two kinds of reason would nowadays be roughly correlated with the distinction between intellect and feeling, and it is now recognized that both of them play an unescapable part in deciding our beliefs. Moreover, the grounds he gave for recognizing the claims of "practical reason"—namely because of the demands of the moral law —accord with the importance we have to attribute to the moral sources of feeling.

The question from which we started, concerning the psychological motives for one or other of these beliefs, has of course been raised before, chiefly, as one would expect, by determinists, since they hold there must be motives or "causes" preceding them. Spinoza, for example, expressed the opinion that man thinks he is free simply because he does not know the causes of his wishes, and Hume made the same point. Hume went further, however, in asserting that people believe in free will (1) because of their objection to the idea of constraint, (2) their direct feeling of liberty of choice, and (3) religious influences. This is the beginning of a psychological inquiry.

Psycho-analysis from its study of the unconscious mind can make the following contributions to the problem. In the first place it is in a position to reveal the apparently unknown causes of our wishes, the feature pointed out by Spinoza and Hume. Its investigations have shown that man is only imperfectly aware of his whole personality and that consciousness is but a selection of the total mentality. The source from which all our motives and wishes spring, trivial or serious, is the unconscious mind, and we are aware only of the end products of complex mental trains. By the free association technique one can over and again demonstrate that a choice felt by the individual to be a purely spontaneous one on his part is in fact related to various past thoughts and interests—ultimately of a very personal order. You may carry out this interesting experiment by following up the old play "Think of a name" or "think of a number", by then passively allowing its associations to enter your mind. The upshot of this work is the conclusion that ignorance of the causes of our choice is no longer a reason for believing that it is uncaused, or that our will is free to initiate any thought or decision without being influenced by previous experiences.

The second contribution psycho-analysis can make is to point out that ratiocination has but a limited power outside consciousness. Unconscious attitudes, whether they are tantamount to belief or disbelief, are beyond its influence. A good example of this is the question of immortality. Many people are convinced, on what they would hold are rational grounds, that a human being is as perishable as any other animal and that after his death nothing remains of his personality except the memory in other people of the influence and activity he had exerted in his life. This, however, has no effect on the unconscious, which is quite unable to apprehend the idea of personal extinction. Even in consciousness our ability to picture being dead is a very limited one despite any rational grounds to the contrary.

The third contribution of psycho-analysis concerns the motives actuating the various beliefs about freedom of the will. There are deep sources for both sets of beliefs, and which of the two is accepted in consciousness largely depends on what interpretation the unconscious gives to the question, i.e., what it comes to *mean* to the unconscious.

The sense of self-ness is the most typical attribute of what we call the ego, and it is commonly believed that this ego is a sharply defined unity, as it were a pin-point of consciousness in the universe. Investigations of the deeper layers of the mind, however, reveal that the ego is not only a complex structure, one which is even liable in certain morbid states to disintegrate into its elements, but is a product of many factors. It is a part only of the mind, one elaborated by degrees out of the primordial unconscious which Freud has recently termed the *id*. Furthermore, an important part of the ego, appropriately termed the super-ego, is set apart with certain defensive functions such as warning the ego against the dangers of being overpowered by irruptive impulses from the *id*; in favourable circumstances the super-ego becomes the conscience, and from the beginning it has a moral nature far harsher than any conscience. These considerations have, as will presently be seen, an important bearing on our question of motivation.

When I remarked just now that all turns on the interpretation given by the unconscious, I meant to indicate that everything depends on the relation between the ego and the super-ego. When the latter is functioning successfully it reassures the ego that it need not fear the terrible dangers emanating from the repressed unconscious. What the person ought to do or is wise to do then becomes much the same as the wish to do it. There is little or no conflict between the sense of free will and the belief in determinism, and the person will show little interest in the problem. It is a type that suffers little from anxiety, because the strongly organized ego has confidence in its ability to hearken to a friendly warning super-ego and to defend itself without any difficulty from any danger.

There are, however, other graver possibilities. If the ego is intimidated by the warnings of the super-ego and yet is unwilling to trust the defensive powers of the latter we have the type of person to whom "self-control" (including the belief in free will) becomes obsessive. Such people cannot relax, they are often afraid of "losing control" and going mad, they are afraid of hypnotism or of being deprived of their conscious control through the administration of an anæsthetic, and are apt to suffer from insomnia, due to the fear of "letting go". An opposite type to this nevertheless arrives at the same belief in free will. It is one where the harshness of the super-ego is so great as to lead to a defiant rebellion on the part of the ego, which so to speak insists on having its own way and being its own master. They are the people Hume had in mind when he spoke of the objection to compulsion and loss of freedom (confounded with loss of political or social liberty) which the concept of determinism seems to imply. In yet another type unconscious fear may make the person feel safer at the idea of determinism. The notion of a break in the uniformity of natural law brings a dread of chaos. If they are religious people they may feel it impious, as the Calvinists do, to deny the omnipotence and omniscience of God by daring to assert any claim to individual initiative independently of Him. "God's will be done" is a familiar phrase of resigned submission.

I have been dealing here, in an extremely condensed way, with some advanced and only recently developed psychological conceptions, all relating to the unconscious mind which is very unfamiliar territory. The interplay between the different parts of the mind is much more complex than I have just sketched, so that the final influence of the various conflicts on the conscious attitude towards the problem of free will is hard to predict without knowing something of the relative strength of the forces concerned. But the main consideration I have tried to convey is that the matter of *internal security*, which is striven for by devious routes, is probably the key to extreme attitudes concerning free will and determinism. There are of course philosophical and rational grounds for believing in one or the other of these, but I am persuaded that even philosophers may be influenced by unconscious motives the nature of which I have endeavoured to indicate.

The concept of "causality" is at present undergoing important modifications, and the use of it will probably be replaced by the simpler one of "correlation". Psychological science, any more than any other, cannot do without the latter concept, and in its postulate of orderly relationship subsisting between phenomena must therefore be as deterministic as the rest of science. The irruptions of spontaneous and unrelated phenomena supposedly emanating from "free will" would make nonsense of its scientific pretensions, and I have indicated that investigation of the unconscious has made it unnecessary to postulate any such unrelatedness. It has, however, the special feature in this connection that it has to take into account the phenomenon of a belief in this unrelated spontaneity, i.e., free will. Psycho-analysis of the unconscious shows that, whatever the conscious attitude towards the matter may be, there exist in the deeper layers of the mind the strongest, and probably ineradicable, motives creating what may be called the "sense of free will", closely connected with the sense of personality itself and retained so long as this is retained, i.e., until insanity, delirium or death dissolve it. That from the point of view of scientific objectivity this belief is illusory is irrelevant to the fact of its existence, and in a way to the necessity of its existence.

We come back therefore to Kant's two forms of truth, to his "critical reason" and "practical reason", but we see, much better than he had the opportunity of doing, a chance of reconciliation between the two in place of regarding them as an insoluble antinomy. When there is internal harmony in the mind the sense of free will becomes fused with the sense of inevitability, as with Luther's pronouncement which I mentioned earlier. This internal harmony may be expressed in religious terms, such as Spinoza's statement that the highest liberty consists in the service of God. Or it may be expressed in secular terms as when Leibnitz, not a determinist like Spinoza, proclaimed that freedom meant self-realization. Which of these two you prefer will depend again on other things.

Postscript

More recently some arguments derived from atomic physics have given a fresh turn to this ancient controversy and have illustrated once again how in the endeavour to sustain belief in the objectivity of free will support is sought in every possible direction. Starting from Planck's quantum theory and Heisenberg's uncertainty principle some physicists, notably Sir Arthur Eddington and in more ambiguous ways Sir James Jeans, hold that determinism is absent on the atomic plane and apparently present on the macrocosmic one only because of the effect of statistical averages. The basis of this conclusion would seem to be the awkward fact—no doubt inherent in the peculiar conditions of experimentation—that while the speed of an electron can be measured and its position in space determined it is impossible to make both these observations simultaneously. The authors rather leap from this to the conclusion that the movement of an individual atom is quite unrelated to any other event, i.e., that it is unconditional. Then the further step is taken to assert that since the material world is not deterministic therefore the mind need not be, so we have the right to claim free will for it. Eddington writes: "A complete determinism of the material universe cannot be divorced from determinism of the mind. . . . Conversely if we wish (*sic*) to emancipate mind we must to some extent emancipate the material world also."

The arguments transcend the sphere of psychology, which was the theme of my address, but I note that Susan Stebbing in a book devoted to the subject has published a trenchant criticism, one widely acknowledged to be valid, of the philosophical principles and dialectics employed by the group of physicists in question. Furthermore I note that Planck himself, in spite of his believing in free will on moral grounds, has with superb integrity resisted the temptation to join them in exploiting—shall one say?—the facts of atomic physics, and that Einstein agrees with him in ranging himself against the conclusion that determinism does not hold good in external nature.

The most comprehensive and profound study of this modern aspect of the problem is to be found in E. Cassirer's *Determinismus und Indeterminismus in der modernen Physik*, 1937. He writes: "From the significance of freedom as a mere possibility limited by natural laws there is no avenue to that 'reality' of volition and freedom of decision with which ethics is concerned. To mistake the 'choice' (*Auswahl*) which an electron has between different quantum orbits with a 'choice' (*Wahl*) in the ethical sense of this word would signify becoming the victim of a purely linguistic equivocality. To speak of an ethical 'choice' there must be not only different possibilities but also a conscious distinction between them and furthermore a conscious decision about them. To attribute such acts to an electron would be a relapse into a gross type of anthropomorphism." He sums up: "It is of no avail whether causality in nature is regarded in the form of rigorous 'dynamical' laws or of merely statistical laws. . . . In neither case does there remain open any access to that sphere of 'freedom' which is claimed by ethics."

VIII

THE PSYCHOLOGY OF RELIGION[1]

In spite of the excellent work done by the pioneers in this field some quarter of a century ago—I need only mention the names of Coe, Davenport, Flournoy, Frazer, Höffding, King, Starbuck, and, above all, Leuba—the claim they advanced that religious phenomena can be brought within the orbit of science has not yet been generally, or even widely, conceded. It is fully intelligible that we should meet here the last ditch of the anti-evolutionary. The belief in a miraculous special creation, which has been given up by all modern thinkers in respect of man's body and is gradually being renounced in respect of the greater part of his mind, is tenaciously clung to when the question of his religious activities is raised. The crudest form that this takes is the view that man's soul, comprising his "religious faculty", is divinely implanted as such, so that it is both impious and fruitless to inquire into its origin: this naturally goes together with the idea that it is peculiar to man and not to be correlated with any manifestations such as fear, respect and awe which we may find in other animals. The alternative view, indicated by the very existence of this symposium, is the genetic one that religious manifestations, like all other human ones, must have developed out of simpler, and ultimately non-religious, forms of mental life. The arguments that have been adduced in support of this standpoint, and of the justification for the psychological study of religion,

[1] Read before the International Congress of Psychology at Groningen, 7th September, 1926. Published in the *British Journal of Medical Psychology*, Vol. VI.

particularly those advanced by Coe and Leuba, appear to me so cogent that I shall waste no words in dwelling on them here. It only remains to make the obvious comment that even for those who adopt the genetic standpoint it is still possible to maintain philosophically that the evolution of religion is merely one of the mysterious ways, like the other evolutionary ones, which the Creator has employed in order to bring about an appreciation and worship of His greatness. The problem of the existence or non-existence of such a Creator is not open to direct investigation as such, and will always be decided solely by the operation of internal mental processes, on the nature of which, however, much light can now be thrown.

In the attempt to get as near as we can to the meaning of religion we are met at the outset by a very imperfect agreement about what is to be included under the term. Any psychological theory of religion, therefore, is open to the criticism that it does not comprehend this or that feature which is alleged to be essential. Some criticisms of this kind are merely factious and prove nothing more than that the theory in question is incomplete, which the author himself would in most cases admit: to seek to define religion exactly would be, like defining sexuality, a presumptuous undertaking in the present state of our knowledge and we must be content with the fact that after all we have a very good general idea of what is meant by the word. There is a wide agreement that any comprehensive theory must take into account at least the following aspects of the problem: (1) Other-worldliness, the relation to the supernatural. This has been described as "the consciousness of our practical relation to an invisible spiritual order". The spiritual order is invested with the attributes of power and sacredness. The emotional attitudes towards it vary, those of dependence, fear, love and reverence being the most characteristic; the first-named is perhaps the most constant. Propitiation is common, though not invariable. (2) The effort to cope with the various problems surrounding death, both emotionally and intellectually. (3) The pursuit and conservation of values, especially those felt to be the highest and most permanent. (4) A constant association with the ideals of ethics and morality. Religion is rarely found apart from these ideals, though they are often found, especially among civilized peoples, independently of religion. (5) The connection between religion and the sense of inadequacy in coping with the difficulties of life, whether these difficulties be external or, more characteristically, internal ones such as the conviction of sin and guilt.

Each of these features has been singled out at various times as constituting the central kernel of religion. Thus, to mention but a few, we have Statius' famous "primus in orbe Deos fecit timor"; Herbert Spencer's attempt to trace the beginning of religion to the necessity of propitiating dead ancestors and his other view of it as an hypothesis to render the universe comprehensible; the stress laid on sacredness by Durckheim; Feuerbach's reduction of religion to the "instinct for happiness"; Frazer's definition of religion as "a propitiation and conciliation of powers superior to man"; Höffding's conception of it as a conservation of values, and so on. Leuba sees in this endless attempt to find a unitary explanation of religion the chief obstacle to constructing a proper psychology of it, and he has come to the important conclusion that the various manifestations and aspects of religion must have been derived from different, and presumably disparate, sources. Personally I regard this conclusion as an unnecessary counsel of despair, though we might learn from it the wisdom of prefacing any attempt at generalization by a more patient analysis of the individual phenomena.

The attempt to translate religious manifestations into terms of the primary emotions and instincts has not met with much better success, probably because the psychology of the instinctual life is itself so insecurely founded. Fear has been made to play a central part by many writers, but evidences of it are present in only certain groups of religious phenomena, being apparently quite absent in others. Irving King and others have laid stress on the cultural and social sources of religion, and Trotter's hint of the connection between it and the herd instinct should also be mentioned. The so-called instincts of self-assertiveness and self-submission evidently play a part in some manifestations. The connection between religion and sexuality has been warmly debated, but the discussions of it have been largely vitiated by the tendency to take up extreme positions. Leuba, for instance, in his standard text-book on the subject, makes no reference to the connection, while William James positively denies that any exists. The evidence for the connection, however, is too unequivocal to be ignored and is indeed far more extensive than is generally known. But most advocates of the supposed erotogenesis of religion have stated their views in much too simplistic terms to carry conviction.

The last discussion of the psychology of religion held before this Congress, at the Sixth Meeting that was held at Geneva in 1909, represented the high-water mark of our knowledge at that time, and perhaps the furthest point to which academic psychology was able to take us. Since then, however, a revolution in our knowledge has taken place, one which demands attention in considering the problems of religion. I refer to the increasing realization, primarily due to the writings of Freud and his school, of the enormous importance of the unconscious mental life. The view taken by this school, and supported by a formidable mass of evidence, is that the primordial and essential part of our mental life is unconscious, whereas consciousness, the part which was formerly taken for the whole, is seen to constitute only a carefully selected portion of this whole. What was previously regarded as primary elements in our consciousness we now know to be the highly elaborated end-products of a complicated chain of imperceptible (unconscious) mental processes. Since religious manifestations give every sign of proceeding from the very depths of the personality it would not be surprising if the patient elucidation of the processes that go on in these depths, their nature, strength and interaction, were to throw light on the mysteries of religion. Freud himself and several of his followers, including Reik, Róheim, Pfister, Löwenstein, Kinkel, Levy, Dukes, the present writer and others, have published a number of detailed studies on various aspects of religion. Up to the present, however, there has been no comprehensive presentation of the bearing of these studies on the psychology of religion as a whole, nor can such a task be attempted in the short space at my disposal here. Nevertheless some indication must be offered of the main principles along which such a presentation would proceed.

Psycho-analysis has called attention to a region which should logically be investigated before recourse is had to the more obscure and remote region of the inherited instincts. I refer to the infantile mind, which is continued in later life as the unconscious mind and constitutes the essence of the latter. Both the content and the mode of functioning of the infantile mind differ widely from those of the adult conscious one and the greater part of it becomes buried in later life, "repressed" and inaccessible to consciousness, as the result of powerful forces acting in this direction. There is the strongest possible tendency to depreciate the significance of infantile mental processes, which are felt to be merely "childish", so that any attempt to correlate them with important adult ones meets with instinctive incredulity. To take a simple illustration of this. If one were to correlate the abject fear of supernatural agencies that has been experienced so many countless times, and the fear that can still be experienced of the awful wrath of God, with the fear that a child may feel for his father, no one can well appreciate the significance of this who has not had personal experience, through psycho-analysis of the unconscious, of how intense the child's dread of the father can be.

In the past quarter of a century a vast experience has accumulated from psycho-analytic investigation of the religious life of individuals, and in addition, as was mentioned above, a great number of works have been published containing psycho-analytic studies of various aspects of religious beliefs and other phenomena. The outstanding conclusion that emerges from all this investigation is that *the religious life represents a dramatization on a cosmic plane of the emotions, fears and longings which arose in the child's relation to his parents.* This is a sentence which must remain without much meaning for those who have not taken cognizance of the modern study of the unconscious mind, but it is pregnant for those who have.

The five aspects of the problem of religion enumerated above may now be commented on in that order.

(1) Relation to a supernatural spiritual order, characteristically to supernatural beings. The attributes of power and taboo connected with these, and the varying emotional attitudes, notably those of dependence, fear, love and reverence, are all direct reproductions of the child's attitude towards his parents. The child's sense of the absolute as felt in its original attitude towards his own importance is, when it becomes impaired by contact with reality, partly continued as the anthropocentric view of the universe implicit in all religions and partly displaced, first on to the parents and then, when this also fails, on to divine beings; the earthly father is replaced by the Heavenly Father. The conflicts with the parents that necessarily arise during the

process of upbringing, the essence of which consists in the regulation of—or interference with—the infantile sexuality (or child's love life, if the phrase be preferred), are for the greater part unconscious even at the time. They lead to repressed death wishes against the parents, with a consequent fear of retaliation, and from this comes the familiar religious impulse to propitiate the spirits of dead ancestors or other spiritual beings. The accompanying love leads to the desire for forgiveness, reconciliation, help and succour.

(2) All the emotional problems surrounding death arise, not from the philosophical contemplation of dead strangers, but from ambivalence towards the person's loved ones. Dread of death invariably proves clinically to be the expression of repressed death wishes against loved objects. It is further found that the themes of death and castration (or the equivalent withdrawal of the loved object) are extremely closely associated and that anxiety concerning indefinite survival of the personality constantly expresses the fear of a punitive impotence.

(3) The primal self-love and self-importance of the child, which more nearly approaches the absolute than any other experience in life, is commonly displaced on to a selected portion of the mind called the super-ego, an ideal of what the ego longs to be as the result of its moral education. The sense of supreme values, of a rich "meaning" in life, which plays a cardinal part in all the higher religions, is a typical manifestation of this striving. It is, of course, related to the desire to be reconciled with God and to be approved of by Him.

(4) The constant association of religion with morality is another aspect of this same feature.

(5) The sense of inadequacy in coping with life, Janet's "*sentiment d'incomplétude*", Freud's "inferiority complex", may appear in any aspect of life, physically, morally, intellectually, and so on. Psycho-analysis of the pheno-

menon, however, reveals a unitary origin, namely in the sense of sin or guilt aroused in the child in his endeavour to make all his impulses conform with adult moral standards. It is thus psychologically comprehensible that all manifestations of inadequacy, in whatever sphere, can be allayed by dealing with their origin by religious means; to be reconciled with the Father is the same thing as to obtain assistance from him. It is well known what a central part the conviction of sin plays in religion; without it, and the consequent necessity for salvation, the Christian religion, for instance, would be well-nigh emptied of meaning.

In conclusion I would ask that the simplistic appearance of the foregoing propositions be not taken as a token of their nature. It is an inevitable result of the attempt to present in a few words an exceedingly complicated and novel body of doctrine.

IX

PSYCHO-ANALYSIS AND THE CHRISTIAN RELIGION[1]

I PRESUME I owe the invitation to speak to you on this topic to the interest aroused by the current series of Broadcast talks on Science and Religion.[2] In looking through the list of speakers I was specially struck by one thing: there is no psychologist among them. Perhaps your invitation is the result of making the same observation. Theologians debate with anthropologists, biologists, and even physicists, but no one mentions the simple fact that after all religious beliefs and emotions are in themselves mental phenomena. Whether they are brought about by mundane or by supernatural agents they are in either case susceptible to study by those accustomed to investigate mental phenomena, i.e., psychologists. Moreover, many such studies have already been carried out, with very interesting results, as will be known by those who have access to the various periodicals entirely devoted to the subject or to the many books by such authors as William James, Starbuck, Leuba, etc. The first of these studies were on a purely descriptive plane and had no pretensions to offering any explanation of the facts observed. Even so, when it was shown that such familiar phenomena as sudden religious conversion could be positively correlated with matters like age, sex, surroundings, previous mental state of the subject, and so on, it could no longer be maintained that supernatural agencies were the only ones concerned.

[1] Read before the Lotus Club, Oxford University, 22nd November, 1930.
[2] *The Listener*, October-December, 1930.

From such humble beginnings as this, however, religious psychology has in the last forty years made great strides and is now in a position to give some scientific answers to some of the most fundamental theological problems.

I intend to confine myself here to only a part of this vast subject, namely to the contributions that psycho-analysis has made to our understanding the meaning of religions, and more particularly to that of the Christian one. The first of them was made in 1908 when Freud called attention to the psychological resemblances between religious rituals and the ceremonials of obsessional neurotics, the unconscious genesis of which he had recently unravelled. The great differences are of course evident enough, the social nature of the one as contrasted with the private individualism of the other, the sense of high value in the one case and of futile worthlessness in the other. Both are carried out with the same sense of conscientiousness and with both there is a dread of pangs of conscience if they are omitted. Both depend on a renunciation of primitive impulses, sexual or aggressive. Both are prepared to avoid a feared calamity. With religious rituals the calamity is evidently a punishment by God, either in this world or more certainly in the next. If they are carried out successfully then not only will God refrain from punishing or damning one eternally but may bless and love one. There is here a difference from the obsessional ritual, where the person can hope only for the former of these two benefits. His psychology is based on repressed hatred of his father, with a consequent fear of retaliatory punishment, and his rituals symbolize acts of appeasement or restitution only; love is beyond him.

This comparison of the religious devotee with an obsessional neurotic raises at once two important questions. What really is the dreaded calamity that has to be warded off by semi-magical means? And what is the source of the disagreement with the Father or with God that demands such penance or reconciliation? The remarkable state of affairs with the obsessional neurotic is not to be accounted for by any current situation. The man may be in fact on excellent terms with his father, or he may even not have a father, yet the neurosis when its apparently unintelligible manifestations are analysed has the meaning I have just mentioned—a conflict of emotions concerning the subject's attitude to his father, or rather his idea of a father. The key to the riddle lies in the words: the unconscious and infancy. The person has never emancipated himself from emotions he experienced in infancy, which we have all experienced in varying degrees of intensity, and which belong to the unconscious system of the mind quite remote from consciousness.

The conscious mind radiates over a thousand interests and activities, the mind of the young infant does not extend far from a few immediate concerns. Its emotions, before they have been more or less disciplined during growth, are of a passionate and uncontrolled intensity such as are seldom met with in later life except in the outbursts of insanity. They relate essentially to the parents, or whoever stands *in loco parentis*, and they are of the opposite kinds. On the one hand the baby, born without the experience of frustrated wishes and in consequence of this with a feeling of omnipotence, soon has to cope with numerous experiences of being thwarted and of being helpless in the face of them. Its only hope of countering this situation by getting its wishes gratified, and in that way recapturing some sense of power, is to appeal to the apparently omnipotent parent. The omnipotence is thus displaced and an attitude of love and awe developed towards the parent. This brings with it, however, the great disadvantage of dependence. All is well so long as its wishes and the parent's friendly response coincide, but the awful possibility remains of the latter being withdrawn and the situation of helplessness being re-established, this time without any hope left. The danger of this is related to the infant's own feelings of resentment, anger and hostility that are aroused whenever the parent's response to its needs is not immediate or positive, as must inevitably happen from time to time. Hostile feelings at that age are still in terms of the absolute: that is, they are equivalent to the instant destruction of the hated object, and this in turn means the disappearance of the person on which the infant is so dependent. Later on the word "disappearance" becomes softened into "turning away from" or "disapproval" on the parent's part, but that is in itself bad enough. The theme I have just touched on is far more complex in fact—I have for instance not yet mentioned the important part played by sexual sensations and sex jealousy—but I would maintain that no psychology of religion is possible without taking into serious account the psychological relation of infant to parent.

We cannot get away from the simple facts that God is commonly called God the Father; that His official representatives on earth bear the same title, Pope, Padre, Father, and so on; that, so we are told, we are all "Children of God"; and thus His benevolence, His mercy and loving care for each of us is just what we all craved for from our own parent and mostly experienced—at least to begin with. When our own parents' limitations and imperfections begin to become evident, it is no wonder that those who are unable to sustain life without help and who are still dependent on an outside source, should seek for an all-powerful and all-loving Person who should stand above all the vexations of this earth and who should never fail one. Never, that is to say, as long as one's relation to Him was satisfactory, one of dutiful love and obedience.

This proviso is all important and indeed contains the key to any understanding of religion. For why should one's relation to one's Father, whether earthly or heavenly, not be satisfactory? Much of the story of mankind lies in the answer to that question: the conflict of the generations, the fight between the new and the old, the struggle between subordinate and superior, between subject and ruler, and between the unsuccessful and the successful in life. Unfortunately love and friendliness do not dominate our life, certainly not exclusively. There are also rebellious and aggressive tendencies which in the depth of the mind are more poisonous in their hostility than as a rule we allow ourselves to become aware of. They are in themselves unconsciously felt to be dangerous, both to oneself and to other people, and we have developed a "bad conscience" about them in the hope of thus checking their activity. This is especially so, and for obvious reasons, when they are experienced *vis-à-vis* those whom we most love and on whom we are also dependent—in the first place our parents. The bad conscience, which can also be described as a sense of moral unworthiness, leads to all sorts of feelings of inferiority from which few people are altogether exempt. We come here to the origin of "sin", which may be defined theologically as disobedience to God's will.

Failure to remedy the discord between oneself and God is naturally believed to entail terrible consequences. Here the sadistic phantasies of the infant's unconscious can obtain free play; the horrors and eternal tortures of hell know no limits. For obvious reasons the wrath of God is thought more likely to find expression in the after life than in this one, so that dread of death, or what Hamlet more accurately calls "the dread of something after death", has always been a matter of the greatest concern to mankind. In the broadcast symposium Professor Malinowski, the anthropologist, described the essence of religion in rather intellectualistic terms as preoccupation with the problem of survival after death and the desire to ascertain the Divine Purpose in the universe. This is the burning question, for both are in essence one; what one really wants to know about the Divine Purpose is its intention towards *oneself*, how to discover the way to be well treated in the next world. Then Professor Huxley, the biologist, strikes a deeper note in finding the attitude of awe to be the essence of religion. From this is derived on the one hand love of God, with the desire to know His will and the sense of mystery that accompanies this search, and on the other hand fear, with the feeling of dependence on unknown powers and the need to attain some degree of harmony with them. Canon Streeter holds the distinction between religion and science to be that the former is concerned with moral values and the desire to ascertain God's conception of them—again the Divine Purpose in slightly different terms. The study of comparative religion has shown such variety in the results of this search that he suspects man himself has had a considerable share in establishing moral ideals, which brings us back to the psychological problem of the origin of man's ideals—and psychology is after all a branch of science.

The comparison between religion and the obsessional neurosis, which must have seemed absurdly far-fetched at first sight, is thus becoming more significant. Both emanate from the feeling of moral badness due to hostility against the Father, in the one case the earthly one, in the other the heavenly one; and both are desperately concerned with the urgent need of coming to terms with him. The obsessional neurotic has the lowlier aim of the two. His complicated ritualistic restitutions have merely the aim, like that of those contemplated by Johannes Agricola as striving

> . . . to win
> If not love like God's love for me,
> At least to keep his anger in.

Other forms of neurosis, e.g., hysteria, have more positive aims, the achievement not only of forgiveness but also of love, and of course this is the ultimate goal of religious endeavour.

There are those who do not feel much need of this salvation, whether because of their good conscience or because they have somehow come to terms with their inner nature. Such people ask wonderingly "what are we to be saved from?" and are still more puzzled on being told that they are in danger of the wrath of God which will express itself in the next world in terms of torture, mutilation and damnation. What sin can be commensurate with such bloodthirsty treatment? As I have already mentioned, the tortures and damnation emanate from the infant's lively and unrestrained sadistic phantasies and are of the same nature as his own hostile wishes against his father for which the punishments are (projected) retaliations. Why is all this so savage? Because the essential sin against the father (or mother according to the sex) originates in the most intimate region of the personality—in the sexual instinct. The boy's jealous wish to castrate or kill his rival and so obtain possession of his mother, with unrestricted access to her body, has been given the name of Œdipus complex after the unfortunate hero (mythologically derived from the son of the Earth-Mother goddess, Demeter) who suffered so grievously after committing both these sinful acts. There are of course innumerable ways of expressing these wishes, various forms of rebellion against authority or the moral code or of desecration of the holy places (altar, etc.) sacred to God. But if we bear constantly in mind this profound Œdipus origin of the sense of sin we shall be in a better position to understand the various ways in which mankind has sought to evade its dreaded consequences, i.e., to be "saved".

The mind has only a very limited capacity for apprehending the idea of personal death in its literal meaning of extinction and bodily disintegration. In its deeper layers the idea of consciousness being abrogated, as for instance during sleep or death, always becomes equated with return to the ante-conscious period of existence, to pre-natal life, from which waking life may again arise. These womb phantasies may be either agreeable or horrifying, according to the associations, innocent or guilty, that have been made with the idea of the mother's genitals. They are often projected on a cosmic scale to the picture of the next world, and they then give us when we awake from the sleep of death the image of heaven or hell accordingly.

Man seems always to have known that, broadly speaking, there are only two ways of achieving salvation and of thus assuring that one's after-life will be one of bliss and not torment. They are via mother-love and father-love respectively. The former is doubtless the more attractive, but the latter appears to be the more efficacious. Which is chosen probably depends on the type of civilization present, whether light or serious minded, and on whether its predominant note is matriarchal or patriarchal. In the Near East, on the confines of Europe and Asia, a number of religions developed in which the Great Mother played a central part, and later on in Rome they competed for a time very seriously with early Christianity. The typical version of the story they incorporated was that of the Dying God, the God who fell a victim to malign influences, but whose body was always found and resuscitated by the Great Mother. Thus the priests of Cybele, often self-castrated, would hold a recurrent festival in which on the third day Attis, her son, would again be brought to life through the ministrations and intercession of his mother. This gave the believers the assurance that they would have the same fate, and the blood of the frenzied priests was held in Roman days to be more potent to save than the blood of the Lamb adored by Christians. Isis of Egypt displayed a similar beneficence to Serapis-Osiris, periodically restoring him to life. Many features of her religion are reminiscent of the Christian ritualism. There was holy water, there were tonsured priests (now only symbolically castrated), and the Goddess herself was known as the "Mother of Tenderness" and the "Mother of Sorrows" (Mater Dolorosa!). The believers achieved the assurance of a happy immortality through identifying themselves with the risen Osiris.

At the other extreme from this were the patriarchal and monotheistic Jews who repudiated all commerce with goddesses and sought to come to terms directly with God. By entering into "covenants" with Him, and obeying His commandments, they hoped if not for tender love, at least for a benevolent attitude on His part. While Catholicism appears to represent a compromise between the two modes of salvation—intercession by the Madonna plays a very important part in it—Protestantism has reverted to the more patriarchal solution.

There is, however, between the two already mentioned a third possibility, one in which the Dying God is not simply a passive agent, being resuscitated by a powerful and tender Mother-Goddess, but takes an important active part himself in the process of salvation. There were adumbrations of this idea in various Eastern religions, but it was central in the two that ran such a close race for acceptance in Rome, Mithraism and Christianity. With the former of these, characteristically the religion of soldiers, the young Son-God resolutely opposes the father and becomes the Master of his own fate. Early in his career he struggled with the Sun and forced him to do him homage. In the central ceremony of the Mithraic religion he faces a bull, a typical father-symbol—here representing the Persian deity Ahura-Mazda—and slays him. It is significant that he is represented as doing this unwillingly, averting his gaze as he deals the fatal blow with his knife as if to indicate some regret for the parricidal deed. After accomplishing it he ascended to heaven, and doubtless ruled there, whence he succours those who believe in his heroic powers. There was also a Eucharist in Mithraism. The fact, however, that women were excluded from Mithraic ceremonies seems to have been fatal to the future prospects of the religion when it had to compete with the more tender and appealing Christian one.

With Jesus, another son of God, we meet with an almost exactly opposite solution. So far from defying the Father, he laid all possible emphasis on submitting oneself to his will. If this be done whole-heartedly enough, as Jesus himself taught by his example, then a state of reconciliation, or even At-One-Ment, with the Father could be attained. More than this, one would win his personal love and care. As with the other Eastern religions, this desirable goal was to be reached by following the example of the Son-God and identifying oneself with him as far as possible by "believing" in him. It was also necessary to identify oneself with all fellow-believers, brethren and sisters in Christ. This identification re-establishes the loving harmony of the primal family situation and abolishes all the jealousy, rivalry and hostility latent in it.

So far this is familiar ground, but Christianity is an extraordinarily rich and complex religion which has incorporated many diverse elements from earlier ones. To this feature it probably owes much of its success. Some Christians, but they are in the minority, are content with the Eastern form of salvation described earlier. One will be saved if one adopts the Saviour's attitude of submission to the Almighty Father and endeavours to follow his example in obeying the Divine precepts of ethical behaviour. Most Christians, however, consider that the road to salvation is harder than this. To begin with, it is necessary that the priestly representatives of God perform a ceremony that symbolizes re-birth; one has to be "born anew in Christ". In this relic of Mother salvation holy Water, the most typical accompaniment of birth symbolism, is of course essential. It is far from being the only relic of the kind in Christianity. Jesus's gentleness and tenderness, for instance, are among his most prominent features and according to our hymns surpass the devotion and tenderness of a mother to her child.

Nevertheless the great question still arises whether the primordial sinfulness of mankind is not so facinorous as to be beyond the powers of an unaided mortal, even a regenerate one, to redeem, and it is generally held that Divine assistance is needed. This grace from above, so Catholics teach, will co-operate with the believer's own efforts, although Calvinists hold it to be independent of such efforts—the final state having been predestined long before the individual's birth, Grace is to be obtained partly by invoking by prayer the Almighty's mercy, but more effectively through the ceremony of the mass or holy communion. This must have meant originally, as indeed it still does in the Catholic Church, eating the flesh and blood of the Saviour, an incorporation which portrays the closest imaginable identification with him. In the Dionysian frenzies the worshippers used actually to tear and devour the raw flesh of an ox or goat who represented the god. This reinforced the Divine element in man, who had first been created by Zeus, the father of Dionysius, out of the Titans who had slain the Son-God, boiled his limbs, devoured them and had thus incorporated that element.[1] The method of identification here employed corresponds with infantile phantasies of devouring a parent and so acquiring strength, phantasies with which we are very familiar in psycho-

[1] For the historical precursors of the Mass *see* Preserved Smith, *A Short History of Christian Theophagy*, 1922.

analytic work. It no doubt has an ancient history, going back to the savage custom of killing and eating one's parents when they get too old to work—a primeval form of inheriting. Doubtless these pious customs have more sinister sources still in the cannibalistic tendencies of early man, now for the most part, though by no means entirely, repressed.

Jesus functioned as a Saviour in yet another way. Those believing in him may assuage God's wrath at their sins, and even win His love, not only by following His son's submissive attitude towards Him and by a mystical union with Him. For Jesus also performed the tremendous deed of taking of himself the sins of mankind and by a vicarious sacrifice propitiated God his Father through in that way expiating those sins—a deed which naturally evokes profound gratitude and adoration from those who might otherwise be damned. We cannot here enter into the ethics of those who thus divest themselves of moral responsibility, but it is of interest to recollect both that the scheme of the scapegoat-god is itself an ancient one and also that to take the blame for others is a laudable tendency which is to be met with even in childhood, as is the less desirable, and far more frequent, one of ascribing the blame to others.

In most Eastern religions the Godhead consists of a Trinity—Father, Mother and Son—which appropriately reproduces the family situation where all the conflicts are born that religion sets out to alleviate or remedy. For centuries the Jews, with their pronounced and patriarchal monotheistic tendencies, strove, with varying success, to abolish Mother-worship, and it is doubtless because of its Jewish component that it plays only a veiled part in Christianity. So, although the idea of the Trinity is maintained, the third member of it has an ambiguously nebulous character, in spite of a probable derivation from the Spirit that moved upon the face of the waters in the beginning of the world and who must originally have been a brooding Mother. In the Spirit's relationship to the Virgin Mary he unmistakably performs the fertilizing functions of the Father, and yet the comfort and tenderness the grace of the Holy Spirit brings to believers has plainly a maternal quality.

Ever since Christianity achieved its dominating position in Europe it has contained two opposed trends over the part to be played by the feminine element in it. On the one hand the North of Europe has reverted on the whole to the Hebrew tradition of patriarchalism with its subordination of that element. There are even Protestant circles where the mention of the Virgin Mary is almost anathema, and the general attitude is to regard her as a purely passive agent who was rather unfortunately necessary for the purpose of introducing Jesus to a mundane existence. To denigrate the mother is one of the most effective ways of denying the incestuous wishes that lie behind the conflict with the father, the real sin against him. On the other hand, in Southern countries, and notably in the Catholic Church, the status of the Virgin Mary has steadily risen and the primordial Trinity is not far from being re-established. The devotion felt for the tenderness of her personality, and her powers of intercession to procure salvation, do not fall far short of the attributes of the original Mother Goddess. Her virginity when bearing Jesus, however, is not so much a tribute to her purity as a derivation from the son's Œdipus complex. The common infantile phantasy of one's mother being virginal signifies a repudiation of any part played by the father in one's birth—the wish to be independent of him—and the jealous distaste felt at the idea of sexual inter-course between the parents. At the time of Jesus's birth such phantasies could be generally accepted in adult life; most gods, heroes, and great men were accorded the privi-lege of virgin birth. Even in the last century the Catholic

Church could proclaim that the Virgin Mary herself had also been born parthogenetically, emphasizing both her purity and her remoteness from male activities.

We have been concerned here only with the beliefs of Christianity, not with the important part it has played in history. Nor has it been possible to consider the remarkable ethical and spiritual ideals it has inculcated. As to the beliefs themselves psycho-analytic investigation of the unconscious mental life reveals that they correspond closely with the phantasies of infantile life, mainly unconscious ones, concerning the sexual life of one's parents and the conflicts this gives rise to. The Christian story, an elaborate attempt to deal on a cosmic plane with these universal conflicts, can be fully accounted for on human grounds alone without the necessity of invoking supernatural intervention. Whether, nevertheless, such intervention took place as well must remain a matter of opinion, but the story itself is no proof of it.

X

THE SIGNIFICANCE OF CHRISTMAS[1]

To ask why we keep Christmas is to ask a good question, i.e., one which one does not usually ask because of taking something for granted. Yet a moment's reflection will show that there is much worth asking in the question. To begin with, we might wonder why Christmas is the only one of the Christian religious festivals that makes any appeal to people who are not Christians. If someone becomes a sceptic or atheist he is apt to lose interest in the important Christian dates; he is likely to forget what ideas are commemorated by the words Epiphany, Whitsun, Advent or Palm Sunday; Eastertide loses its emotional significance and becomes merely a Spring holiday. But Christmas commonly retains as much meaning as ever. And the same is often true of people with other religions who live in contact with Christians. I remember when crossing to America a couple of years ago in December finding that nearly half of the passengers were American Jews rushing through in order to be "home for Christmas"; and no doubt the same observation could be made in any other year. There must therefore be something in the idea of Christmas that appeals to far more than interest in the date, or even the fact, of Christ's birth.

Perhaps we ought to begin further back in our inquiry and raise the question of why mankind keeps festivals at all on particular dates. It was Sir Isaac Newton, in 1730, who

---

[1] Expanded from an article written by request, in October 1931, in answer to the question: "Why do we keep Christmas?" for an American magazine, the name of which I forget—perhaps because it did not publish the article!

first drew attention to the astronomical associations of Christmas and other festivals. Many years ago General Furlong, the distinguished anthropologist, in his famous *Rivers of Life*, took the trouble to collect the dates of festivals in all parts of the world and to construct a curve indicating the times of year in which they most often occurred. The curve revealed the unmistakable fact that by far the greatest number of festivals was held at one or other of the four cardinal points in the earth's journey round the sun. The most favoured times are those of the summer and winter solstice, towards the end of June and December respectively, when the sun begins to wane or wax, when the days begin to shorten or lengthen. The times of year next in favour are those of the spring or autumn equinox, towards the end of March or of September. There can be little doubt that man has always tended, sometimes even consciously so, to associate his aspirations and emotions with these fundamental changes relating to the source of all life, the sun. It is well known how extensively the idea of the sun has permeated the religions of the world, He being the most visible and striking emblem of both the life-giving and the life-destroying forces of the universe.

We can further divide the innumerable religious festivals of the world into two broad groups, happy and unhappy ones or—to speak more accurately—into cheerful and solemn ones. There are festivals of celebration, of rejoicing; there are occasions of sheer merriment and they have at times passed over into bacchanalian orgies. Christmas plainly belongs to this group. On the other hand there are festivals which mark man's periodic need to search his heart, to make a serious review of his position in the Universe or to question his purpose in life and take a strict account with himself. The former group indicate moods of easy conscience, the latter of uneasy conscience.

To get back to the particular festival of Christmas. Before

trying to ascertain what it stands for it is necessary to know something of its historical background. Literally, of course, it signifies the date of Christ's birthday. But actually we have no knowledge of what time of the year that fell on, and even the year itself is uncertain, so there must have been some other reason for choosing a particular day on which to celebrate it. In spite of hints in the New Testament that the birth took place at the beginning of the Jewish New Year, i.e., at about the time of the autumn equinox, there was in early Christian times a number of sects who proclaimed the spring equinox as the most suitable date. Most Christians, however, seem at first to have regarded the matter of His physical birth as too mundane or even desecrating a thought to dwell on; in A.D. 245, for instance, Origen declared it to be a sin even to think of celebrating the birthday of Christ "as if he were a King Pharaoh". They confined their attention to the date when the Holy Spirit took possession of Him; that was His real Divine birth. This moment they regarded as the occasion of His baptism, and to commemorate it they chose the date of 6th January, now called Epiphany. We do not know why they chose that date, but it was one when many festivals were held in the Ancient World—probably on astronomical grounds, it being the first day on which the morning hours begin to lengthen. Epiphany and Baptism were for many centuries closely associated. By the fourth century the date of 6th January was universally accepted in the Eastern World as the time to celebrate the birth of Christ, whether the human or the divine one, and, in the oldest Christian nation, (the Armenian), that is still the date adhered to.

The theological controversies on the nature of Christ decided, however, that His divinity began at birth, so that attention was directed there. Discarding some earlier forgeries we can say that the first authentic date when Christmas Day was recorded in connection with the physical birth of Christ was A.D. 354. The matter seems to have been settled in A.D. 329 at a Council known by the name of Dionysius the little. In A.D. 400 an Imperial rescript ordered all theatres to be closed on that day (as well as at Epiphany and Easter), and in the course of the fifth century 25th December was firmly established in both East and West as the proper time to celebrate the anniversary of Christ.

The reasons why the festival was established at all, and why that particular date was selected for the purpose, are both interesting and complex. A Syrian writer of the period (a Christian) is quoted for the following frank description of the motives. "The reason why the fathers transferred the celebration of 6th January to 25th December was this. It was a custom of the heathen to celebrate on the same 25th December the birthday of the Sun, at which they kindled lights in token of festivity. In these solemnities and festivities the Christians also took part. Accordingly when the doctors of the Church perceived that the Christians had a leaning to this festival, they took counsel and resolved that the true Nativity should be solemnized on that day." This political reason had of course to be denied by the Church, and both St. Augustine and the Pope Leo the Great found it necessary to rebuke Christians for still associating Christmas with the rebirth of the Sun. The fact remains that the date had already been established in innumerable pagan religions in just this sense. The 25th December was the birthday of many a Persian, Phœnician, Egyptian, and even Teutonic Sun-God. And the decision was in line with the general syncretizing activities of the Church in the early centuries when it was combating paganism: it cannot be coincidence that—to quote a few examples—the date of Easter coincides with the similar celebration of the Phrygian god Attis (so popular in Rome) at the vernal equinox; that the festival of the Assumption of the Virgin in August has replaced the festival of the goddess Diana; the festival of St. George in April has replaced the ancient festival of the goddess Pales (one which the Romans later combined with that of Dea Roma); that the festival of St. John the Baptist in June has succeeded to the water festivals of Adonis in midsummer; that the feast of All Souls in November continues the Keltic Feast of the Dead at that time (the beginning of their New Year), and so on.

The matter was, however, a good deal more complex than the Syrian writer supposed, and can be elucidated only by considering the life-and-death struggle that Christianity was going through in the first three or four centuries in Rome. When faith in the orthodox Roman religion began to wane a number of competing Oriental ones crowded in to secure the succession, one of which was the Christian one. The general characteristic of them was the theme of a young Saviour-God who dies, either periodically or once for all, and thereby assures the eternal salvation (from the wrath of the Almighty) of those who believe in him. The series included Attis, Osiris, Adonis, Mithra, and Jesus himself. With all of them except the last two mentioned the belief in a powerful Mother Goddess, whose help secured the reassuring Resurrection of the dying God, played an important part. And it was just those two that were ahead in the struggle for general acceptance, the only two, incidentally, in which the young God died only once and afterwards reigned in heaven. There is little doubt that Mithraism, the religion especially of the army, was the most dangerous rival to Christianity, and the issue of the conflict between the two faiths appears for a time to have hung in the balance. There was much similarity in their beliefs, rituals and moral aspirations:[1] virginity, baptism, holy communion, purity, etc. But Mithraism had one serious weakness, on which the Christians seized and

[1] Kipling, in his *The Church that was at Antioch* (Limits and Renewals) equates in a vivid fashion the moral standards of the two religions.

216

thereby ensured their ultimate success. Its attitude and beliefs were exclusively masculine. In its ritual the young God took up the challenge of the wrathful father, slew him and reigned in his stead, whereas in Christianity he submits in a more feminine fashion to the will of the Father and by sacrificing himself assuages His wrath. Consistently with this solution Mithraism made the conflict one entirely between two males; there was no feminine element, no goddess, in its theology, and women were excluded from its worship. Christianity here saw its chance and incorporated from the other religions the element that had been missing in both itself and Mithraism. Isis, Cybele, Rhea, Astarte and the rest began a new lease of life. Mary, who had been little but the necessary vehicle for the begetting of a son, was rapidly raised in status and from being the Mother of God was given in the fourth century the exalted title of Queen of Heaven. Her virginal conception, the usual belief then attaching to the birth of heroes and gods, had long been established. From then on the increasing Mariolatry demanded that more attention be paid, not only to her intercessory and saving powers, but especially to her maternal role. Mother and Infant, resembling Isis and Horus, began to play a more central part in Christianity, as it still does in Roman Catholicism, so that the circumstances of the birth, including its date and the appropriate festival, assumed a cardinal importance. One might even wonder whether Christianity would have survived had it not instituted the festival of Christmas with all that it signified!

In the crisis the Roman Christians would not have been long in doubt about choosing the actual date. It was indeed dictated by the situation. In the Julian calendar 25th December was reckoned as the winter solstice and hence as the Nativity of the Sun when the day begins to lengthen and the power of the sun to increase. In Eastern countries the pagan celebrants of the Nativity had retired to inner shrines or caves, from which at midnight they issued with cries of "The Virgin has brought forth! The light is wax-ing!" The Egyptians even represented the new-born sun by the image of an infant which on his birthday, the winter solstice, they exhibited to the worshippers. The Virgin who thus bore a son on that day was of course the great Oriental Mother-Goddess, who had many forms and names in different countries. Mithra after conquering the sun had become a Sun-God himself with the title of Solus Invictus, and his festival, the Mithrakana, was appropriately cele-brated on 25th December. If, therefore, the Christians had to compete with such a formidable rival they had to assert that it was *their* God who had been born on that significant date, and surely of a Heavenly Virgin.

From the vast importance of the sun in earlier days one might suppose that man was anxiously concerned lest he might fail them, since it was evident that without his heat and light life could not go on. This might occasionally have been so, to judge by the anxiety displayed during an eclipse and the human efforts (tom-toms, etc.) made to assist him in his fight with the monster apparently swallowing him. But I am persuaded that the case was really otherwise, and that the sun was on the contrary much more a source of security. One must remember that, in the East particularly, celestial phenomena were observed with astonishing accur-acy, and that the motions of the stars and planets were known in great detail; astronomy was in fact the first of the sciences. Those people knew perfectly well that the sun would wax after 25th December just as surely as he would wane before then and that day would infallibly follow night. Uncertain human happenings could therefore be referred to his activities as a means of obtaining reassurance. We still say, as an expression of the utmost certainty, "It is as sure as that the sun will rise to-morrow." The sun, therefore, belonged to the external absolutes of the universe, like God, and human uncertainties that could be brought into association with him, or better still identification, would to that extent be dispelled.

Comparative anthropology has clearly shown that man has always tended to identify the changes in the sun's apparent powers with the most vital of his own activities. The waxing young sun of spring brings times for confident rejoicing which culminate in the mad triumph of Mid-summer Eve, the German's Johannisnacht. Then the bon-fires shoot upward and proclaim the apothegm of human and divine power. How wise were the Fathers of the Revolution to choose the beginning of July to declare their independence and thus provide a whole nation with the opportunity of perpetuating man's delight in the crackling of fire at that time of the year! On the other hand, the diminishing strength of the sun arouses by association the deep fears man always nurses of his own failing powers, of impotence, old age, and death—with the terrors of what may follow this. The re-birth of the sun, therefore, has often been the greatest reassurance he can receive of eternal hope, always provided—and that was vital—that he was identi-fied with the Deity. That a God, however powerful, should periodically, (most often annually), die, to be constantly re-born, is the central theme of many religions. It is fitting that this re-birth should take place on what, according to Bede, the pagan Anglo-Saxons called "Mother-Night", i.e., Christmas Eve, the date from which their new year commenced. The Sun and the God may die, but they will surely be eternally re-born, so all is well.

The most natural expression of the re-birth idea is the association with a new-born babe, and to Christians it is the birth of the babe Jesus that is the central emblem of all that Christmas stands for. In the Roman Catholic Church, in particular, there is no moment of the year in which the

Madonna and Babe are more adored; they then occupy the centre of interest to the exclusion of all other theological preoccupations. In Catholic countries Christmas is little else; the more mundane accompaniments and ceremonies of Northern Christmases are postponed to another date.

The feeling, however, that Christmas is in some deep sense a pagan festival has evinced itself with a strange persistence throughout the ages. The Western Church was responsible for its incorporation in the Christian religion, and the Eastern Church for long protested against what they regarded as a pagan innovation. Behind this word "pagan" surely lies the idea of Mother-Goddess worship, the attraction of which so often seduced the patriarchal monotheistic Hebrews and indeed the Christian Church itself. It is perhaps fundamentally what Protestantism protested against, following the Hebrew prophets. Our own Puritans have felt very strongly on the matter, and an Act of Parliament in 1644 forbade the celebration of Christmas as being a heathen festival, until the Merry Monarch once more sanctioned it. To this day many Protestant sects, notably in Scotland, look distinctly askance at Christmas as being something alien to the pure faith. Ever since the Reformation this attitude of suspicion has connected Christmas with what has often been called the "paganism" of the Roman Catholic Church. An amusing example is recorded of a fanatical member of Parliament moving that, in order to eliminate any association with the Mass, the word itself be purified by being changed to Christ-tide; by way of answer, however, he was exhorted to initiate the change by altering his own name from Thomas Massey Massey to Thotide Tidey Tidey!

To return to the concept of the sacrificial God. It is probable that this was preceded by the custom of sacrificing a king from time to time, either when he grew old or even, as Frazer has expounded in his *Golden Bough*, annually.

However much such a king may have acquiesced in the proceeding, sharing the belief of his people that it would accrue to the good of the community, it was inevitable that he should also feel some objection to it; so it was not surprising that an alternative procedure should be sought for. Two were found. One was to displace his majesty to the skies in the form either of a God like Adonis or an actual Sun-God. That the Sun should decline almost to death every year and then arise refreshed in his glory and strength was a solution satisfying to all concerned and was a relatively innocent form of regicide (i.e., parricide). The other, and perhaps more obvious, solution was to provide a substitute, a mock king. Here we touch on the vast theme of the scapegoat in mythology. In Babylonia, for example, the king originally had to die at the end of his year's rule, ostensibly so as to go and help the God Marduk in his periodical struggle with the monsters of chaos in the regions below, but after a time a criminal was set up for a few days as a "mock king" and then executed in the king's stead. The periodical rebellion against authority (ultimately the Father) implied in the ceremony is attested by the general licence of the rejoicings and by the curious reversal of slaves and masters so characteristic of the Roman Saturnalia (15th December to 1st January) and before that the Persian Sacaea and the Babylonian Zagmuk festivals. Relics of the mock king idea have persisted into historical times. In the early centuries of our era the Roman soldiers stationed in the Balkans had the custom of choosing by lot one of their number to preside over the Saturnalia as king of the revels. After he was feted and boisterously paid court to he had to complete his career by standing at the altar and killing himself. St. Dasius is said to have achieved his fame (and martyrdom) by refusing to play this part on the ground of its being a pagan custom. In parts of central Europe a troupe of masqueraders are still headed by a "fool" or "wild man" who leads their carol singing, but with less lethal results than formerly. In the Middle Ages the "Feast of Fools" was similarly presided over by someone who was given the various titles of "Lord of Misrule", "Abbot of Unreason", "King of the Bean", etc., and who reigned from All Hallows' Eve till Christmas. His position was abrogated in Scotland by Act of Parliament in 1555. A mock service was held in the Church, with an imitation Mass, robes were worn inside out and music sheets held upside down—a general reversal very reminiscent of the Satanic Black Mass and like that indicating a violent reaction against divine authority. The only trace left of it all nowadays is the licence of kissing anyone encountered under the mistletoe, as part of the jollification of a Merry Christmas.

Perhaps the last emblem of the sacrificed god or king was the ceremony of the boar's head at the Christmas banquet, thus turning it into a totemistic feast. For the boar, sacred to the God Frey in the north and to others in the East, is one of the patriarchal symbols in the unconscious; in his parricidal ritual Mithra slew sometimes a bull, sometimes a boar. And he was treated as a royal personage, his entry to the banqueting hall being preceded by a flourish of trumpets and similar rituals. In the Balkans and in Scandinavia cakes or loaves in the form of a pig are still sold at Christmas, reminding the anthropologist how long the impulse to cannibalistic parricide persists in the folklore of the people.

The many other constituents of the Christmas festival accord with its significance as just described. Some date from Rome, but more have been added as Christianity advanced northward and in doing so incorporated pre-existing customs and rituals. Some of them have just been mentioned. Others are the Yule log, cut down by a young man and burned ceremoniously to rekindle the sun; holly and evergreens to show that there is still life in nature; the

Christmas tree, which was added only in the seventeenth century but which has an ancient tradition from the days of tree worship (may trees, etc.); the Christmas candles which replace the old Feast of Lights. All life will surely be somehow renewed and one need not fear extinction.

It is hard to determine how and when Christmas became so predominantly the children's festival it now is—at least in Northern countries. The birth of a babe is, it is true, its central feature, and in this connection it is interesting that to receive a present—which is what Christmas means to children—is in the unconscious mind always associated with the idea of the birth of a baby—the primordial gift *par excellence*. Oddly enough, in Catholic countries this custom is usually postponed to 1st January, such as with the French *étrennes* on the *jour de l'an*. The giver, Father Christmas—evidently Father Time himself—has in the past century got fused with the figure of St. Nicholas, the Archbishop of Myra, the children's saint, famous for his habit of giving presents; and Santa Klaus—the American corruption of the Dutch Colonists' San Nicolaas—is now his accepted name in all English-speaking countries. In Germany he was identified, as Knecht Rupprecht, with Odin himself, the god who sacrificed himself by hanging on a tree, his side pierced by a spear, for nine days; and so St. Nicholas wears his broad-brimmed hat and rides his white horse. In Holland hay has to be put out for the white horse on 6th December, St. Nicholas's own Day; on this day also Perchta, the companion of Odin, comes to inspect households to see if they have been properly managed.

Historically expressed, the festival of Christmas is thus a fusion of many strains of pagan customs and beliefs, but one which Christianity has inspired with a fresh spiritual significance. Psychologically it represents the ideal of resolving all family discord in a happy reunion, and to this it owes its perennial attraction. These two points of view are seen to be identical when one remembers that the ultimate significance of all religions is the attempted solution on a cosmic stage of the loves and hatreds that take their source in the complicated relations of children and parents.

XI

RATIONALISM AND PSYCHO-ANALYSIS[1]

RATIONALISM and Psycho-Analysis would appear at first sight to have so much in common that the most instructive way I can find to introduce what I have to say in this lecture is to begin by remarking on the curious fact that in practice they prove—to put it mildly—to be distinctly unsympathetic to each other.

Freedom of thought is a necessary prerequisite of psycho-analytic work, as indeed of all scientific work. Knowing, however, that this prerequisite is not always to be reckoned with, psycho-analysts aim at furthering freedom of thought by countering in certain ways various emotional obstacles, which we term "resistances", some of which are very familiar to you under such terms as prejudices, super-stitions and the like. The Rationalist cause, in its turn, is closely akin to what may be called the Free Thought move-ment. Let me quote your official definition, laid down by F. J. Gould in 1899: "Rationalism may be defined as the mental attitude which unreservedly accepts the supremacy of reason and aims at establishing a system of philosophy and ethics verifiable by experience and independent of all arbitrary assumptions or authority." You would probably not quarrel much with the *Oxford Dictionary* definition of Rationalism as "the principle of regarding reason as the chief or only guide in matters of religion". We note at once two differences. Rationalism and Psycho-Analysis have different ways of achieving freedom of thought, and

[1] Read before the Glasgow Rationalist Press Association, 29th November, 1936, and the Rationalist Press Association, London, 5th January, 1937.

Rationalism also differs in concentrating on one sphere—on what is commonly called the spiritual side of man, namely religion and ethics. Nevertheless the conception of Freedom of Thought in general is fundamental to both. With aims apparently so similar, therefore, it may seem strange how little co-operation there has ever been between the two.

One might not unfairly describe the attitude of most psycho-analysts to Rationalism as one of cold criticism, any benevolent approval they might feel on general grounds being tempered by considerable scepticism. The attitude of Rationalists to Psycho-Analysis, on the other side, appears to be even cooler and, so far as it has come to public expression, to be definitely antagonistic. We have thus a very interesting, and in a sense paradoxical, problem before us, and I intend to make it the main theme of this lecture in the hope of throwing some light on it and perhaps clearing up some misunderstandings.

It will be safer if I begin by not assuming any knowledge of psycho-analysis, but by explaining shortly what it is. Psycho-Analysis consists primarily in a method of investigation, a particular technique devised by Freud for exploring the deeper and more hidden layers of the mind, layers otherwise inaccessible whose existence was only in small part previously suspected. It is concerned especially with studying the influence of the Unconscious, as these deeper layers are nowadays called, on the conscious mind and on behaviour. In a larger sense psycho-analysis also means the findings that have been made by the use of this method and whatever theory of the mind that seems to yield itself in the endeavour to codify these findings. It is in short a branch of science, using the principles, methods and premisses of science and none other whatsoever. It is our contention that the conclusions we have reached concerning the nature of the mind, however strange they may appear, emerge from scientific investigation alone and have not been imported from elsewhere—least of all from any *a priori* assumptions. So far, therefore, we have merely intensified the puzzle of our problem, since Rationalism has always been an ardent supporter of scientific research.

Let me select a couple of the conclusions arrived at in the course of psycho-analytic work, on the subject of Free Will and Evolution respectively. There is a very formidable case to be made out from a philosophical point of view in favour of the existence of Free Will, but I am concerned here only with certain psychological aspects of the problem. There is also the important observation that almost all people have an intense personal conviction that they as individuals possess Free Will. This belief has played an essential part in most religions, especially those where the ethical aspects are predominant. The apparent contradiction between it and the belief in Divine omniscience has never been satisfactorily resolved and forms a staple topic of theological discussion. Some varieties of Christianity, e.g., the Calvinistic, have on this ground subordinated the former belief to the latter. However all this may be, I take it that Rationalists tend to discard belief in the existence of Free Will as interfering with their preference for a mechanistic, or even materialistic, view of the Universe. If this is so it is open to them to acquire support for their attitude in the matter from certain findings of psycho-analysis. Naturally any minute investigation into the problems of cause and effect may be expected to reduce the sphere in which non-specific agencies, such as Free Will, are said to operate: the narrowing down of Vitalism by modern physiology is a case in point. In the present matter, however, Psycho-Analysis has not only done this: it has added two considerations of fundamental importance. By its exploration of the Unconscious it has constantly been able to show how various mental processes, such as decisions in behaviour, specific interests, ethical attitudes and so on, in regard to which no determining factor may be visible, have nevertheless been powerfully influenced—and perhaps altogether determined —by unconscious factors of which the individual was entirely unaware. These observations, the truth of which is confirmed every day, have inevitably had the effect of narrowing the field of Free Will and make it easier for those so inclined to deny its existence altogether.

The second consideration I alluded to is that psycho-analysis has been able to throw some light on the meaning of the belief itself and to make more intelligible why the conviction of Free Will is so strong and so important to the personality. It is part of the general striving of the person-ality for freedom. Incidentally, I may remark here that the driving force behind the Rationalist movement is pretty evidently, and indeed avowedly, the desire to achieve free-dom from constraint. It is at first sight paradoxical that a body of people moved by a passionate desire for freedom should at the same time be eager to renounce such a supreme expression of it as the belief in Free Will, but perhaps we can understand it better if we contrast them with religious believers. The latter retain the belief in question by subordinating their personality to an external power—the Deity—whereas Rationalists in their endeavour to replace the latter by human reason are able to identify Reason with their own personality and thus to dispense with the individual conviction of Free Will.

The connection between these remarks and the second theme I mentioned, namely Evolution, is probably not very evident. Let me start afresh. As you doubtless know, psycho-analysis took its departure from the study of a curious and widespread class of phenomena the common feature of which is inefficiency in mental functioning. I refer to neurotic symptoms and what may be called every-day slips—slips of the tongue or pen, forgetting, mislaying, and the like; in a sense dreams might also be included here.

For these phenomena science had previously had the "explanation" that they were either completely meaningless, i.e., were effects without causes, or else the result of some hypothetical maladjustment in brain functioning. It was reserved for Freud to demonstrate that they all had a precise signification and motivation. The reason why this had been previously unknown was that the causative factors operated in a region of the mind called the "unconscious", one which—although its existence was often surmised—was inaccessible to scientific examination until Freud discovered a method to investigate it. The concept of unconscious mental processes has been sometimes objected to as being a contradiction, the argument being that mental means conscious and nothing else. This both drags in the red herring about mind and body, thus confusing the issue, and also begs the question. What psycho-analysis asserts is that processes of the same order as those we call mental, wishes, fears, and so on, can occur without one's being conscious of them and so are conveniently called unconscious mental processes. What their nature is, and how they are related to physiological processes, are matters irrelevant to the present topic.

Freud found that existence of the unconscious is bound up with a process called repression, i.e., the keeping from consciousness of mental processes incompatible—on moral, æsthetic, or other grounds—with it. This division dates from infancy, and the processes operative in the unconscious represent either the persistence of infantile ones or derivations from them. With neurotic symptoms, and other failures in normal functioning, the operative processes have been little changed from infancy, so that the study of them provides a unique opportunity for ascertaining the earliest stages in mental development—stages so primitive as to show great similarity not only among normal as well as neurotic but among all races of mankind; incidentally, one may mention that samples from all these races have now been examined from this point of view.

Psycho-Analysis is thus essentially a genetic study. It follows in detail the development of mental processes from the most primitive beginnings to their most sophisticated manifestations. Furthermore, the agencies at work are all conceived of biologically, in terms of innate instincts. With this genetic study of the development of the mind from biological instincts, all of which are common to man and other animals, Freud has filled in the gap in the theory of human evolution which Darwin had perforce to leave. The opponents of the doctrine of evolution have always been able to make a comfortable reservation concerning the mind or soul of man, to claim a privileged status for it in the universe, one well deserving for its creation a special act of interposition on the part of Providence. One result of psycho-analysis is that such reservation will be less easy to make and such interposition less needful to postulate.

This leads us on to the matter of Religion in general, one with which both Rationalism and Psycho-Analysis have to do. Before developing this theme, however, I should like to say a few words on the more general one of the relationship between Science and Religion.

Until psychology appeared on the scene, within the last few years only, this relationship has mainly concerned the more intellectual, cosmological and theological aspects of Religion. It is hard to estimate the relative importance of these aspects, but in my opinion Religion as a whole contains much more significant ones than them, and I feel sure that those Rationalists err who tend to take the part for the whole. They are, however, right in their contention that there is an inevitable conflict between science and those aspects of Religion, and further that their influence has had a deterrent effect on the progress of Science. It is surely evident that if one is brought up to answer as an act of piety such questions as "why has the heart four chambers?" "why does an epidemic of plague occur in this year and not in that?" "why is the moon at the full only once a month?" and so on by the simple statement that it is because God has so willed it, then any further inquiry is at once stifled as both superfluous and impious. Wherever religious feeling chooses to concentrate on any of these mundane questions and make a test case of it, as has happened over and over again in history, then a series of events regularly happens. The scientific investigators who dare to prosecute their inquiries in the face of the ban are assailed as atheists in spite of their being for the most part themselves religiously-minded; they produce their non-theological explanation of the phenomena in question; and more or less slowly the Church accepts the explanation and no longer feels that the case was a vital religious issue. These recurrent happenings naturally began in the fields of astronomy and physics, since they were the more easily investigated aspects of nature. When Copernicus and Newton showed that the movements of the solar system could be correlated with simple mathematical statements and with the familiar processes of gravitation, it became unnecessary to postulate an immediate interposition of the Deity to account for the observed facts. When a little over a century ago Wöhler manufactured a substance, urea, which previously had been inseparably connected with vital processes, he dealt the first blow at the fundamental distinction so important to theologians between animate and inanimate matter. When the evolutionary biologists, culminating in Darwin, showed that man's body was, in spite of its differences, of the same order as that of other animals and in all probability derived from them, then man's pride was badly wounded at the thought that it was no longer necessary to invoke an act of special Divine creation to account for his existence on the earth.

Although such events as these might be said to displace God to a greater distance from man by rendering unnecessary the idea of miraculous interposition on His part, two things prevented the religiously-minded from having their faith profoundly disturbed thereby. One was—and this was decisive—that they *felt* God to be as near as ever. The other was that Science, despite Keats's view to the contrary, does not destroy the sense of wonder and awe. In many ways, indeed, Science heightens this by displaying the orderly and grandiose scale of the way in which things work in the universe. A theist with a capacity for imagination can feel more uplifted, even if less flattered, by the reflection that the creation of man has proceeded by a more remarkable, though more devious, fashion than he had previously supposed. The primitive belief in the miraculous is replaced by the more mature and profound sense of wonder.

Science, however, cannot stop at the intellectual aspects of Religion, and in the last forty or fifty years it has taken an objective interest in other aspects also. William James has studied the nature of the psychological harmony induced by the event of religious conversion, and other psychologists have correlated the intensity of religious phenomena with many individual and environmental factors. Any searching investigation of the human mind, such as psycho-analysis, must concern itself with such a fundamental constituent of it as Religion is, especially since it is so often involved in neurotic conflicts. It was soon found, as indeed might have been expected, that the sources of religious feeling arise very early in the course of mental development, though we see no reason for according it, as some writers have done, the status of a biological instinct which its universality might at first sight appear to demand. Thinkers have drawn two opposite conclusions from this feature of universality, a feature the existence of which psycho-analysis with few exceptions confirms. Some have inferred that it shows the existence of a supernatural world which the mind more or less clearly perceives. Others have inferred that it indicates a prevalent quality in the mind itself, although hitherto only very vague and general guesses have been made about the nature of this quality. In other words, some infer from it an external source of religion, others an internal. The discoveries of psycho-analysis are necessarily concerned with the latter, since it is not in a position to throw any light on the former. They have added greatly to the psychology of religious feeling, a study which has of course already been under-taken from several points of view. If the sources of religious feelings are traced to their origins in the unconscious mind it will be found that they are there always interwoven with the child's conflicting emotions about his parents. Here I touch on a theme so vast that it could not be expounded in any single volume or series of lectures. It would not be a gross exaggeration to say that psycho-analysis is essentially a detailed study of the relations between a child and his parents. At the moment I can only assert in a single sentence that the conflicting emotions in question are far more complex, and far more important for the whole mental development, than can easily be imagined. Returning to the matter of religion, we should say that we find all the numerous mental attitudes that man has at different times displayed towards his various gods—love, hate, dread, adoration, awe, yearning, helplessness, exaltation—to be without exception copies or derivatives of corresponding feelings he has at an earlier age experienced, consciously or unconsciously, towards his parents or their substitutes. When the Christian says we are all children of one Father he is using a metaphorical parallel, but to the psycho-analyst he is indicating a truly genetic description of his belief. We can go even further and assert that the precise ways by which these earlier feelings become translated on to the plane of Religion are also fairly well understood. It is therefore hard to avoid the conclusion that even if there were no Divine Being in reality the human mind is so constituted that it would inevitably build such a conception together with the characteristic attitudes accompanying it.

This is a tremendous conclusion, and one would have expected Rationalists to have exploited it pretty extensively. It surprises me that they have not. Yet I think the scientifically-minded should be careful not to be carried away beyond the actual evidence before us. To infer that a given belief has a subjective origin is not the same thing as to say it is therefore untrue objectively. That is quite another matter, not to be confounded with the first one. On the contrary, our analytical experience of subjective beliefs is that they have an uncanny way of piercing through to an external reality. When, for instance, a madman is for subjective reasons possessed of the idea that someone wishes his destruction or that his wife is disloyal to him he may have reached these ideas on purely internal grounds, but they are not always untrue in fact. Whether they are or are not has to be determined by quite another type of investigation. So to say that men must believe in the existence of God for purely internal reasons, reasons which would be operative whether He existed or not, is not the same as asserting that therefore God does not exist. There are those who argue thus, but in my opinion they are not reasoning scientifically in so doing. The question is not one for any scientific specialist as such, but for the philosophic thinker, if anyone.

The Christian Church learned in time, not only to adapt itself to, but even to assimilate, the teachings of Copernicus and Darwin, although these flatly contradicted some of its most important doctrines. I expect that it will be able to do the same with the teachings of Freud. The view will probably be put forward that the grandeur of God is more fully brought to expression by recognizing the extraordinarily complex—one might even say subtle—harmony of His works than by upholding the primitive ideas of His particulate intrusion into their details.

Let us now review the situation so far. Rationalism and Psycho-Analysis both profess adherence to the principles of scientific method and to the value of free thought. They both find reasons for criticizing the doctrine of Free Will and for accepting the theory of natural evolution. They both consider that human factors are adequate to account for the genesis of religious beliefs. Rationalism is apt to take the further step of declaring that these do not correspond with any external reality. There would thus appear to be a great deal of common ground between Rationalism and Psycho-Analysis and we recur to our original question concerning the manifest lack of sympathy between them.

I can naturally say more about this matter from the side of the Psycho-Analyst, but I will first state what I perceive of the Rationalist's attitude. He shares of course the general doubt about psycho-analysis, the feeling that its conclusions are exaggerated and improbable. I seem to have noted two special features in the criticisms passed by Rationalist writers, and they are of considerable interest. We have been very accustomed to the epithet of "gross materialism"; a variety of abusive adjectives may be attached to it, of which "carnal" and "earthy" are the mildest. This is perhaps not very surprising when one remembers the work psycho-analysis has done on the animal nature of man and its conclusions that many of his "higher" attributes are derived from "lowly" impulses, such as the sexual ones. It is not very hard to distort psycho-analytic work into a picture of latitudinarian lewdness or of mundane coarseness; some people feel about it, as Keats did about physics and the rainbow, that it robs the soul of man of all its fineness and spirituality. We have, as I say, been so accustomed to this sort of un-understanding abuse that the news of certain rationalists taking just the opposite view came with a certain sense of novelty. Here we found ourselves, to our equal bewilderment, assailed as being merely another variety of spiritualist who under the guise of the word "psychological" tried to undo the progress of biology and physical medicine by reverting to ideological conceptions about the immaterial. So much has the simple word "psychical" been debased by that unfortunate phrase "psychical research" that it seems hard for many people to dissociate it from the supernatural, and to such people Freud's conception of the psyche gets at once confounded with theological conceptions of the soul. To this I would say in reply that those who are guilty of this misunderstanding seem to be still so affected by theological preoccupations as to find it hard to conceive of a scientific attitude towards mental phenomena. And by this term I simply mean the phenomena which we discuss in a language called mental—using words like "grief", "distress", "thoughts", etc.—for the very good reason that we have as yet no other language in which to discuss them. In doing so no particular system of philosophy, idealistic, parallelistic, or materialistic, is implied. Our work is purely scientific, not philosophical. Speaking for myself only, however, (and in no way committing psycho-analysis itself as a branch of study), I will say freely that I know of no reason for believing that mental phenomena can occur anywhere apart from bodily ones, and furthermore I see no reason to believe that such an entity as "mind" exists at all, whether attached to the body or not. If the time comes when we can correlate our mental language with descriptions of neurotic processes in the cerebrum I should expect to find that the two modes of the description are merely different languages depicting the same processes. So much for the supposed "spiritualism" of psycho-analysis!

A second, perhaps less characteristic, feature is the distaste many rationalist writers have evinced for the evidently irrational modes of thought which are so much the concern of the psycho-analyst. When we describe what we find in the unconscious mind, its illogicalities, its self-contradictions, its contempt for reason, its grotesque suppositions and pseudo-ratiocinations, it must and does produce on the conscious mind an impression of nightmarish improbability. Many Rationalists seem to shrink back from this picture with a peculiar horror as if they wished to protest that the mind of man surely could not be so irrational as all that. I suppose their abhorrence for such irrationality is so great that they would fain deny its existence until they are driven to recognize it. Yet a cooler reflection might make them more willing to admit the strength of the enemy they have devoted their lives to fighting. Sometimes I think that their animus goes even further and that they are inclined to blame the psycho-analysts for the existence of the extensive irrationality to which we have called attention, just as in former times kings were wont to execute the bringers of bad tidings.

Now for the other side of the question—the Psycho-Analyst's criticism of the Rationalist's position. I can best introduce this by reverting to our starting-point—the topic of free thought. Psycho-Analysis not only demands for its work as much freedom of thought as is available, but it is also concerned with the difficulties in the way of achieving freedom of thought. In investigating them it recognizes that freedom of thought is only one form of psychological freedom and that one cannot properly consider the part without the whole. To deal with freedom of the intellect only, as Rationalists sometimes do, is unnecessarily to limit oneself. This is especially so because in our judgement freedom of thought is not so much the prerequisite of freedom in general—although it can plausibly be described as such—as a *sign* or *index* that the wider freedom of the personality in general has already been attained. The problem of what constitutes this freedom of the personality, on which the capacity for free thought very largely depends, is one that greatly exercises psycho-analysis. It has furthermore concerned itself with the significance of freedom itself, with the question of why the subjective feeling of freedom is so tremendously important to men and with the interesting fact that its importance seems to vary so much at different periods. The feeling in question is evidently bound up with the sense of security, and may even be regarded as one aspect of this. It is certainly striking how often men will prize some form or other of freedom above all else and will gladly sacrifice their lives in the endeavour to achieve it. Even more astonishing is the way the same men will at other times tamely submit to the most extraordinary regimentation of their daily lives and interference with every detail of their personal freedom, especially at the behest of their fellow-countrymen. Italy, for instance, has shown us several examples of both these reactions in less than a century. At the present time it is only too easy to point to numerous examples of extreme renunciation of liberty, whereas I should be hard put to it to find a good example of the contrary—outside, of course, the ranks of the Rationalist Press Association.

But the first thing that strikes an outsider about the laudable campaign Rationalists are conducting on behalf of freedom is the remarkable localization of their aim. Confining ourselves for the moment to the external barriers against freedom, and still further to the barriers against intellectual freedom to the neglect of other perhaps equally important forms of freedom—social, political, economic, and so on—one cannot help wondering why Rationalists concentrate so much on the theological obstacles. In the definition I quoted earlier it is stated that "Rationalism ... aims at establishing a system of philosophy and ethics ...

independent of all arbitrary assumptions or authority". Well, I should have doubted very much that any Church, with the exception of that in Austria and Ireland, could nowadays be called an authority that hinders one from establishing such a system if one wants to. Matters were of course different in bygone ages, and, as I just hinted, are still different in a few countries of Europe, but I should have thought the Rationalist Press Association has survived long enough to discover that there are other much more formidable obstacles to intellectual freedom than organized religion. A very short residence in either Germany or Russia should be enough to convince one of this, and of the disturbing consideration that opposition to freedom can proceed not only from blind tradition but also from a consistent and up-to-date efficiency. Even in England I should anticipate that anyone wishing to inculcate a new system of ethics would encounter at least as much opposition or prejudice from the legal and political worlds as from the clerical, nor do I think that most of it would be religious in its origin. At your annual dinner a year after the war William Archer said: "To the historian of a thousand years hence this greatest of wars will rank as a mere skirmish in the never-ending battle of Rationalism against irrationalism." Assuming that by Rationalism he meant freedom of thought we have to record the painful fact that the great victory won for freedom and democracy has led to far firmer shackles being put on freedom of thought throughout Europe than had existed for centuries previously, and that even in this country the number of those who admire and yearn for those shackles is unfortunately in the ascendant. And no one could maintain that organized religion has played any serious part in this restriction; if anything, its influence has been on the other side.

The investigations of psycho-analysis have thrown a great deal of light on the problem of freedom and have also been able to some extent to explain the curious oscillation in man's attitude towards it. It has been forced to concentrate on this problem because in its therapeutic work its main endeavour is to bring about freedom from the bonds that have cramped the personality, or—to put it more modestly—to diminish the number of influences that have restricted its freedom. One important conclusion issuing from these investigations is that there exist internal bonds, i.e., bonds *inside* the personality, which are much more potent in their restrictive power than any external ones. Anyone, therefore, who is seriously interested in achieving mental freedom would do well to turn his attention to the nature of these bonds. It is not possible for me here to expound the psychology of the unconscious, that region where the tumult of the instincts releases emotional forces of which consciousness perceives only a faint mirror, but I should say very emphatically that the restrictive bonds in question are essentially due to the massive layers of guiltiness and fear that are always present in the unconscious mind. And I would add, what I am sure is an unexpected conclusion, that this guiltiness and fear is only in small part imposed on the child from without, its main source being quite endogenous. So important do we consider these layers of the mind, arising as I say mainly from within the growing personality itself, that we should not find it a very gross exaggeration if anyone tried to describe the whole of human life as a series of infinitely varied endeavours to alleviate the distress they would cause if allowed to function unchecked. These endeavours we term *defences*. Like the more familiar defences against external dangers they may be either active or passive. Instances of the first kind are: aggressiveness, intolerance, pugnacity and—curiously enough—often the struggle for freedom from external barriers. Instances of the second are: flight of all kinds, inhibitions, denial, shame, aversion and a clamour for security. We now begin perhaps to see why mankind oscillates between the passion for freedom and the passion for security: each promises help for his fundamental distress. Our social institutions also can be fruitfully regarded from this point of view. The one that has the most direct bearing on these difficulties of the individual is undoubtedly Religion, and it is not hard to see that it functions along both the active and passive lines. When St. Paul spoke of "the liberty wherewith Christ hath made us free" the phrase must seem distinctly unintelligible to a Rationalist, but it is full of meaning to a Psycho-Analyst. The sociological disadvantages, however, of the religious solution are first, that it operates successfully with only a minority of the community, and secondly, that its operation tends to be bound up with certain rather strict limiting conditions—to quote St. Paul again, "being then made free from sin ye become the servants of righteousness", thus opening up the wide question of what constitutes the "righteousness" whose servants we are to become.

When the internal and unconscious restrictions become too painfully tyrannical various reactions of defence against them in turn come into play. Of these I will mention one very important example to which we give the name of "projection". The unconscious restricting influence is identified with a suitable external one, projected on to it, and this is then attacked with an aggressiveness that may culminate in a venomous hostility. Germany, for instance, pursued by world condemnation which she vainly tried to exorcize by repudiating what she called the "war-guilt lie", discovered with relief that the poison in her system could be identified with the Jewish section of her population. The Jews were both the unseen instigators of wars and the arch intriguers of defeatist pacifism, both the bloated upholders of the capitalistic system sucking the life blood of the nation and the evil communists seeking to destroy the sacred rights of property. The action she took in response to this discovery is unfortunately known to all of us. The Priesthood, or any form of organized Religion, has at times been described as the main enemy to freedom, and the frequent justification for this has led many to concentrate on it as the one and only obstacle, an attitude which in my opinion can only lead one astray. I should like here to echo the words of your President, Lord Snell, when he warned you recently that no Movement can live by worship at the tomb of the past. He added: "Let us take care that our Association does not become the sepulchre of an idea rather than its cradle."

Certain signs enable us to say whether a given emotional attitude contains this element of projection and is thus being used as a defence against unconscious internal bonds. They are the combination of hostility and animus with a passionate enthusiasm for an ideal and excessive optimism about attaining it. I will leave it to you to decide whether the Rationalist movement has always been free of these characteristics. Whenever you come across them you may be sure that the clamour for external freedom they accompany is being misused to conceal an internal lack of freedom. True freedom, on the contrary, breeds tolerance, understanding and firmness. I wish, further, to lay stress on the self-righteousness that so often accompanies the projection attitude I have just described. When Thomas Jefferson thundered "I have sworn upon the altar of God eternal hostility towards every form of tyranny over the mind of man" we are naturally impressed by his earnestness, but we might not feel sure that such a categorical assertion of moral cartitude, if seduced by power, could not degenerate into a doctrinaire opinionism. Bernard Shaw once caustically said "Beware of the man whose God is in the skies", meaning of course that a man may become inaccessible when his private prejudices are fortified by projection on to the idea of a supernatural Being. And when William Archer asserted of the human reason that "its genesis is the mystery of mystery, the miracle of miracles" one cannot help being reminded of the error the leaders of the French Revolution fell into when they replaced the worship of the Almighty by that of the Goddess of Reason.

This remark brings me to my last but not least theme, the subject of reason. All I wish to say here is that we have become very familiar in Psycho-Analysis with the deplorable fact that reason, however one may prize it, can be misused like any other faculty when it becomes one of the "defences" about which I have been speaking. By misuse I mean the employing of the intellect not to discover truth, but to conceal it. Nothing is commoner than for a man unwilling to recognize his true motives for an attitude, and unwilling to reveal the underlying feelings from which such motives spring, to prostitute his intellect by using it to invent reasons, quite logical ones, which will serve as an explanation. An unwillingness to face intimate emotions is characteristic of mankind, and yet without feeling reason is powerless to understand the workings of the mind. The theses I am sustaining here are that only by feeling can reason discover truth and that, as was said by a certain Person, "the truth shall make you free."

XII

THE GOD COMPLEX[1]

THE BELIEF THAT ONE IS GOD, AND THE RESULTING CHARACTER TRAITS

EVERY psycho-analyst must have come across patients amongst whose unconscious phantasies is contained the curious one in which the patient identifies himself with God. Such a megalomaniac phantasy would be barely comprehensible did we not know how closely the ideas of God and Father are associated, so much so that, from a purely psychological point of view, the former idea may be regarded as a magnified, idealized, and projected form of the latter. Identification of the self with the loved object occurs to some extent in every affection, and is a regular constituent of a boy's attitude towards his father; every boy imitates his father, pretends to himself that he is the father, and to a varying extent models himself on him. It is therefore only natural that a similar attitude may develop in regard to the more perfect Heavenly Father, and indeed this is in a certain sense directly inculcated in the religious teaching that one should strive to become as like the divine model as is possible (i.e., to imitate it), and in the belief that every man is a copy of God and contains the divine spirit within him. The transition from obedient imitation to identification is often a rapid one, and in the unconscious the two terms are practically synonymous. The function of representing his king or state that is

[1] Published in the *Internationale Zeitschrift für Psychoanalyse*, 1913, Bd. I, S. 313.

244

entrusted to an ambassador in a foreign country or to a governor in a foreign province has many a time been transgressed in history by opportunity allowing it to be exchanged for one of greater power; the Roman Empire, for instance, was perpetually exposed to this menace. In religion we see indications of the same process, though of course they are less evident. To the common people the figures of Buddha, Mahomet, Peter, and Moses mean something more than mere representatives of God, and we find even minor prophets and preachers speaking in the name of God with an authority so astounding as to preclude the idea of its arising solely in learning; in other words one feels sure that their conscious attitude is generally the product of an unconscious phantasy in which they identify their personality with that of God.

This phantasy is not at all rare, and possibly occurs here and there in all men; it is naturally far commoner with men than with women, where the corresponding one seems to be the idea of being the Mother of God. There is, however, a class of men with whom it is much stronger than is usual, so that it forms a constant and integral part of their unconscious. When such men become insane they are apt to express openly the delusion that they actually are God, and instances of the kind are to be met with in every asylum.[1] In a state of sanity, that is to say when the feeling for reality and the normal inhibitions of consciousness are operative, the phantasy can express itself only after passage through this censorship, and therefore only in a modified, weakened, and indirect form. It is with these external manifestations that we are here concerned, and it will be the object of the present paper to indicate how from them the presence of what may be called a "God-

---

[1] A well-known medical anecdote, *ben trovato*, relates how an inquisitive visitor approached one such patient with a perplexing problem in theology. The patient turned away haughtily with the remark, "I never talk shop."

complex" in the unconscious may be inferred. This unconscious complex, like any other important one, leaves permanent traces of its influence on conscious attitudes and reactions, and analysis of a number of individuals with whom it is strongly pronounced shows that the character traits[1] thus produced constitute a fairly typical picture, one clear enough to be applicable for diagnostic purposes. It is intelligible that they necessarily resemble those characteristic of the father-complex in general, being indeed simply a magnification of these; they form in fact a part of this broader group, but one sufficiently peculiar in itself to deserve to be singled out and distinguished from the rest of the group.

The inductive generalizations arrived at on the basis of my observations do not altogether coincide with those that might have been expected from deductive consideration of the attributes popularly ascribed to God. A main distinction between them, for instance, is this: Whereas the aspect of God as the Creator is perhaps the most impressive in the ordinary mind, as illustrated by the conclusiveness with which the existence of God is commonly held to be settled by the question "who else could have created the world?" or by more abstract ratiocinations about the necessity for a "first cause", this aspect is far from being either the most prominent or the most typical to be represented amongst the phantasies belonging to a God-complex. The most striking and characteristic of these would seem to be the ones relating to effective power in the broadest sense (omnipotence), and most of the external

[1] When George Meredith, in *The Egoist*, endowed the chief figure of the book with certain peculiarly human attributes, his friends individually reproached him for having laid bare to the world their hidden weaknesses, each seeing in the novelist's description a mirror of his own heart. The character-traits pointed out in the present paper are so widely spread that I run the risk of laying myself open to a similar charge, as indeed does everyone who attempts to contribute something to our stock of psycho-analytical knowledge.

manifestations of the complex can best be stated in terms of this. In my experience the main foundation of the complex is to be discovered in a colossal *narcissism*, and this I regard as the most typical feature of the personalities in question. All the character-traits presently to be described can either be directly derived from narcissism, or else stand in the closest connection with it.

Excessive narcissism leads inevitably to an excessive admiration for and confidence in one's own powers, knowledge, and qualities, both physical and mental. Two psycho-sexual tendencies are especially closely correlated with it, the auto-erotic and exhibitionistic,[1] two of the most primitive in the life of the individual, and we shall see that they play a highly important part in the genesis of the character-traits. With the second of these, the exhibitionistic, there is always associated its counterpart, the instinct of curiosity and knowledge, and this also produces some of the end-results. From the intimate inter-association, therefore, of these impulses, the narcissistic, auto-erotic, exhibitionistic, and curiosity ones, it is comprehensible why any sharp separation of the character-traits from one another according to their origin is quite impossible, for many of them could be equally well described under any one of the four, being related to all. It will thus be convenient to describe them as a whole, and not separately.

One other general remark may be made before we proceed to the details, and that is to call attention to the characteristically negative way in which these instincts are manifested in the syndrome in question; for instance, excessive modesty is more often met with than pronounced vanity. The reason for this is that the unusual strength of the primitive tendencies has called forth an unusually

---

[1] *See* Stekel, "Zur Psychologie des Exhibitionismus," *Zentralblatt für Psychoanalyse*, Jahrg. I., S. 494.

ESSAYS IN APPLIED PSYCHO-ANALYSIS

strong series of reaction-formations, and it is these that, being more superficial in the mind and more in harmony with social feelings, manifest themselves most directly. In fact one can often infer the strength of the underlying impulses only through noting how intense are the reactions they have evoked.

We may begin the series by mentioning some manifestations of narcissistic exhibitionism, i.e., the wish to display the own person or a certain part of it, combined with the belief in the irresistible power of this. This power, which is the same as that ascribed to the tabu king[1] or to the sun and lion symbols of mythology, is for either good or evil, creation or destruction, being thus typically ambivalent. In the instances under consideration the harmful element predominates, another interesting difference between this phantasy and the (modern) conception of God.

These first manifestations, like those throughout the whole complex, are most typically reaction-products. Thus obvious self-conceit or vanity is not so frequent or so characteristic as an excessive self-modesty, which at times is so pronounced as to be truly a *self-effacement*. The man advances his strongest convictions in the most tentative manner possible, avoids the word "I" in both conversation and writing, and refuses to take any prominent or active part in the affairs of life. Already the exaggeratedness of this betrays it as being an affectation, not a primary character-tendency but a reaction to one, and this becomes still more evident when we observe the more extreme forms of the trait. These constitute what I consider to be the most characteristic manifestations of all—namely, a tendency to *aloofness*. The man is not the same as other mortals, he is something apart, and a certain distance must be preserved between him and them. He makes himself as *inaccessible* as possible, and surrounds his personality with

[1] *See* Freud, *Imago*, 1912, Bd. I, S. 306-15.

248

a *cloud of mystery*. To begin with, he will not live near
other people if he can avoid it. One such man told me
with pride he lived in the last house of his town (a Metro-
polis) and that he found this already too near to the
throng, so he intended to move farther away. Such men
naturally prefer to live in the country, and if their work
prevents this they try to have a home outside the town to
which they can retire, either every evening or every week-
end. They may come in daily to their work and never
mention their home address to their friends, using when
necessary clubs and restaurants for whatever social purposes they need. They rarely invite friends to their home,
where they reign in solitary grandeur. They lay the
greatest stress on privacy in general, this being of course
both a direct expression of auto-erotism (masturbation) and
a reaction against repressed exhibitionism. There are thus
two elements in the tendency in question, the wish not to
be seen, and the wish to be distant or inaccessible; sometimes the accent is on the one, sometimes on the other.
Both are well illustrated in the following phantasy that a
patient once confessed to me: his darling wish was to own
a castle in a distant mountain at the very extremity of the
country (near the sea); as he drove up to it he was to sound
a terrific horn in his automobile so that the blast would
reverberate along the hills (thunders of Jehovah and Zeus,
paternal flatus), and on hearing it the servants and re-
tainers were to disappear to their underground chambers,
leaving everything prepared for him in the castle; under no
circumstances were they ever to see him. Such men in
actual life interpose all manner of difficulties in the way of
being seen, even on business; appointments have to be
made long beforehand or secretaries have to be interviewed,
and when the time arrives they are either late or are "too
busy" to come at all. How prominent this feature of
inaccessibility is with the nobility, kings, popes (!) and even

important business men[1] is well known. A by-product of the desire for distance, one which has also other roots, is a keen interest in the matter of communication and in improved means for enabling them to annihilate distance; they invariably travel first-class or else by automobile, thus keeping apart from the mob, insist on having the best system of telephones (which presents the advantage of allowing them to communicate without being seen), and so on. This trait is in striking contrast with the fact that such people do not willingly travel long distances, especially out of their own country. They always feel best at home, dislike going to the world and insist on making it come to them.

The sense of this desire for inaccessibility is at once seen when we consider its extreme exaggerations, as met with in insanity. The late paranoic King Lewis of Bavaria would seem to have shown a typical case of this. It is said that he began by imitating Louis XIV ("obligation of the name"—Stekel), and proceeded to identify himself formally with Le Roi Soleil. It is further related that at this stage he refused to interview people unless there was a screen between him and them, and that when he went out his guards had to warn people of his approach, to get them to hide in time and shelter themselves from his magnificent presence. Such behaviour can only indicate the belief that the rays emanating from this presence were charged with power of destruction, and the king's solicitude possibly covered repressed death-wishes. We have here a recrudescence of the old Egyptian, Persian and Grecian projection of the father as a sun-god, one that played an important part also in early Christianity. The significance of it in

[1] H. G. Wells, in his novel *Tono-Bungay*, gives an amusing description of the difficulties in obtaining an audience with a successful financier. The applicants are sorted out in room after room by one secretary after the other, and only a very few are fortunate enough to penetrate to the Holy of Holies and come face to face with the great man himself.

paranoia, as well as of the interesting and not rare "aiglon" phantasy, was pointed out by Freud in his Schreber analysis.[1] In insanity the patient may identify both his father and himself with the sun, as in the instance just mentioned, or else only the former, as with a paraphrenic patient of mine who spent the greater part of ten years defiantly staring at the sun. In more normal people such phantasies remain in the unconscious, and only a refined form of them can penetrate through to consciousness, such as the desire for aloofness. This desire, therefore, seems mainly to express, in an indirect way, a colossal narcissistic-exhibitionistic tendency, being based on the person's belief that his proximity is fraught with tremendous power on other people, and that the glory of his presence may dazzle or even blind them; as a precaution against such terrible consequences he withdraws to a distance whenever possible. A repressed tendency that also plays a part in determining this attitude is revealed by consideration of the fear of blinding others. This of course symbolizes the fear, i.e., the repressed wish, that he may castrate them, and we shall see later that both this wish and the accompanying fear of being castrated are prominent characteristics of the group of complexes under consideration.

The other trait of *mystery*, mentioned above in conjunction with that of inaccessibility, may be regarded as the mental correlate of this; thus the broad tendency of aloofness displays itself by the desires, on the physical side of being inaccessible, on the mental side of being mysterious. The person aims at wrapping himself in an impenetrable cloud of mystery and privacy. Even the most trivial pieces of information about himself, those which an ordinary man sees no object in keeping to himself, are invested with a sense of high importance, and are parted with only under some pressure. Such a man is very loth to let his age be

[1] Freud, "Nachtrag," *Jahrbuch der Psychoanalyse*, Bd. III, S. 588.

known, or to divulge his name or his profession to strangers, let alone to talk about his private affairs. I know of a man who has lived for eight years in a town in Western America without any of his friends there being able to find out whether he is married or not; anyone who knows something of the publicity of American private life will realize what a feat this is. Some little characteristics about writing are derivatives of the same tendency. A man of this kind writes unwillingly, particularly letters.[1] He dislikes to part with such expressions of his personality, and also finds the not-answering of letters of other people to be a convenient way of indicating his opinion of their importance.[2] In spite of a great interest in accurate language, of which we will speak later, he rarely expresses his thought clearly and directly. Very characteristic is a lengthy, involved and circuitous form of diction that at times becomes so turgid and obscure as to render it really impossible for the reader to discover what is meant. The more important is the topic (to the writer) the more difficulty does he have in parting with his valuable secret. The most important part is often not written at all, but instead is constantly hinted at with repeated promises that it will be disclosed on a further occasion. In striking contrast with this is the fact that the actual handwriting is typically clear and distinct. With some such men it is the opposite, quite illegible, but with both kinds the person is inordinately proud of it, whether of the distinctness or of the obscurity. In any event he insists that it is peculiar to himself, apart, and unique. (In general nothing offends such a man as the suggestion that he resembles someone else, whether it be in hand-

[1] It need hardly be said that there are many other causes for this inhibition besides the ones here mentioned.

[2] Napoleon expounded this contemptuous attitude very wittily. He is said to have formed the rule, particularly during busy times, of never answering a letter until it was three months old. On being once criticized for this, he remarked that it saved much trouble for he found that most letters answered themselves in this time.

writing, in personal appearance, in capacity, or in conduct.) The veil of mystery and obscurity that he casts over himself is naturally extended so as to cover all those pertaining to him. Thus he never spontaneously refers to his family, speaking of them reluctantly when any inquiries are made about them, and the same applies to any affairs in which he may have become concerned. That all this privacy refers not only to narcissistic self-importance, but also to auto-erotism[1] in general, and particularly to masturbation, is too well-known to need special emphasis here. The primary narcissistic tendency leaks through in the curious trait that when the reticence is abrogated, as during psycho-analysis or during a confidential chat with an intimate friend, the person takes the greatest pleasure in talking about himself in the fullest minuteness and is never weary of discussing and dissecting his own mental attributes. He is apt to be a successful lecturer and after-dinner speaker, showing a fondness for this that contrasts with his other reactions to exhibitionism.

The tendency to aloofness also manifests itself on the purely mental side quite directly. Such men are both un-sociable and unsocial, in the wider sense. They adapt themselves with difficulty to any activity in common with others, whether it be of a political, scientific or business kind. They make bad citizens as judged by the usual standards;[2] how-ever interested they may be in public affairs they take no part in them, and never even vote, such a plebeian function being beneath their dignity. Any influence they exert is done so quite indirectly, by means of stimulating more

[1] The prominence of this in the present group of complexes explains the frequency with which the type under consideration presents the two character-traits of an interest in philosophic discussions on the nature of truth (prag-matism, etc.), with a low personal standard of honour in the matter of probity and truthfulness.

[2] Very characteristic is the combination of bad citizenship in a practical sense with a keen theoretical interest in social reform, which will be spoken of later.

active admirers. Their ideal is to be "the man behind the throne", directing affairs from above while being invisible to the crowd. To follow, to participate, or even to lead, in a general movement, whether social or scientific, is repugnant to them, and they use every effort to maintain a policy of magnificent isolation. In this they may achieve, as Nietzsche did, true grandeur, but more often they present merely a churlish egotism.

As is to be expected, such a strong exhibitionistic tendency as that indicated by the traits just mentioned must have a counterpart in a strongly developed complementary instinct—namely, the pleasure in visual curiosity ("scoptolagnia"), though there are fewer characteristic manifestations of these in the syndrome. They differ from the previous ones in being more often of direct origin, and not reaction-formations. There is usually present a quite womanish curiosity about trivial personalities, gossip and the like, though generally this is concealed and is betrayed only on occasion. More often a higher form of sublimation occurs, and this typically takes the form of *interest in psychology*. If the person in question is endowed with a natural intuition for divining the minds of others, is a judge of human nature, he will make use of this in his profession whatever it may be; if he is not so endowed he tends to become a professional psychologist or psychiatrist, or at least to take a considerable abstract interest in the subject. This desire to compensate a natural defect furnishes no doubt one of the explanations for the notorious circumstance that professional psychologists so often display a striking ignorance of the human mind. It also accounts for their constant endeavour to remedy their deficiency by the invention of "objective" methods of studying the mind that are to make them independent of intuition, and their antagonism to methods, such as psycho-analysis, which deliberately cultivate this; the flood of curves and statistics that threatens to suffocate the science of psychology bears witness to the needs of such men. To revert to our typical man: he takes a particular interest in any methods that promise a "short-cut" to the knowledge of other people's minds, and is apt to apply such methods as the Binet-Simon scale, the psycho-galvanic phenomenon, word-association reactions, or graphology in a mechanical and literal manner, always hoping to find one that will give automatic results.[1] The more unusual the method the more it attracts him, giving him the feeling of possessing a key that is accessible only to the elect. For this reason he is apt to display great interest in the various forms of thought-reading, cheiromancy, divination, and even astrology, as well as in occultism and mysticism in all their branches. This topic connects itself with that of religion on the one hand, and the various manifestations of omniscience on the other, both of which will presently be discussed.

Certain less direct products of narcissistic exhibitionism may be grouped under the heading of *omnipotence phantasies*. These may extend over every field where power can be exhibited, so that it becomes impossible to discuss them in detail; they are particularly apt to apply to unusual ones, therefore claiming powers possessed by the few. Perhaps the commonest is that relating to money, a matter closely connected, in fact and fancy, with the idea of power. The person imagines himself a multi-millionaire, and revels in the thought of what he would do with all the power then at his disposal. This phantasy is usually associated with a pretended contempt for money in real life, and sometimes with an actual generosity and freedom in the use of it; the amount actually possessed is so infinitesimal in comparison with what he possesses in his imagination that it is too small to treasure.

---

[1] The complicated mathematical analysis of questionnaires, so much the vogue nowadays, evidently lends itself readily to such an attitude.

The most characteristic sub-group in the present connection, however, are those relating to *omniscience*. This may be regarded as simply a form of omnipotence, for whoever can do everything can also know everything. The passage from the one to the other is clearly seen in the case of foretelling; to know beforehand when something is going to happen is in itself a kind of control, merely a weakened form of actually bringing the thing about, and the transition between a deity and a prophet is historically often a very gradual one (!).

One of the most distressing character-traits of the type under consideration is the *attitude of disinclination towards the acceptance of new knowledge*. This follows quite logically from the idea of omniscience, for anyone who already knows everything naturally cannot be taught anything new; still less can he admit that he has ever made a mistake in his knowledge. We touch here on a general human tendency, one of which the psycho-analytical movement has already had much practical experience, but it is so pronounced in the present character that it cannot be passed over without a few words being devoted to it. In the first place, men with this type of character talk even more than other men about their capacity to assimilate new ideas, and are sometimes lavish in their abstract admiration for the new. But when put to the test of being confronted with a new idea that doesn't proceed from themselves, they offer an uncompromising resistance to it. This follows on the usual well-known lines, being merely exaggerated in intensity. The most interesting manifestations are the modes of acceptance, when this does occur. There are two typical forms of these. The first is to modify the new idea, re-phrase it in their own terms, and then give it out as entirely their own; the differences between their description and that given by the discoverer of the new idea they naturally maintain to be of vital importance. When the modifications made are considerable they are always of the nature of a weakening of the original idea, and in this case the author of them usually adheres to the new conclusion. Sometimes the resistance to the new idea is indicated by the modifications being simply changes in nomenclature, or even in spelling (!), and then later reactions of the person show that he has never seriously accepted the new idea, so that his old repugnance to it will sooner or later be again evident. The second mode, closely allied to the first and often combined with it, is to devalue the new idea by describing it in such a way as to lay all the stress on the links between it and older ones, thus putting into the background whatever is essentially new in it, and then claiming that they had always been familiar with it.[1]

Of especial importance is the subject's *attitude towards time*. The idea of time and its passage is so intimately bound up with such fundamental matters as old age and death, potency, ambitions, hopes, in short with the essence of life itself, that it is necessarily of the greatest importance to anyone who claims omnipotence and omniscience. Like all lesser things it must therefore be under his control, and this belief is revealed in a number of little traits and reactions. His own time is naturally the correct one, therefore his watch is always right and any suggestion to the contrary is not merely repudiated, but resented; this confidence is sometimes maintained in the face of the strongest evidence against it. *His* time is also exceedingly valuable in comparison with that of others, so that, quite consistently, he is usually unpunctual at an appointment, but is most impatient when others keep him waiting; time in general belonging to his domain, it is for him to dispose of,

---

[1] A beautiful instance of this performance occurred recently. I had written a paper on Freud's theory of the neuroses, dealing principally, of course, with the importance of infantile conflicts, repressed sexual perversions, etc. A very distorted abstract of it appeared in a French journal, finishing with the assurance that "since Janet's works all these ideas had long been current in France".

not for others. An exception is provided by those members of the group that adopt the definition of punctuality as "la politesse des rois", and who find pleasure in demonstrating their perfect control over time by being absolutely exact (one thinks of Kant's daily four o'clock walk).

The attitude towards *past time* chiefly concerns their personal memory. This they regard, like their watch, as infallible, and they will stoutly defend the accuracy of it to the last lengths; in support of this they cultivate with attention an exactitude in such things as quotations, dates, etc., which can easily be checked. In some cases they are proud of their excellent memory, but more typically they regard it as something obvious and are annoyed when any of their success is attributed to it.

The capacity to foretell demonstrates the power over *future time*, and this occupies a great deal of their interest. To speculate about the future of an acquaintance, an enterprise, a nation, or even the whole human race, is a matter of quite personal concern, and they freely give vent to all manner of predictions, most often of a sinister kind. One of the most characteristic of all the present series of character-traits is the person's firm belief in his ability to *foretell the weather*, and particularly rain or thunder. The vagaries of weather have always played a prominent part in the phantasy of mankind, not only on account of their obvious importance for his welfare, but because the utter variability of them seemed to point directly to the activity of supernatural beings, whether good or evil. Christian congregations that would consider it unreasonable to expect the Deity to improve the landscape at their request, or even to change the temperature, still pray earnestly for modifications of the weather, and almost the last belief about witches to die out was that they were responsible for the production of inclement weather. The weather is the part of nature that most flagrantly defies both the prescience and the control of modern science, rivalling in this respect the human mind itself; one may say that the chief evidences of spontaneity and free will to be found in the universe occur in these two spheres, so that it is little wonder that they are equally regarded as conspicuous exceptions to the natural laws of determinism and order and as manifestations of an external agency. In addition to all this, it is easy to show that the various elements have always possessed considerable symbolic significance, rain, wind, and thunder in particular being taken to represent grand sexual-excremental performances; a thunderstorm is in this connection of especial importance, because it comprises all of the three. In view of these considerations it is not surprising that the present type should take the greatest interest in the subject of the weather, and should arrogate to himself special powers of prediction in regard to it. It is practically pathognomonic of the God-complex when a man maintains that he can invariably foretell a thunderstorm, relying on signs and methods that cannot be explained to anyone else, and regards as "false prophets" all those who use other ones.

Such men also take a great interest in the subject of *language*, one which bears a symbolic relation to the last-mentioned. They pose as authorities on literary style, and often are so, claiming a "mastery" of their mother-tongue. The style they affect is usually good, exact but not pedantic, but tends to be involved and even obscure; lucidity is not its virtue, and they find it difficult to express clearly what they have to say. With the thorough knowledge of their own tongue goes an aversion to foreign ones, which they often refuse to learn; their own is *the* tongue, the only one worthy to be noticed. They are fond of talking, especially in monologue, and usually excel in lecturing, speech-making, and conversation.

Two character-traits that bear an even more direct

relation to narcissism are those concerning the attitude towards advice and judgement. They are very unwilling to give *advice*, the responsibility being too great. Any advice that they gave would be so precious and important that not to follow it would surely be disastrous. Rather than expose their friends to this risk they prefer to withhold their advice, another instance of apparent altruism. It goes without saying that any advice tendered to them by others is contemptuously rejected as worthless.

The attitude towards *judging* is also characteristic. It is a double one, consisting of an alternation of extreme tolerance and extreme intolerance. The question of which of the two is shown seems to depend on whether the infringement to be judged is of their own will or merely of that of other people. In the former case no punishment is too harsh for the offender; I have heard such men describe, just like a child, how they would execute various people who disobeyed them, tradesmen who were behind time, and the like. In the second case, on the other hand, they are always in favour of the greatest leniency and broad-minded tolerance. They thus advocate the abolition of capital punishment, the more humane and understanding treating of criminals, and so on.

The subject of *religion* is usually one of the greatest interest to such men, both from the theological and historical side and from the psychological; this sometimes degenerates into an interest in mysticism. As a rule they are atheists, and naturally so because they cannot suffer the existence of any other God.

We may now briefly mention a few character traits that, though pronounced, are less distinctive, inasmuch as they are of such general occurrence; they only belong here because they are almost always prominent features of the present type. One of these is an exaggerated *desire to be loved*. This is rarely shown directly, or at most by a desire for praise and admiration rather than for love. It is commonly replaced by its opposite, an apparent indifference to and independence of the opinion of others, and the repressed need often betrays itself in such ways as a theoretical interest in the action of crowd suggestion, intense belief in the importance of public opinion, pliant yielding to convention in deeds in spite of a rejection of this in words.

Like all other human beings, they are convinced in their unconscious of their own *immortality*, whether this be ensured through direct continuity or through an eternal series of rebirths; they have thus neither beginning nor end. The belief in their *creative power*, as was mentioned above, is more subordinate, at all events in comparison with other ones, than might have been expected, yet it is often pronounced enough. The belief in self-creation, and rebirth phantasies, are practically constant features. It is further revealed in such phantasies as visions of a vastly improved or altogether ideal world, naturally created by the person in question, or even of the birth of a new planet where everything is "remoulded nearer to the heart's desire";[1] far-reaching schemes of social reform also belong here. In general there is in such men a vein of romantic idealism, often covered by a show of either materialism or realism.

The idea of *castration* always plays with our type a part of quite special importance, both in the form of castration-wishes against the father (authorities) and of fear of castration (talion) on the part of the younger generation. The latter is as a rule the more pronounced of the two, and naturally leads to a fear and jealousy of younger rivals, this being in some cases remarkably intense. Beyond the constancy with which a strong castration-complex is

---

[1] English readers will at once think here of the numerous works of H. G. Wells that excellently illustrate this phantasy; he does not appear, however, to present any other characteristics of our type, at least not in a striking degree.

present there is nothing characteristic about its numerous manifestations in this type, so that I will refrain from mentioning these, particularly as they are fairly well known. The resentment with which these men observe the growing prominence of younger rivals forms a curious contrast to another character-trait, namely their *desire to protect*. They are fond of helping, of acting as patron or guardian, and so on. All this, however, happens only under the strict condition that the person to be protected acknowledges his helpless position and appeals to them as the weak to the strong; such an appeal they often find irresistible.

The reader will probably have realized the difficulty I have experienced in grouping such multiple traits and will therefore allow me to repeat them now in a more concise fashion. Thus, the type in question is characterized by a desire for aloofness, inaccessibility, and mysteriousness, often also by a modesty and self-effacement. They are happiest in their own home, in privacy and seclusion, and like to withdraw to a distance. They surround themselves and their opinions with a cloud of mystery, exert only an indirect influence on external affairs, never join in any common action, and are generally unsocial. They take great interest in psychology, particularly in the so-called objective methods of mind-study that are eclectic and which dispense with the necessity for intuition. Phantasies of power are common, especially the idea of possessing great wealth. They believe themselves to be omniscient, and tend to reject all new knowledge. The attitude towards time and towards the foretelling of weather, particularly thunderstorms, is highly characteristic. The subjects of language and religion greatly interest them, and they have an ambivalent attitude towards those of giving advice and of judging (e.g., punishment). Constant, but less characteristic, attributes are the desire for appreciation, the wish to protect the weak, the belief in their own immortality, the fondness for creative schemes, e.g., for social reform, and above all, a pronounced castration-complex.

An obvious consideration, and one important not to forget, is the fact that all Gods have not the same attributes—although there is much that is common to them all—so that the God-type will vary according to the particular God with whom the person identifies himself. By far the most important of these variations is that depending on the idea of the Son of God, therefore in Europe of Christ. This gives a special stamp to the type in question, which must shortly be indicated. The three chief characteristics are: revolution against the father, saving phantasies, and masochism, or in other words, an Œdipus situation in which the hero-son is a suffering saviour. With this type the mother plays a part of quite special importance, and her influence is often shown in the particular attributes described by Freud in his harlot-saving type.[1] Saving phantasies, where what is to be saved from the "wicked father" varies from a given person (e.g., Shelley's first wife) to the whole of mankind (democratic reform, etc.), are thus extremely common here. The salvation is often to be effected at the expense of a terrific self-sacrifice, where the masochistic tendencies come to full satisfaction. These also reveal themselves in the trait of extreme humility and altruism, especially striking in men who originally were unusually virile and aggressive, e.g., St. Francis of Assisi. Second only to the importance of the mother who has to be rescued is that of the oppressive father. There is thus constantly present an intolerance of authority of any kind, and any person invested with this, or even only with seniority or pre-eminence, may be viewed in the light of this complex so that his figure is artificially distorted into the *imago* of

---

[1] Freud, "Beiträge zur Psychologie des Liebeslebens," I, *Jahrbuch der Psychoanalyse*, Bd. II, S. 389.

JUNG

the wicked father. With this Christ type there invariably goes also an anti-semitic tendency, the two religions being contrasted and the old Hebraic Jehovah being replaced by the young Christ. The castration-complex is if possible even more pronounced in this variety than in the main type described above.

It is interesting to see that the character evolved through the influence of the God-complex in general tends to belong to one or the other of two extreme kinds. On the one hand, if the complex is guided and controlled by valuable higher factors, it may give us a man who is truly God-like in his grandeur and sublimity; Nietzsche and Shelley are perhaps good instances of this. On the other hand—what unfortunately we see more commonly, particularly in patients during analysis—we find characters that are highly unsatisfactory, with exaggerated self-conceit, difficulty in adapting themselves to life in common with ordinary men, and therefore of no great use for social purposes. Probably this can be correlated with the unconscious basis of the complex, the enormous narcissism and exhibitionism. The last named instinct is of all the sexual components the one most closely related to the social instincts, being in a sense a definition of the individual's attitude towards his fellow man, and one can see a similar ambivalence in the value of its products; on the one side, by giving a greater self-confidence and self-estimation, and a powerful motive to achieve a good standing in the estimation of others, it supplies a driving force that greatly contributes towards successfully coming forward in life, while on the other side when either exaggerated or not properly directed it gives rise to difficulties in social adjustment through a false sense of values.

In conclusion we may refer to a few considerations, which though evident have to be mentioned so as to avoid the possibility of misunderstanding. In the first place, the picture sketched above is a composite one, just like any other clinical picture. The individual details are from separate studies and artificially fused, just as a text-book description of typhoid fever is. I have never seen anyone who presented all the attributes mentioned above, and it is very possible that such people do not exist; at all events in every case some of the attributes are more prominent than others. Then I would further emphasize the fact that the present description is quite tentative, necessarily so because it is based on only one person's experience of about a dozen analyses bearing on the problem,[1] in other words on evidence that is certainly insufficient to establish a sharply drawn syndrome. I am convinced that there is such a thing as a God-complex, and that some of the attributes above mentioned belong to it, but am equally convinced that the present account of it needs modification, and probably both expansion in some directions and limiting in others. The present paper is thus published mainly as an incentive to the further investigation of an interesting series of character-traits.

Postscript. The close resemblance between the character traits here described and those derived from what Melanie Klein has termed the "manic" phase of infantile development will be evident to present-day psycho-analysts.

---

[1] Experience of many more cases since this paper was written has only confirmed the main outlines here sketched so that no alterations have been made in it.

XIII

THE MADONNA'S CONCEPTION THROUGH THE EAR

A CONTRIBUTION TO THE RELATION BETWEEN AESTHETICS AND RELIGION[1]

Introduction — The Legend of the Virgin Mary's Conception through the Ear — Breath and Fertilization — The Dove and the Annunciation — The Ear as the Receptive Organ — Conclusion

I. INTRODUCTION

THE object of the present essay is to illustrate, by the analysis of a single example, the following thesis: that the close relation of æsthetics to religion is due to the intimate connection between their respective roots.

The closeness of the relation, which is perhaps more striking with the higher religions, is shown in manifold ways: sometimes by the diametrical opposition of the two, as in the iconoclastic outbursts of Savonarola or the English Puritans against art, but more frequently by the remarkable union between the two. The latter may be manifested both positively, as when art and religion are fused in worship (religious dancing, painting, music, singing, architecture; "The works of the Lord are lovely to behold," "God is lovely in his holiness," etc.), and negatively, as when religion condemns the same piece of conduct, now as sinful, now as ugly or disgusting.

It is widely recognized that the ultimate sources of

[1] Published in the *Jahrbuch der Psychoanalyse*, 1914, Band VI.

artistic creativeness lie in that region of the mind outside consciousness, and it may be said with some accuracy that the deeper the artist reaches in his unconscious in the search for his inspiration the more profound is the resulting conception likely to be. It is also well known that among these ultimate sources the most important are psycho-sexual phantasies. Artistic creation serves for the expression of many emotions and ideas, love of power, sympathy at suffering, desire for ideal beauty, and so on, but—unless the term be extended so as to include admiration for any form whatever of perfection—it is with the last of these, beauty, that æsthetics is principally concerned; so much so that æsthetic feeling may well be defined as that which is evoked by the contemplation of beauty. Now, analysis of this aspiration reveals that the chief source of its stimuli is not so much a primary impulse as a reaction, a rebellion against the coarser and more repellent aspects of material existence, one which psychogenetically arises from the reaction of the young child against its original excremental interests. When we remember how extensively these repressed coprophilic tendencies contribute, in their sub-limated forms, to every variety of artistic activity—to painting, sculpture, and architecture on the one hand, and to music and poetry on the other—it becomes evident that in the artist's striving for beauty the fundamental part played by these primitive infantile interests (including their later derivatives) is not to be ignored: the reaction against them lies behind the striving, and the sublimation of them behind the forms that the striving takes.

When on the other hand religious activities, interests and rites, are traced to their unconscious source it is found that, although—as I have pointed out in the case of baptism[1]—they make extensive use of the same psychical material as that indicated above, they differ from æsthetic

[1] *See* Chapter II, pp. 34, 70, 71.

interests especially in that the main motives are derived not so much from this sphere as from another group of infantile interests, that concerned with incestuous phantasies.[1] At first sight, therefore, æsthetics and religion would appear to have on the whole disparate biological origins. Freud's[2] researches have demonstrated, however—and this is not the least far-reaching of their conclusions—that infantile coprophilia belongs essentially to the as yet unco-ordinated infantile sexuality, constituting as it does a prominent part of the auto-erotic stage which precedes that of incestuous object-love. From this point of view we obtain a deeper insight into the present topic, and indeed a satisfactory explanation of the problem, for, since æsthetic and religious activities are derived from merely different components of a biologically unitary instinct, components which are inextricably intertwined at their very roots, it becomes throughout intelligible that even in their most developed forms they should stand in close relationship to each other.

II. THE LEGEND OF THE MADONNA'S CONCEPTION THROUGH THE EAR

A belief, often forgotten nowadays, but preserved in the legends and traditions of the Catholic Church, is that the conception of Jesus in the Virgin Mary was brought about by the introduction into her ear of the breath of the Holy Ghost. I do not know if this is now held as an official tenet of the Church, but in past ages it was not only depicted by numerous religious artists, but also maintained by many of the Fathers and by at least one of the Popes, namely Felix.

[1] See Freud, Totem und Tabu, 1913.
[2] Freud, Drei Abhandlungen zur Sexualtheorie, 4e Aufl., 1920

St. Augustine[1] writes: "Deus per angelum loquebatur et Virgo per aurem imprægnebatur," St. Agobard[2] "Descendit de cœlis missus ab arce patris, introivit per aurem Virginis in regionem nostram indutus stola purpurea et exivit per auream portam lux et Deus universæ fabricæ mundi", and St. Ephrem of Syria[3] "Per novam Mariæ aurem intravit atque infusa est vita"; similar passages could be quoted from various other Fathers, such as St. Proclus, St. Ruffinus of Aquileia, etc. In the Breviary of the Maronites one reads: "Verbum patris per aurem benedictæ intravit," and a hymn,[4] ascribed by some to St. Thomas à Becket, by others to St. Bonaventure, contains the following verse:

> Gaude, Virgo, mater Christi,
> Quae per aurem concepisti,
> > Gabriele nuntio.
> Gaude, quia Deo plena
> Peperisti sine pena
> > Cum pudoris lilio.

There were many versions of this current in the Middle Ages; Langlois[5] quotes the following one from the seventeenth century:

> Rejouyssez-vous, Vièrge, et Mère bienheureuse,
> Qui dans vos chastes flancs conçeutes par l'ouyr,
> L'Esprit-Sainct opérant d'un très-ardent désir,
> Est l'Ange l'annonçant d'une voix amoureuse.

The event was often portrayed by religious artists in the Middle Ages. For instance, in a painting of Filippo

---

[1] St. Augustine, *Sermo de Tempore*, XXII.
[2] St. Agobard, *De Correctione antiphonarii*, Cap. viii.
[3] St. Ephrem, *De Divers Serm.* I, Opp. Syr., Vol. III, p. 607.
[4] Bodley MS., *Latin Liturgy*, X, Fol. 91 vo.
[5] Langlois, *Essai sur la Peinture sur Verre*, 1832, p. 157.

Lippi's in the convent of San Marco in Florence, in one of Gaddi's in the Santa Maria Novella, in one of Benozzo Gozzoli's in the Campo Santa of Pisa, and in an old mosaic —no longer extant[1]—in Santa Maria Maggiore in Rome, the Holy Dove is seen almost entering the Virgin's ear. In the first named of these the Dove emanates from the right hand of the Father, in the second from his bosom; more typically, however, as in the picture of Simone Martini's here reproduced,[2] one which will presently be more fully discussed, the Dove emanates from the mouth of the Father. The Dove may either constitute a part of the Father's breath—as it were a concrete condensation of this—or it may itself repeat the emission of breath: in the Florence Bargello there are three examples of this (by Verrocchio and the Della Robbias), and it may also be seen in a picture of the Ferrarese school in the Wallace Collection, London, as well as in Martini's picture.

The connection between the fertilizing breath of the Dove and the child to be conceived is made plainly evident in an old panel that used to stand in the Cathedral of Saint-Leu, of which Langlois gives the following description: "Du bec du St-Esprit jaillissait un rayon lumineux aboutissant à l'oreille de Marie, dans laquelle descendait s'introduire, dirigé par ce même rayon, un très-jeune enfant tenant une petite croix."[3] A similar picture, by Meister des Marialebens, in which also the infant is seen descending along a ray of light, may be seen in the German-isches Museum in Nuremberg. We note that here it is a ray of light that issues from the mouth of the Dove, instead of the more appropriate breath. This equating of radiating breath and rays of light is an interesting matter to which we shall have to return later. It may have been partly deter-

[1] Gori, *Thesaurus*, Tab. XXX, Vol. III.
[2] *See* Frontispiece.
[3] Langlois, loc. cit.

mined by the greater technical facility with which rays of light can be represented by the painter, but it also has its theological aspects, since it is related to the doctrine of the monophysite Churches of Armenia and Syria (which split off from the Byzantine in the fifth century) that Jesus's body, originating in an emission of light from heaven, was made of ethereal fire and had neither bodily structure nor functions. Another example of this equation occurs in an old stained-glass window which was formerly in the sacristy of the Pistoia Cathedral,[1] also representing rays issuing from the Dove's mouth and bearing an embryo in the direction of the Virgin's head; the picture is surmounted by the lines:

Gaude Virgo Mater Christi
Quae per Aurem concepisti.

In a sculpture now in the Fränkisches Luitpoldmuseum at Würzburg[2] a little child carrying a crucifix is seen in the midst of the Father's radiating breath and aiming at the Virgin's right ear; the Dove here stands aside, at the right side of the head. The presence of the infant at this stage was denounced as heretical by the Catholic Church, for it contradicted the belief that He took his flesh from the Virgin Mary and so was really man.

As a counterpart to the accompanying picture of Martini's where the sacred words "Ave Gratia plena dominus tecum" are designated passing from Gabriel's lips to the Virgin's ear—converging thus with the breath of the Dove—may be mentioned a twelfth-century altarpiece at Klosterneuburg,[3] by Nicolas Verdun, in which two rays escape from the tips of the fingers of Gabriel's right hand and are directed towards the Virgin's ear. The anomalous

---

[1] Cicognara, *Storia della Scultura*, 1813-1818, Vol. I, p. 324.
[2] Nr. 6 Portalstein der Hauskapelle des Hofes Rödelsee in Würzburg, 1484.
[3] Arneth, *Das Niello-Antipendium zu Klosterneuburg*, 1844, S. 11.

termination of light rays in the *ear* demonstrates the strength of the main idea, that of impregnation by means of breath—here replaced by its symbolic equivalent of rays of light—entering the ear.

Much discussion took place in subsequent centuries over the delicate questions pertaining to the mode of birth of the Holy Babe, of whether He left His mother's body by the natural route or emerged between the breasts or from the ear itself, whether the hymen was ruptured, and if so whether its integrity was restored later, and so on.[1] It is not proposed, however, to discuss these matters here, our attention being confined to the initial stage of the process.

This remarkable conception of the process of impregnation, so foreign to all human experience,[2] must arouse the desire to investigate its meaning, for it evidently represents a symbolic expression of some obscure idea rather than a mere literal description of a matter-of-fact occurrence. Lecky[3] asserts that it "of course was suggested by the title Logos", but we shall find grounds for doubting whether this rationalistic explanation does not reverse the actual order of genesis of the two ideas.

Our interest is further increased when we learn that the story is in no way peculiar to Christianity, though perhaps it is here that it reaches its most finished and elaborate form. Anticipating a little of our later discussion, we may mention at this point the legend of Chigemouni, the Mongolian Saviour, who chose the most perfect virgin on earth, Mahaenna or Maya, and impregnated her by

[1] *See* Guillaume Herzog, *La Sainte Vierge dans l'Histoire*, 1908, Ch. III, "La Virginité 'in partu'," pp. 38-51.

[2] So foreign that Molière uses it to indicate the utmost limit of ignorance on sexual topics. In the *Ecole des Femmes* he makes Anolphe say that Agnes has asked him

> Avec une innocence à nulle autre pareille,
> Si les enfants qu'on fait se faisoient par l'oreille.

[3] Lecky, *History of the Rise and Influence of the Spirit of Rationalism in Europe*, Cheaper Edition, Vol. I, p. 212.

penetrating into her right ear during sleep.[1] We shall see
also that when the Mary legend is dissected into its elements
each of these can be richly paralleled from extra-Christian
sources, and that the main ones have proved to be of
almost universal interest. It is therefore certain that we
are concerned, not with a purely local problem of early
Christian theology, but with a theme of general human
significance.

For the sake of convenience the subject will be divided
up, and an attempt made to answer in order the following
questions: Why is the creative material represented as
emanating from the mouth, and why as breath in particular? Why is it a dove that conveys it? And why is the
ear chosen to be the receptive organ?

III. BREATH AND FERTILIZATION

In anthropological, mythological and individual symbolism, instances of which are too numerous in the literature
to need quoting here, the *mouth* has more frequently a
female significance, being naturally adapted to represent a
receptive organ. Its capacity, however, to emit fluids
(saliva and breath), and the circumstance of its containing
the tongue, the symbolic significance of which will presently
be considered, render it also suitable for portraying a male
aperture; the idea of spitting, in particular, is one of the
commonest symbolisms in folk-lore for the male act (hence,
for instance, the expression "the very spit of his father").

[1] Norlk, *Biblische Mythologie*, 1843, Bd. II, S. 64. Jung (*Jahrbuch der
Psychoanalyse*, Bd. IV, S. 204) makes the interesting statement, for which
however he gives no authority, that the Mongolian Buddha was also born
from his mother's ear; the accounts I have read, on the contrary, say that he
was conceived by the ear, but born by the mouth. In a silk banner painted
about A.D. 1100 and recently discovered in the Cave of the Thousand Buddhas,
the first appearance of the babe is depicted as being within his mother's sleeve
(*See* Stein, *Ruins of Desert Cathay*, 1912, Vol. II, p. 199), a fact to which
Mr. Alfred Ela of Boston kindly directed my attention.

The idea of the *breath* as a life-giving agent is familiar to us from the passages in the Old Testament: "And the Lord God formed man of the dust of the ground, and breathed into his nostrils the breath of life; and man became a living soul" (Genesis ii. 7); "The heavens by the Word of God did their beginning take; And by the breathing of his mouth he all their hosts did make" (Psalms xxxiii. 6). Mohammedan tradition ascribes the miraculous impregnation of the Virgin Mary to Gabriel having opened the bosom of her garment and breathed upon her womb.[1] One of the various legends of the birth of the Aztec divinity Quetzalcoatl relates that the Lord of Existence, Tonacatecutli, appeared to Chimalma and breathed upon her, with the result that she conceived the divine child.[2]

Further than this, the idea of breath has played a remarkably extensive part in religion and philosophy, in the lowest as well as in the highest beliefs of mankind. In Brahmanism it becomes formally identified with the Eternal Being,[3] and all over the world it has furnished one of the main constituent components of the idea of the soul (*Hauchseele*).[4]

Now when we ask what is the source of this intense interest and importance with which the idea in question has been invested, such an inquiry may seem almost superfluous, for it will be said that the importance attached to the idea of breathing is inherent in the act itself. Breath, as a symbol of life, is felt to be a natural and appropriate choice. No manifest act is more continuously essential to life than that of breathing, and the presence or absence of it is the simplest and most primitive test of death; the

---

[1] Sale, *Koran*, 1734, Note to Ch. XIX, citing various Arabian authors.

[2] Bancroft, *The Native Races of the Pacific States of North America*, 1876, Vol. III, p. 271. *See* also Preuss, *Globus*, Bd. LXXXVI, S. 302.

[3] Deussen, *The Philosophy of the Upanishads*, Engl. Transl. 1906, pp. 39, 110.

[4] Wundt, *Völkerpsychologie*, Bd. II, 'Mythus und Religion," 1906, Zweiter Teil, S. 42 et. seq.

mysterious invisibility of breath finds a meet counterpart in that of the soul.

Psycho-Analysis, however, has by now become familiar with the experience of finding various matters taken for granted as being something obvious and in no need of explanation—infantile amnesia affords one of the most striking examples of this—and then nevertheless discovered that behind this attitude of indifference may lie most important problems, just where there was thought to be no problem at all. So that, sharpened by such experiences in the past, we should not be content to adopt a current estimate of mental phenomena until an unbiassed examination of the facts confirms the accuracy of it. With the matter under consideration this is, in my opinion, not so. In spite of the obvious reflections just mentioned, the thesis will here be maintained that the current conclusion indicated above furnishes only a part answer to the question asked, and that much of the significance attached to the idea of breath is primarily derived from a source extraneous to it. In other words, it is maintained that we have here another example of the familiar process of displacement, whereby various affects that originally belonged to another idea altogether have become secondarily associated with that of breath.

I have two reasons for venturing to differ from the generally accepted opinion on this matter, first because this seems to me to be based on an erroneous estimate of the amount of psychical interest normally attaching to the idea of breath, and secondly because it is in open disaccord with the principles of psychogenesis. To make the idea in question the centre of an elaborate religion, philosophy or *Weltanschauung*, as has been done many times in history, seems to me to presuppose an amount of primary interest in it which transcends that taken by anyone not in the throes of mortal illness. And when we explore the Unconscious, that region where so many philosophic and religious ideas have their source, we find that the idea of breath is much less important even than in consciousness, occupying a rank of almost subordinate inferiority. In the numerous cases, for instance, of neurotic symptoms centring about the act of breathing or speaking, analysis always shows that the primary importance of the act has been over-determined by extraneous factors. There is reason, it is true, to think that if we could apply the libido theory more extensively to somatic processes, along the lines opened up by Ferenczi, the act of breathing would assume an importance hard to overestimate, but there is no evidence—at all events as yet—to indicate that any serious amount of what may be termed ideational interest results from this organic importance of the act.

In the second place, it is a law of psychogenesis, founded now on extensive experience, that an idea can become psychically important in adult life only through becoming associated with, and reinforcing, an earlier chain of ideas reaching back into childhood, and that much, or even most, of its psychical (as apart from intrinsic) significance is derived from these. Thus whenever we find such an idea dating mainly from adult life we may be sure that it represents much more than itself—namely, earlier groups of important ideas with which it has become associated. These considerations are much more extensively applicable, and should therefore be regarded as correspondingly more potent, with ideas concerned with the adaptation to the world of inner, psychical reality than with those relating to the outer world, and the religious and philosophic ideas referred to—as also those concerning the act of breathing—certainly enter into the former category. Now in the present instance it must be admitted that the ideational interest attaching to the act of breathing arises for the most part relatively late, for the infant is usually unaware of the act as such, which it performs automatically, and which arouses almost as little interest as the beating of the heart; even with difficult breathing in disease it is rather the sensations of distress (precordial, etc.) that are important than the idea itself of the act of breathing. This whole argument will not perhaps be very convincing to those who have not realized through psycho-analytical experience the ontogenetic antiquity of our affective processes, but with those who have it must, in my judgement, carry considerable weight.

To trace the origin of the various affects that in later life invest the idea of breath, or of course those of any other idea, is a matter of detailed individual-psychological studies and of noting the different displacements that have occurred during the growth of the mind. If this is done, it will be found, as I pointed out some time ago,[1] that much of the interest and affect attaching to this particular idea has been derived from that of an excreted air other than breath—namely, the gas resulting from intestinal decomposition. This conclusion may seem at first sight repellent, highly improbable, and above all unnecessary, but the truth of it is supported not only by the preceding theoretical considerations and the results of actual individual analyses, but by a large amount of very definite evidence of a purely external nature. Psycho-analytic investigation has shown that from the beginning children take a far greater interest in the act referred to than is commonly supposed, as is true of all excretory functions,[2] and that they are apt in various ways to attach great significance to it, most of which of course becomes in later years displaced on to other, associated ideas. From this point of view the extensive part played by the idea in the

---

[1] *Jahrbuch der Psychoanalyse*, Bd. IV, S. 588 et seq.

[2] It should not be forgotten that the interest in question is a manifestation of the sexual instinct. The part played by breath in infantile sexuality is certainly less important than that played by the rectal excretions.

obscene jokes of childhood, and indeed in the more allusive ones of later years,[1] becomes for the first time intelligible. It is hardly necessary to add that, owing to the repugnance of the idea, most of the infantile interest in it gets buried in the Unconscious and the phantasies concerning it forgotten.

One of these phantasies, which has a special reference to the main theme of this essay, is the identification of the material in question with the sexual secretion. In their early cogitation about what is done by the father to bring about the production of a baby many children originate the belief, to which I have elsewhere directed attention,[2] that the mysterious act performed by the parents consists in the passage of gas from the father to the mother, just as other children imagine it to consist in the mutual passage of urine. Some children, probably the smaller number, go on to connect this with the swelling of the mother's abdomen during pregnancy, and their personal experience of a swollen abdomen due to dyspepsia and intestinal decomposition may be the starting-point for reproduction phantasies of their own.[3] The possible objection that this

---

[1] Cp. the volumes of Krauss' *Anthropophyteia*, which give some notion of this. Most farcical comedians on the variety stage make almost unconcealed allusions to the act, usually in conjunction with the orchestra.

[2] *Zentralblatt für Psychoanalyse*, Jahrg. I, S. 566. In the *Jahrbuch der Psychoanalyse* (1912, Bd. IV, S. 563) a detailed report is given of one of the cases on which my conclusion was based. The explanation was subsequently, and independently, confirmed by Reitler (*Zentralblatt für Psychoanalyse*, Jahrg. II, S. 114).

[3] Larguier des Bancels (*Arch. de Psychologie*, t. XVII, pp. 64-6), in a criticism of the present essay, holds that my conclusions "se brisent sur un point capital". Quoting the extremely doubtful conclusions of Hartland, to the effect that many savage races are ignorant of any connection between sexual intercourse and fecundation, he asks how one can attribute to young children greater perspicacity in this respect than that possessed by savage adults. My answer is that I attribute to both a greater perspicacity than does my critic. That, quite apart from actual knowledge, young children commonly imagine the begetting of a baby to be dependent on some unknown act between the parents may be news to him, but it is a very familiar fact to me, as to all others who have intimate experience of the child's mind.

is in any way an artificial finding of psycho-analysis, or perhaps one that refers only to present-day civilization, can be at once disposed of by mentioning a single counter-part from antiquity. Thus in the Satapatha-Brâhmana,[1] and in several other passages in the Vedic literature, it is described how the Lord of Existence, Pragapati, who had created the original gods with the "out (and in) breathings of his mouth", proceeded to create the whole of mankind with the "downward breathings that escape from the back part (jaghanat)"; the identity of cosmogonic theories of creation with infantile ones has been amply demonstrated by Otto Rank.[2]

It will be most convenient to continue the discussion at this stage by dissecting the natural associations existing between the two expiratory gases, and grouping—rather artificially, it is true—various topics under each. Air emitted from the body, whether upwards or downwards, has the following attributes: blowing movement, sound, invisibility, moisture, warmth and odour.

1. *Blowing Movement*

The primitive notion that the down-going breath, to use the seemly phrase of the Vedic writers, is a fertilizing principle has frequently been extended to the *wind*, as might readily have been expected. It is significant that the corresponding belief can be traced in every quarter of the world, from Australia to Europe. Perhaps the most familiar example of it is the legend of Hera, who was fertilized by the wind and conceived Hephaistos. In the Algonkin mythology, Mudjekeewis, the West Wind and Father of the other winds, quickens the maiden Wenonah,

---

[1] X. Kânda, I, iii, 1 and 6; Kânda, I, ii, 2.
[2] Otto Rank, "Völkerpsychologische Parallelen zu den infantilen Sexual-theorien," *Zentralblatt für Psychoanalyse*, Jahrg. II, S. 372, 425.

ESSAYS IN APPLIED PSYCHO-ANALYSIS

who then bears the hero Michabo, better known to us under the name of Hiawatha.[1] In Longfellow's well-known poem of this name the courtship is described in terms that indicate the symbolic equivalence of wind, light, speech, odour and music, one which will be discussed later.

> And he wooed her with caresses,
> Wooed her with his smile of sunshine,
> With his flattering words he wooed her,
> With his sighing and his singing,
> Gentlest whispers in the branches,
> Softest music, sweetest odours,
> Till he drew her to his bosom.

The Minahassers of Celebes believe they are descended from a girl in primeval days who was also fecundated by the West Wind.[2] The Aruntas of Central Australia still hold that a storm from the West sometimes brings evil "ratapa", or child-germs, that seek to enter women; as the storm approaches, the women with a loud cry hasten to the shelter of their huts, for if they become impregnated in this fashion twins will result who will die shortly after their birth.[3]

Although this belief is more especially connected with the West Wind, other ones can on occasion display a similar activity. Thus in the Luang-Sermata group of islands in the Moluccas the origin of mankind is traced to a "sky-woman" who climbed down to earth and was impregnated by the South Wind;[4] her children had access to the sky until the Lord Sun forbade it, a belief the onto-genetic significance of which is evident. Again, in the

[1] Brinton, *American Hero-Myths*, 1882, p. 47.
[2] Schwarz, *Internationales Archiv für Ethnographie*, 1907, Jahrg. XVIII, S. 59.
[3] Strehlow, *Die Aranda- und Loritja-Stämme in Zentralaustralien*, 1907, S. 14.
[4] Riedel, *De Sluik- en Kroesharige Rassen tusschen Selebes en Papua*, 1886, p. 312.

Finnish national epic, Kalevala, the virgin Ilmatar is fructified by the East Wind and gives birth to the wizard Väinamöinen; appropriately enough, the latter not only invented the harp and discovered fire, but became the instructor of mankind in poetry and music.[1] In the similar legend of Luminu-ut current in Singapore and the Indian Archipelago[2] it is not stated which wind was responsible. In classical times this belief was especially connected with the Spring Wind, Zephyrus or Flavonius, who, for instance, begot Euphrosyne with Aurora, and it is highly probable that the Floralia included a worship of this wind as well as of flowers; Ovid[3] describes how Chloris, called Flora by the Romans, was ravished by Zephyr. Widespread also are the traditions of whole regions—particularly islands—the inhabitants of which are descended from the wind, or whose women conceive only in this way. In early classical times the latter belief was entertained in regard to Cyprus, and only last century the inhabitants of Lampong, in Sumatra, believed the same of the neighbouring island of Engano.[4] Mohammedan tradition tells of a pre-Adamite race consisting entirely of women, who conceived (daughters only) by the wind, and also of an island of women thus peopled.[5] The Binhyas of India also claim descent from the wind.[6] In an interesting poem by Eduard Mörike entitled "Jung Volkers Lied", the connection is clearly indicated between the belief in question and the tendency to repudiate the male sex; it is probable that all these beliefs in miraculous conception spring from the boy's desire to exclude the father from anything to do with his birth:

---

[1] Abercromby, *The Pre- and Proto-historic Finns*, 1898, Vol. I, pp. 316, 318, 322.

[2] Bab, *Zeitschrift für Ethnologie*, 1906, Jahrg. XXXVIII, S. 280.

[3] Ovid, *Fasti*, v, 195-202.

[4] Marsden, *The History of Sumatra*, 1811, p. 297.

[5] *L'Abrégé des Merveilles*. Translated from the Arabian by De Vaux, 1898, pp. 17, 71.

[6] Saintyves, *Les Vierges Mères*, 1908, p. 143.

Und die mich trug im Mutterleib,
Und die mich schwang im Kissen,
Die war ein schön frech braunes Weib,
Wollte nichts vom Mannsvolk wissen.

Sie scherzte nur und lachte laut
Und liess die Freier stehen:
"Möcht' lieber sein des Windes Braut,
Denn in die Ehe gehen!"

Da kam der Wind, da nahm der Wind
Als Buhle sie gefangen:
Von dem hat sie ein lustig Kind
In ihren Schoss empfangen.[1]

As is quite comprehensible, the same belief was by analogy also extended to animals. Freud[2] has reminded us of the ancient belief that vultures were, like the inhabitants of the islands just referred to, all female, and that they conceived by exposing their genitals to the wind; so accepted was this that Origen appealed to it in support of the credibility of Jesus Christ's virgin birth. Nor was the vulture the only bird that has been supposed to conceive in this way; in Samoa the same thing was related

---

[1] And she who bore me as a child
Who rocked my cradle then,
She was a fine brawn lass so wild
That would know nought of men.

She only scoffed and laughed beside,
And left the men alone,
"I'd rather be the wild wind's bride
Than marry anyone."

The wind he came, the wind so wild,
Bride was she, he the groom,
By him she got a merry child,
A boy child in her womb.

[2] Freud, *Eine Kindheitserinnerung des Leonardo da Vinci*, 1910, S. 25.

of snipe,[1] and both Aristotle[2] and Pliny[3] tell us that partridges can be fecundated when merely standing opposite to the male, provided that the wind is blowing from him to her.[4] St. Augustine[5] gravely relates how the mares in Cappadocia are fertilized by the wind, Virgil[6] says the same of the mares of Boaetia, and Pliny[7] of those of Lusitania. In more modern times this ancient belief is found only in the form of poetic analogy, such as in the following passage from Shakespeare:[8]

When we have laugh'd to see the sails conceive,
And grow big-bellied with the wanton wind;
Which she, with pretty and with swimming gait
Following, (her womb then rich with my young squire)
Would imitate, and sail upon the land.

Not only have the life-bringing powers been ascribed to the outer air, usually in the form of wind, but this has been extensively identified with the principle of life and creation altogether. Something will be said later of the enormous part it has played in Indian and Greek philosophy, where it has been exalted to the rank of the breath and essence of God himself, the fundamental substratum of all material and spiritual existence, the source of all life and activity, the first principle of the universe, and so on. A glance at the extraordinary mass of material collected by Frazer[9] on the subject of "The Magical Control of the Wind" is enough to show the astonishing significance of

[1] Sierich, "Samoanische Märchen," *Internat. Arch. für Ethnographie*, Bd. XVI, S. 90.
[2] Aristotle, *Hist. Anim.*, v, 4.
[3] Pliny, *Hist. Nat.*, x, 51.
[4] *See* also Plutarch, *Moralia*, Lib. VIII, Art. i, Par. 3.
[5] St. Augustinus, *Civ. Dei*, xxi, 5.
[6] Virgil, *Georgics*, iii, 266-76.
[7] Pliny, op. cit., viii, 67.
[8] Shakespeare, *A Midsummer Night's Dream*, Act II, Sc. 2, l. 69.
[9] Frazer, *The Magic Art*, 1911, Vol. I, pp. 319-31.

the idea in anthropology and folk-lore. There remain in
modern times many examples of this over-estimation of the
idea, particularly in poetry, of which the following may be
quoted from Shelley's "Ode to the West Wind", in which
also the association between wind, birth, fire, thoughts, and
words, which will presently be discussed, is well indicated:

> Be thou, Spirit fierce,
> My spirit! Be thou me, impetuous one!
> Drive my dead thoughts over the universe
> Like withered leaves to quicken a new birth!
> And, by the incantation of this verse,
> Scatter, as from an unextinguished hearth
> Ashes and sparks, my words among mankind!

The question why various beliefs in the fertilizing power
of the wind get attached, now to the wind from one cardinal
point, now to another, cannot be completely answered
without a special study. It is plain that a number of
different determining factors enter into the matter. For
instance, it was believed in Thuringia[1] to be advantageous
to sow barley when the West Wind was blowing, and
one gets a clue to the meaning of this on learning further
that the sowing should be done on a Wednesday, i.e. on
Odin's day, since Odin, probably for reasons to do with
the setting sun, had special connections with the west.
A very general factor in the localizing of the belief is its
association with winds of a warm, moist, and "relaxing"
character, which commonly induce a more or less lascivious
mood: a good example is the "Föhnfieber" in Switzerland,
which is certainly a form of sexual excitation. The good
King René of Provence passed the very tolerant law that
those who committed crimes when the mistral was blowing
were not to be punished, since they could not be held

---

[1] Witzschel, *Sagen, Sitten und Gebräuche aus Thüringen*, 1878, Bd. II, S. 215.

responsible in such "irritating" circumstances. All agencies leading to sexual excitation are readily identified, especially in the unconscious, with a fertilizing principle. As winds of this character prevailing blow from the west or south-west over the chief part of Europe, it is not surprising that in this region most of the beliefs in question are related to it. In confirmation of this supposition is the fact that the opposite type of wind, the East Wind, is popularly credited with the contrary effect. There is a saying among German sailors which runs (in Plattdeutsch) as follows:[1] "Oste-Wind makt krus den Buedel un kort den Pint." ("The East Wind makes the scrotum crinkled and the penis short.")

It is nowadays generally recognized, since the belief in mankind's primary interest in physical geography has been largely discredited, that all this significance attaching to the idea of wind must have arisen mainly through a projection outward of thoughts and feelings concerning the air in immediate connection with man's body. In accord with this view is the fact that the beliefs just mentioned concerning the sexual activities of the wind can be extensively paralleled by similar ones relating to the breath. One or two of these may be added to those already cited. The Delphi priestess in her love-embrace with Apollo was filled with his breath, which the God poured into her. In an early Mexican picture[2] a man and woman are represented as having intercourse by mingling their breath.

On the basis, therefore, of present-day views on mythology, which do not need to be expounded here,[3] we may assume that the idea of breath is primary to that of wind, and that the beliefs just related concerning the latter may

---

[1] Private communication from Dr. Karl Abraham.

[2] Reproduced by Seler, "Tierbilder der mexikanischen und Maya-Handschriften," *Zeitschr. f. Ethnologie*, Bd. XLII, S. 67.

[3] *See* Rank and Sachs, *Die Bedeutung der Psychoanalyse für die Geisteswissenschaften*, 1913, Kapitel II.

be taken as some index of how important the former has been in anthropological history. That, however, the idea of another personal gas is still more primary than that of breath is a thesis that an attempt will be made to substantiate in the following pages.

2. Sound

In the description of a fertilizing principle or of the Creative Being himself sound may occur either alone, when it is plainly a symbol, or as the most prominent attribute of some other phenomenon. A clear example of the former is the "Last Trump", which is to wake the dead from their sleep and call them to eternal life. This motif also plays a part in the various miracles of raising people from the dead; it is indicated for instance in a picture by Bronzino (in the Santa Maria Novella, Florence) representing the raising of Jairus's daughter, in which an angel stands at the side blowing a trumpet. Another example of the significance of sound, where the sexual meaning comes to open expression, is afforded by a cameo, dated 1294, in the Florence Bargello, in which a satyr blowing a trumpet surprises a sleeping bacchante.

In the second type, where sound is merely one of the prominent features, the phenomenon is perhaps most often conceived of in the form of *wind*. In the Old Testament the voice of God is described by Ezekiel (iii. 12) as "a great rushing", and in the account of the advent of the Holy Ghost given in the Acts of the Apostles (ii. 2) we read: "And suddenly there came a *sound* from heaven, as of a rushing mighty wind, and it filled all the house where they were sitting." Similarly the South American Indians worshipped "Hurrakan", "the mighty wind", a name supposed to be cognate with our word "hurricane", and the natives of New Zealand regarded the wind as a special indication

286

of God's presence;[1] with this may be compared the Australian fear, mentioned above, of the impregnating storm, the idea of "Father" being common to both. Even in modern times tempests have been regarded as representing God in a dangerous mood, while in all ages the creating of storms and thunder has been considered a special prerogative of the Deity (Odin, Thor, Yahweh, Zeus, etc.).

A Chinese myth[2] relates how Hoang-Ty, or Hiong, the founder of civilization, was born of a virgin, Ching-Mou, and *thunder*. The mythology of thunder is much too extensive to be considered here, but attention should be called to the close association between the ideas of "thunder" and "father", one, indeed, which applies to the whole group under discussion. The Phrygian precursor of Zeus was called both Papas (= Father) and Bronton (= Thunderer). Frazer[3] has shown how extensive has been the connection between Kings and thunder, and has made it probable that the early Roman kings imitated Jupiter's powers in this respect; it is well known that psychologically the idea of king is equivalent to that of father. The old Indian God of Thunder and of Procreation, Parjanya, was represented in the form of a bull,[4] a typical patriarchal symbol. That the idea of thunder is exceedingly apt, in dreams and other products of the unconscious phantasy, to symbolize flatus, particularly paternal flatus, is well known to all psycho-analysts; such psycho-neurotic symptoms as brontephobia are almost constantly related to unconscious thoughts concerning this, and in obscene jests the association is at least as old as Aristophanes.[5]

The association Father—God—Sound has always been

[1] Taylor, *Te Ika a Maui, or New Zealand and its Inhabitants*, Second Edition, 1870, p. 181.

[2] De Prémare, *Vestiges des principaux dogmes chrétiens*, 1878, p. 433.

[3] Frazer, op. cit., Vol. II, pp. 180-3.

[4] *Rigveda* (Griffith's Translation), Vol. II, p. 299.

[5] Aristophanes, *Clouds*, Act V, Sc. 2. Βροντὴ και πορδὴ, ὁμοιω.

a remarkably close one, and the following description of Zeus in this respect would hold good for the majority of Gods: "He gave his oracles through the voices of winds moaning and rustling in his sacred oak grove amidst the murmur of falling waters and the clangor of bronzen vessels struck by wind-moved hammers."[1] By a characteristically human reasoning process it was assumed that supernatural beings, including God himself, could be influenced by sounds, of any kind, and this device has been widely employed in connection with both the purposes for which it was desired to attract the attention, and influence the conduct, of the Divine Being. The beating of tom-toms in African villages to frighten away evil spirits, and the similar Norse procedure to prevent the sun from being swallowed at the time of an eclipse, may be cited as examples of the one kind; in Greece also, loud noises were considered especially effective as apotropaic measures against the malign influences of evil demons. By the side of this Luther's statement[2] may be recalled, according to which the devil is to be driven away through the efficacy of the passage of flatus.

On the other hand, sounds, especially in the form of hymn-singing and music, have been, and still are, favourite means of intercession to obtain benefits from the Deity. A hymn called "haha" (= breath), an invocation to the mystic wind, is pronounced by Maori priests on the initiation of young men.[3] The instrument called the "bull-roarer", "bummel", or "buzzer" is said by Haddon[4] to be the most ancient, widely-spread, and sacred religious symbol in the world. It consists of a slab of wood which, when tied to a piece of string and rapidly whirled around,

[1] Cotterill, *Ancient Greece*, 1913, p. 58.
[2] Schurig, *Chylologia*, 1725, p. 795; *see* also *Les Propos de Table de Luther*, *Trad. franc.* par Brunet, 1846, p. 22.
[3] Andrew Lang, *Custom and Myth*, 1884, p. 36.
[4] Haddon, *The Study of Man*, 1898, p. 327.

emits a roaring, uncanny noise. It is still used in Mexico, Ceylon, British Columbia, New Zealand, the Malay Peninsula, New Guinea, Africa, and Australia.[1] Under the name of the rhombus it figured prominently in the Dionysian mysteries in Ancient Greece, and Pettazoni[2] has recently pointed out that the "rombo" still survives in modern Italy. It is used sometimes to invoke the presence and aid of the Deity, sometimes to drive away evil spirits. A study of the various beliefs surrounding it shows that the three main ideas with which its use is associated are: (1) thunder and wind, (2) reproduction (vegetation cults, initiation ceremonies, danger if seen by women, etc.), (3) ancestor worship (i.e., Father)—in other words, ideas that take a prominent part in the theme under discussion here. There is naturally a close connection between bull-roarers and thunder-weapons in general, which have played an important part in religious rites in most parts of the world except Egypt;[3] the hammer of Thor, the trident of Poseidon, the trisula of Siva, and the keraunos of Zeus are a few of the many variants of it the phallic significance of which is evident. In short, there are innumerable connections between the idea of thunder on the one hand and ideas of paternal power, particularly reproductive power, on the other, a conclusion reached long ago by Schwartz[4] and in full accord with the conclusions of Abraham[5] and Kuhn[6] on the sexual symbolism of lightning.

In ancient times it was believed that the young of lions were born dead and that they were awakened into

---

[1] Frazer gives numerous references to it in the different volumes of his *Golden Bough. See* also Marett, *Hibbert Journal,* January 1910, and Bouvaine, *Journal of the Anthropological Institute,* Vol. II, p. 270.

[2] Pettazoni, "Soppravvivenze del rombo in Italia," *Lares,* 1912, Vol. I p. 63.

[3] *See* Blinkenberg, *The Thunderweapon in Religion and Folklore,* 1911.

[4] Schwartz, *Wolken und Wind, Blitz und Donner,* 1879, S. 186.

[5] Abraham, *Traum und Mythus,* 1909.

[6] Kuhn, *Uber die Herabkunft des Feuers und des Göttertranks,* 1859.

life through the roaring of their sire; this is given as one of the reasons why in the Resurrection Jesus was sometimes represented as a lion, the space of three days being also common to the two beliefs. It may be paralleled by the belief mentioned by Pliny,[1] that a female partridge can be impregnated merely from hearing the *cry* of the male. The general importance of the voice in love-making is well known to biologists. With many animals, e.g., deer, most birds, etc., the love-call of the mate is one of the strongest means of attraction, and even with human beings the *voice*, in both speaking and singing,[2] has by no means lost this primitive effect.

From the sound of the voice it is an easy transition to the idea of *Speech*. The sexual relationships of speech are made plain in every psycho-analysis of neurotic symptoms in which this function is implicated; stammering, self-consciousness concerning speech, and so on. It has been dwelt on by many writers. The philologist Sperber[3] has made out a powerful case for the view that speech originated as a development of the love-call excitation accompanying the search for symbolical sexual gratification. In mythology and folk-lore the function of speech is often treated as equivalent to loving or living, just as its opposite, dumb-

[1] Pliny, op. cit., x, 51.

[2] That infantile interest for the sound accompanying the passage of flatus may be transferred in later life to the subject of *music* was first pointed out by Ferenczi (*Zentralbl. f. Psychoanalyse*, Jahrg. I, S. 395, Anm. 1). The resemblance between the German words "fisteln" (=to sing falsetto) and "fisten" (=to pass flatus) is certainly in accord with this finding. One may in this connection recall the fact that Hermes was God, not only of music, but also of winds, speech, and money. (The anal-erotic association between money, gas, and intestinal contents is indicated by many expressions in English. Thus new words are "coined", while new coins are "uttered". "To stink of money" is to be over-wealthy. "To raise the wind" is slang for "to obtain money", just as "to cough up money" is for parting unwillingly with it. "To have a blow-out" means to have a good meal, while "to blow" money is to spend it extravagantly; the latter expression is often, through confusion with the past tense "blew", corrupted to "to blue money".)

[3] Sperber, "Über den Einfluss sexueller Momente auf die Entstehung der Sprache." *Imago*, 1912, Bd. I, S. 405.

ness, signifies impotence or death; an example of the latter symbolism is to be found in the New Testament story where, to emphasize the supernatural nature of John the Baptist's conception, the earthly father (Zacharias) is said to have been dumb (= impotent) from just before the conception until just after the birth.

Speech was therefore quite naturally considered to be identical with God, i.e., the Creator, and the doctrine of the Logos has played a prominent part in most of the higher religions. One need only recall the familiar passages in St. John (i. 1 and i. 14): "In the beginning was the Word, and the Word was with God, and the Word was God;" "And the Word was made flesh" (embodiment of Jesus Christ). He also relates of his vision of the Being on a White Horse that "his name is called the Word of God" (Apocalypse xix. 13). God seems to have selected with preference mere speech as the means of carrying out his wishes, for instance in the Creation itself ("And God said, Let there be light; and there was light," etc.). The association between the Holy Ghost and speech was just as intimate: the saints "spoke by the Holy Ghost" (St. Mark xii. 36; Acts of the Apostles xiii. 2; xvi. 7), or were "filled by the Holy Ghost and prophesied" (St. Luke i. 67), while St. Paul pointedly says that "no man can say that Jesus is the Lord, but by the Holy Ghost" (1 Corinthians xii. 3).

The sexual equivalency of the idea of speech, or word, comes to especially clear expression in the very legend under discussion. From a number of passages in the writings of the early Fathers that bear this out I will quote two only: St. Zeno[1] writes: "The womb of Mary swells forth with pride, not by conjugal gift, but by faith; by the Word, not by seed," and St. Eleutherius,[2] "O blessed

---

[1] *St. Zeno*, Lib. ii, Tractatus viii and ix, Pat. Lat., Tom. II, p. 413.
[2] *St. Eleutherius Tornacensis*, Serm. in Annunt. Fest., Tom. 65, p. 96.

Virgin . . . made mother without co-operation of man. For here the ear was the wife, and the angelic word the husband." The Virgin's conception has been constantly contrasted by ecclesiastical writers with the fall of Eve, "the second Eve" being a very usual designation for Mary. The following passage, from St. Ephrem,[1] is typical of many: "In the beginning the serpent, getting possession of the ears of Eve, thence spread his poison throughout her whole body; to-day Mary through her ears received the champion of everlasting bliss." It is now generally recognized[2] that the myth of the Fall in Eden represents an expurgated version of a fertilization myth, so that such passages as the one just quoted must be simply regarded as expressing the contrast between forbidden and allowed sexual union, as typified by Eve and Mary.

It is thus plain that at least some of the significance attaching to the idea of speech has arisen in psychosexual affects, and the next question is, in which specific ones? I have elsewhere[3] indicated the probable answer to this— namely, the acts of breathing and speaking are both treated in the Unconscious as equivalents of the act of passing intestinal flatus, and a corresponding displacement of affect is brought about from the latter idea to the former ones. Indications of this association are still preserved in such expressions as "poetic afflatus", "clat-fart" (Staffordshire dialect for "gossip"), "flatulent speech", "a windy discourse", and the contemptuous slang phrases for this, "gas" (English) and "hot air" (American). The word "ventriloquism" (literally "belly-speaking", German *Bauchreden*) is noteworthy in the same connection, and

---

[1] *St. Ephrem*, De Divers. Serm., I, p. 607. *See* also St. Fulgentius; *De laude Mariae ex partu Salvatoris;* St. Zeno: *Ad Pulcheriam Augustam*, etc.

[2] *See*, for instance, Otto Rank, *Zentralbl. f. Psychoanalyse*, Jahrg. II, S. 389, and Ludwig Levy, "Sexualsymbolik in der biblischen Paradiesgeschichte," *Imago*, 1917-19, Bd. V, S. 16.

[3] *Jahrbuch der Psychoanalyse*, 1912, Bd. IV, S. 588, 594.

it is of interest that Ferenczi[1] has pointed out that during analysis the suppression of a remark may be betrayed by a rumbling in the stomach.

Nor is it without significance that of the five Prânas (the sacred breaths in the Vedas) it is the Apâna, or down-breathing, that is the one associated with speech.[2]

3. *Invisibility and Fluidity*

These attributes favour the occurrence of the interesting association between the idea of *Thought* and the group under consideration. Thought is usually imagined as something flowing; one thinks of such expressions as "he poured out his thoughts", "his thoughts ceased to flow", etc., and every psychologist is familiar with William James' famous chapter on "The Stream of Consciousness". The idea of breath, speech and thought are symbolic equivalents and are all unconsciously associated with that of intestinal gas.[3] I have elsewhere[4] brought forward reasons for thinking that the unconscious belief in the omnipotence of thoughts (*Allmacht der Gedanken*), which lies at the root of animism and magic, may be related to this association with the idea of creative power, just as most concrete emblems of power (sceptre, sword, cross, staff, etc.) are well-recognized phallic symbols. The notion of thought as a begetter also occurs, e.g., in the myth of Athene's birth out of the brain of Zeus. There are frequent reports of nuns in the Middle Ages who professed to be pregnant because Jesus had *thought* of them.

We thus see how the unconscious conceives of the *Mind*,

---

[1] Ferenczi, *Contributions to Psycho-Analysis* (Engl. Transl.), 1916, p. 179.

[2] *Khândogya-Upanishad*, iii, 13, 8.

[3] This association is also illustrated in the case already referred to and its relation to the idea of "auto-suggestion" expounded.

[4] *Internationale Zeitschrift für Psychoanalyse*, 1913, Bd. I, S. 429. *See* also Eisler, *International Journal of Psycho-Analysis*, 1921, Vol. II, p. 255 et seq.

regarded as an objective phenomenon. In the Vedic literature[1] the mind is said to be cognate with the Vyâna, or back-going breath, while in another of the Upanishads[2] we read that the Self consists of speech, mind, and breath, and that the Self should be consoled in sacrificing the desire for a wife by remembering that "mind is the husband, speech the wife, and breath the child".[3] Similarly for the Neo-Platonist Plotinus the world-soul is the energy of the intellect and is begotten by the intellect, the father, just as Athene, the Goddess of Wisdom, sprang from the brain of her father. In quoting the following passage from him, "That which lies closed together in the intellect attains full development as the Logos in the world-soul, fills this with meaning and, as it were, makes it drunk with nectar," Jung[4] comments: "Nectar, like soma, is the drink of fertility and life, i.e., sperma." Diogenes[5] also identified the intellect with air; he maintained that air has intelligence, and that human beings are intelligent in virtue of the air that enters in from without. The latter statement is perhaps a highly sublimated expression of the infantile sexual theory described earlier in this essay.

From the ideas of thought and the mind it is but a step to that of the *Soul*, and we shall see that the same group of affects have extensively influenced this concept also. Of the primitive conceptions of the soul,[6] the lower (we do not say the primary) is that of the "bound soul", which was imagined as the vital principle of various internal organs, and was evidently little else than a symbolisation of the vital essence, i.e. sperma. (We are not here concerned with the motives or forces that led mankind to conceive the idea

[1] *Taittiriyaka-Upanishad*, i, 7, 1.
[2] *Brihadâranyaka-Upanishad*, i, 5, 3.
[3] Ibid., i, 4, 17.
[4] Jung, *Jahrbuch der Psychoanalyse*, 1912, Bd. IV, S. 179.
[5] *See* Brett, *A History of Psychology: Ancient and Patristic*, 1912, p. 46.
[6] *See* Wundt, op. cit., S. 1, et seq.

of a soul, a matter on which Freud[1] has thrown considerable light, but simply with the original content out of which this idea was constructed.) If sexual thoughts played such a prominent part in this crude conception of the soul it is reasonable to expect that they have also been operative, though perhaps in a more disguised manner, in regard to the more elaborate ones, and this we find to have been so. The most important part of the concept "Free Soul" is that known as the "Breath Soul" (*Hauchseele*), and it is easy to show that the idea of this belongs to the group under consideration. The evidence for the far-reaching association between the ideas of soul and breath is so familiar that it need not be recounted here; we are constantly reminded of it by the very names for the former, from the Greek "psyche" and the Hebrew "nephesh" to the German "Geist" and the English "ghost" and "spirit". The fact that all these words originally meant simply "breath" also indicates that the latter was the primary idea of the two, which is indeed evident from every point of view, and that we have here a typical example of displacement of significance.

There are at least two reasons for suspecting that the affects here concerned did not all originate in the idea of breath even, but in a still deeper one—namely, in that of intestinal gas. These are, that in the first place the affects and psychical significance which have been attached to the idea of breath, or air or wind, were disproportionate to the inherent psychical importance of the idea and so must have been derived from one of greater psychical significance (such as flatus indubitably is in infantile life and in the adult unconscious), and that in the second place numerous direct connections can be indicated between the idea of intestinal gas and the conception of the Breath-Soul.

The first argument, put in other words, is that, if a mass of feeling flowed over from the idea of breath to

[1] *Totem und Tabu*, 1913, Kap. IV.

that of the soul greater in quantity than the amount inherently belonging to the former, then it follows that this idea must have acted, in part at least, merely as a carrier. Now it is not hard to show that the significance attached to the ideas of wind, air, soul, and breath have been much greater than what might be explicable from the primary psychical importance of the last-named of these, omitting of course its secondary importance as an emblem of life and creation. Confining ourselves solely to Hindu and Greek philosophy, and taking first the former, we note the following beliefs and statements in the Upanishads alone. Prâna (breath) is identified on the one hand with Brâhman, the Supreme Being, and on the other with Atman, the primary essence of the Universe.[1] The origin of the latter is thus described: From Atman came the Other, from this the wind, from this the fire, from this water, and from water came earth; thus the primary four of the series are expressed in terms of a gas. It is unnecessary to cite any further examples, but it may be said that by far the greater part of this whole literature is taken up with this theme, the ideas of breath, wind, and so on, being described in the most exalted language imaginable.

Similarly if we turn to Greece we find that the same group of ideas forms a central starting point for a great part, probably the greater part, of the views on philosophy, medicine, psychology, and general *Weltanschauung*. Many of the earlier monists, including Anaximenes, posited air as their ἀρχή, and the continued existence of the world was explained by a process of cosmic respiration,[2] the conception of which was based in detail on that of bodily respiration. Heidel, in a specially careful study,[3] has further shown that the various atomic theories of the Greeks can

[1] Deussen, op. cit., pp. 110, 194.

[2] Heidel, "Antecedents of the Greek Corpuscular Theories," *Harvard Studies in Classical Philology*, 1911, Vol. XXII, pp. 137-40.

[3] Heidel, op. cit., pp. 111-72.

principally be traced to their views about the act of breathing.[1] Diogenes, in taking air as the most important element in the world, plainly says that the necessity of breath for life is the reason why air is chosen as the primary reality; the interaction between air in the body and the air outside is the type of all vital action.[2] With the Stoics also,[3] the pneuma was of cardinal importance: it was the breath of life, the warm air closely associated with the blood, the vital principle transmitted in generation, and at the same time the soul, which is contained in the body and yet is one in nature with the surrounding World-Soul.[4] The part played by the idea of breath in moulding the Greek conception of the soul is too familiar to need insisting on. The influence of this conception extended far into Christian times: Clement of Alexandria, for instance, as well as Tertullian, maintained that the "rational soul", which is directly imparted by God to man, is identical with that "breath of God"[5] mentioned in Genesis, in contradistinction to the "irrational soul", which is akin to the life-principle of animals. The latter belief may profitably be compared with the Indian one mentioned above (p. 279) concerning the two breaths, upper and lower in a moral as well as in a physical sense, and the juxtaposition here of animal and divine opens up the whole topic of repression.

The pneuma concept was also one of the highest significance in Greek medicine and retained much of its importance until about a century ago, gradually fading away

[1] It is interesting to note that prominent ideas in nineteenth century physical science, the atomic theory and the conception of ether, both of which were anticipated in Greek philosophy, represent in both cases sublimated projections of the complex under discussion.

[2] Brett, op. cit., pp. 45, 46.

[3] Brett, op. cit., pp. 166, 167.

[4] It is clear that the idea of "cosmic consciousness", of which we hear so much in modern pseudo-philosophy, is psychologically equivalent to ideas concerning the outer air, which have been projected from more personal sources.

[5] The Hebrew "ruach" denoted both the human soul and the breath of God.

via the doctrine of "humour" and "diathesis"; its memory is perpetuated in such expressions as "to be in a bad humour", "in good spirits". All causes of disease other than those relating to food and drink were summarized under the generic term "air", a pernicious relic of which attitude we still retain in the almost universal superstition that draughts are dangerous to health (not to mention the special risks ascribed to specific forms of air such as "night air", "damp air", air coming through holes, etc.), and the therapeutic value ascribed to a "change of air", or a "change of climate" was even greater than that obtaining in our own days.[1] For centuries most physicians were attached to one or other school of philosophy, and the most important group were those constituting the school of Pneumatists, who subscribed to the Stoic doctrines; physiology and philosophy thus exerted a mutual influence on each other. The pneuma coursed through the entire body, regulated nutrition, generated thought and semen,[2] and, according to Aristotle, conveyed to the heart the movements of sensation that had been transmitted to it from without through the medium of the sense organs; on the state of it depended the health of the individual. An interesting example of the strength of the pneuma doctrine

[1] One should also think of the excessive significance which is still attached by many people to respiratory exercises. In the description of my patient referred to above there are some beautiful examples of the mystical application of these. Nor can orthodox medicine be entirely exempted from this reproach; I may cite the following examples taken at random from a medical catalogue:
  1. Fletcher: The law of the Rhythmic Breath, Teaching the Generation, Conservation and Control of Vital Force.
  2. Arnulphy: La Santé par la science de la respiration. (La respiration est un des principaux procédés au moyen desquels on arrive à développer sa force magnétique, sa volonté.)
  3. Durville: Pour combattre la peur, la crainte, l'anxiété, la timidité, développer la volonté, guérir ou soulager certaines maladies par la Respiration Profonde.

[2] The view was, for instance, expressed that Hephaistos took the form of pneuma that coursed through the arteries of Zeus to his brain and thus led him to generate thought, i.e., to procreate Athene. (*See* Creuzer, *Symbolik und Mythologie*, 2e Aufl., 1819-23, Bd. II, S. 763 et seq.)

was the way in which it was able totally to obscure the significance of the discovery of the nerves,[1] it being insisted, in spite of all the evidence to the contrary, that these were merely ramifications of the pneuma-carrying arteries; even later, when the relation of the nerves to the brain and to muscular action had been established, Augustine maintained that they were tubes of air which transmitted to the limbs the actions commanded by the will. The following passages from Brett[2] well illustrate the general significance of the pneuma doctrine: "To one who thinks of the body as irrigated throughout by air, who attributes the cause of pulsation to the shock of air meeting blood, who moreover feels dimly that man is in direct connection with the whole universe through the continuity of this air, the importance of this factor must have assumed the greatest proportions."

There is abundant evidence to show that the idea of breath could not have been by any means the sole source of this series of doctrines, readily as this seems generally to be assumed. Proceeding first with the Greek views, we note two considerations: that the pneuma was not always brought into connection with breath as one would have expected from the current opinion, and further that their conception of respiration was a singularly broad one, many processes being included under this term besides that of breathing. Aristotle, for example, positively states that the pneuma of the body, the importance of which we have just noted, is not derived from the breath, but is a secretion resulting from processes going on within the body itself (primarily in the intestine), and Galen says, even more explicitly, that the psychic pneuma is derived in part from

[1] Brett (op. cit., p. 284) gives a striking description of the prejudices due to the tenaciousness with which the pneuma doctrine was held, and of the difficulty with which these were overcome before the value of the discovery could be properly appreciated.

[2] Brett, op. cit., pp. 52, 53.

the vapours of digested food.[1] This association, which appears to be still active in the unconscious, is also embodied in our daily speech: we talk of *"expressing* our thoughts", of being given "food for thought", and so on. It would seem possible that the association has played some part in the development of certain forms of materialistic philosophy; one is struck, for instance, by the simile employed in such dicta as that of Cabanis, "the brain secretes thought as the liver secretes bile". We see an interesting revival of this attitude in the current materialistic trends of present-day psychiatry, which would derive the greater part of mental disorder from toxins due to intestinal disturbances—quite logically, if this organ were the source of thought, as the Greeks believed; the absence of any evidence in support of this ætiology makes no difference to the belief in it.

In the second place, a little study of the accounts given by various writers makes it plain that the Greeks thought of the respiratory and alimentary systems as being throughout closely connected,[2] which is the main point we are trying here to establish. On the one hand respiration was not restricted to breathing, but included also perspiration (a perfectly scientific view), while on the other hand respiration was regarded as a variety of nutrition, which indeed it is. They not only identified the absorption of air, its subsequent changes within the body, and its final excretion,[3] with those of food, but ascribed to the influence of the former the process whereby the latter becomes sufficiently rarefied to be carried over the body; the underlying idea, with of course many modifications, seems to have

[1] Brett, op. cit., pp. 118, 291.
[2] *See* Heidel, op. cit., pp. 131-7.
[3] Hippocrates in describing the foetus says that it draws in breath through the umbilical cord, and that when it is filled with breath this "breaks", makes a passage for itself outward through the middle of the foetus, and in this way escapes. (*See* Heidel, op. cit., S. 135, 136.)

been that the inspired air reached the stomach, either through the blood stream or through the œsophagus (which they believed led to the heart), and there digested the food, the internal pneuma being the product of this and thus representing a combination of air and food. From this point of view it is clear that pneuma was not merely a symbolic equivalent of intestinal gas, but was actually and grossly identical with it. The world-wide belief that the soul escapes through the mouth[1] probably refers, therefore, to ideas concerning not only the respiratory system, but the alimentary one also; this conclusion is supported by the existence, among many tribes, of various precautions and taboos designed to prevent the escape of the soul through the mouth during eating.[2]

Study of the Vedic literature shows that the conceptions of the Indian philosophers on this matter were fundamentally similar to those of the Greeks. They devoted an extraordinary attention to the subject of the five Prânas, or breaths, but the accounts given of these in the various passages are so overlapping that it is not always easy to define the precise differences between them; in fact it is known that the definitions shifted to some extent at different periods. In spite of this, however, it is possible to determine the main outlines of the conceptions, and we may consider them in order. Prâna, the "up-breathing", means essentially the breath proper. Where it stands alone it frequently denotes the sense of smell, consequently inspiration, but sometimes when used in conjunction with Apâna it means expiration and the latter inspiration.[3] Apâna, the "down-breathing", though it also sometimes denotes smell and inspiration, usually means the wind of digestion residing in the bowels. It originates in the navel

---

[1] *See* Frazer, *Taboo and the Perils of the Soul,* 1911, pp. 30-3.
[2] Frazer, op. cit., p. 116.
[3] *See* Deussen, op. cit., pp. 276-9, where this matter is discussed in detail.

of the primeval man.[1] It carries off the intestinal excrements;[2] it dwells in the bowels,[3] and presides over the organs of evacuation and generation.[4] The Vyâna, or "backgoing" breath, unites the breath proper to the wind of digestion,[5] and courses through the blood-vessels.[6] The Samâna, or all-breathing, also unites the Prâna to the Apâna,[7] and carries the food over the body.[8] These two last-mentioned breaths evidently make up together the Greek "internal pneuma". Finally the Udâna, the "up- or out-breathing", sometimes called the "wind of exit",[9] dwells in the throat,[10] and either brings up again or swallows down that which is eaten or drunk.[11] The Udâna, which evidently denotes gas regurgitating from a flatulent stomach, is an interesting counterpart to the Apâna, for while the latter is formally identified with death itself[12] the former carries away the soul from the body after death;[13] the connection between them is naturally a close one, since they both represent intestinal gas, which may escape either upwards or downwards. The idea of death and of intestinal decomposition are here, as so often,[14] brought near together, an additional explanation being thus afforded for the belief that the soul escapes from an alimentary orifice after death.

Consideration of these accounts reveals the striking fact that four out of the five Prânas are much more closely

[1] Aitareya-Âranyaka, ii, 4, 1, 6. (I refer throughout to the notation in Müller's edition.)
[2] Ibid, ii, 4, 3, 2. Also *Maitrâyana-Upanishad*, II, 6 and *Garbha-Upanishad*, I.
[3] *Amritabindhu*, 34.
[4] *Prasña-Upanishad*, iii, 5.
[5] *Maitrâyana-Upanishad*, ii, 6.
[6] *Prasña-Upanishad*, iii, 6.
[7] *Prasña-Upanishad*, iv, 4.
[8] *Maitrâyana-Upanishad*, ii, 6. *Prasña-Upanishad*, iii, 5.
[9] *Vedântasâra*, 97.
[10] *Aimritabindhu*, 34.
[11] *Maitrâyana-Upanishad*, ii, 6.
[12] *Aitareya-Âranyaka*, ii, 4, 2, 4.
[13] *Prasña-Upanishad*, iii, 7.
[14] *See* Vol. I, p. 11.

related to the alimentary system than to the respiratory, being primarily concerned with the movement of food, either within the alimentary canal itself or in the body at large; even the fifth, the Prâna in the narrowest sense, does not altogether dispense with this connection, for on the one hand it is doubly united to the Apâna (flatus) and on the other hand it has to do with the sense of smell, which biologically is nearly related to both sexuality and coprophilia.

It seems to me, therefore, a hardy venture for anyone who has reviewed the evidence just brought forward still to maintain that no other bodily gas than breath has played a part in developing the conception of the "Breath-Soul".

4. *Moisture*

It is well known that the idea of water has played an extraordinarily extensive part in anthropological symbolism, and especially in connection with the ideas of creation and birth. The symbolic significance of water is mainly derived from its unconscious equivalency with uterine fluid, urine, and semen; it is probably the commonest symbol, both male and female, employed in birth phantasies. It is therefore quite intelligible that the ideas of water and of gas should frequently be found in proximity in these phantasies, and that they should even be treated as symbolic equivalents. A simple example is that in the myth of Prometheus, who created mankind out of water and sound. One nearer to the principal theme of this essay is that of the relation between the Holy Ghost and Baptism. In a previous essay[1] I have tried to show that the psychological symbolism of the baptismal rite signifies "rebirth through purification", and that purification is an idea unconsciously equivalent to fertilization. It is thus noteworthy that the

[1] Chapter II, p. 70.

two ideas of baptismal water and the Holy Ghost (in infantile terms, urine and gas) are frequently brought together in the New Testament in relation to the idea of re-birth. Jesus, in his reply to Nicodemus, says: "Verily, verily, I say unto thee, Except a man be born of water and of the Spirit, he cannot enter into the kingdom of God. That which is born of the flesh is flesh; and that which is born of the Spirit is spirit. Marvel not that I said unto thee, Ye must be born again. The wind bloweth where it listeth, and thou hearest the sound thereof, but canst not tell whence it cometh, and whither it goeth; so is every one that is born of the Spirit" (St. John iii. 5 et seq.), and again, "For John truly baptised with water; but ye shall be baptised with the Holy Ghost" (Acts i. 5). The replacement of the desire for earthly (i.e., incestuous) re-birth by that for spiritual re-birth is equivalent to the wish to be purified from sin, sin (of which incest is the great archetype) and death being opposed to re-birth and life; St. Paul writes (Romans viii. 2): "For the law of the spirit of life in Christ Jesus hath made me free from the law of sin and death."

The tertium comparationis between water and gas is evidently fluidity, and in the idea of *vapour* we get a fusion of the two. For this reason vapour has always played an important part in connection with the various topics discussed above, and the process of evaporation, whereby water is converted through vapour into gas, has extensively engaged the interest and attention of mankind. In Ancient Greece the Plutonia, Charonia, or hell-gates, where vapours issued from the earth, were sacred, because the exhalations were regarded as the spirits of the dead[1] (cp. the relation mentioned above between death and Apâna and Udâna). These spirits were looked to for increase of flocks and

[1] Rohde, *Psyche*, 6. Aufl., 1910, Bd. I, S. 213. Also Preller-Robert, *Griechische Mythologie*, Bd. I, S. 283, 811.

herds[1] and for the fruitfulness of the soil, while women worshipped them to obtain offspring.[2] Such beliefs are still current in Syria:[3] for example, at the Baths of Solomon in northern Palestine, blasts of hot air escape from the ground, and one of them, named Abu Rabah, is a famous resort of childless wives who wish to satisfy their maternal longings; they let the hot air stream up over their bodies and really believe that children born to them after such a visit are begotten by the saint of the shrine. In ancient Italy issuing vapours were personified as a goddess, Mefitis, whose chief temple was in the valley of Amsanctus. The exhalations here, supposed to be the breath of Pluto himself, are known to consist of warm, noisy blasts of sulphuretted hydrogen[4] (i.e., had the odour of flatus); the association between intestinal functions and Pluto, the god of the lower world, is brought to our consciousness by the title of the well-known purgative, Pluto water!

Heidel[5] says that "probably no other natural phenomenon played so important a role in Greek philosophy as evaporation". Rohde has abundantly shown that to the Greeks the soul was essentially a vapour;[6] the later conception of the soul, however, for instance that of the Stoics, would seem to have been that of an invisible, gaseous medium which owed both its origin and its continued activities to the vapours, derived from the mixture of blood and air, that coursed through the body. The process of evaporation or distillation was evidently of cardinal importance in effecting this change from the material to the immaterial, and thus helps to explain the significance

---

[1] Many passages in Dieterich, *Mutter Erde*, 1905.

[2] Rohde, op. cit., S. 297-9.

[3] Curtiss, *Primitive Semitic Religion To-Day*, 1902, pp. 116 et seq.

[4] Frazer, *Adonis, Attis, Osiris*, 2nd Edition, 1907, p. 170.

[5] Heidel, op. cit., p. 122. *See* also Gilbert, *Die meteorologischen Theorien des griechischen Altertums*, 1907, S. 439 et seq.

[6] It may be mentioned that our word "breath" is cognate with the German *Brodem* (steam, odour).

attaching to bodily heat that brought it about, of which we shall speak later. From this point of view it is also easy to grasp Diogenes' notion that thought is an activity of *dry* air, that moisture is detrimental to thinking, and that excess of moisture is the reason why the young lack intelligence.[1] The same train of thought was applied to the life of the universe, cosmic respiration being imagined in terms of moisture, the earth and sea giving forth vapour and receiving back rain.[2] It dominated further the greater part of physiology, for digestion, absorption and nutrition were essentially problems of the conversion of food into the internal pneuma and the distribution of this through the body.

The inter-relation of moisture and air in both respiratory and intestinal breath affords a physiological basis for these conceptions, the psychological origin of which, however, goes back, as was indicated above, to infantile life.

5. *Warmth*

In relating the variants of the idea of the Virgin Mary's conception, as portrayed in art, we noted the curious fact that rays of light were sometimes treated as the equivalent of radiating breath, issuing from the mouth, entering into the ear, and so on, and we take this as a starting point for the discussion of warmth as an attribute common to the upper and the lower breaths. The belief in question finds many parallels outside of Christianity: the legends of virgins that have been impregnated by rays of light, usually from the sun or by fire, are exceedingly numerous and wide-spread. Bab,[3] Frazer,[4] Hartland,[5] and others have collected many dozens of such stories, with customs based on the belief, and it is not necessary to quote any specific

[1] Brett, op. cit., p. 46.   [2] Heidel, op. cit., p. 134.
[3] Bab, op. cit., S. 279 et seq.
[4] Frazer, *The Golden Bough*, 1900, Vol. III, pp. 204 et seq., 244, 270, 305, 314.
[5] Hartland, *Primitive Paternity*, 1909, Vol. I, pp. 11-13, 18, 25, 26, 89-100.

examples here. They show the usual characteristics of supernatural births, the child proving to be a Messiah, a great Emperor, or what not. One rather striking feature is the frequency with which water is made to play a part in the event; the virgin is the daughter of a river-god, a star falls into water which she drinks, and so on. That the making of fire is commonly conceived of by the primitive mind as a sexual performance is well established.[1]

But beyond the symbolic equivalency just signified, an inherent connection between breath and fire (or light) is often predicated. To breathe on a fire, especially a holy one, is strictly tabooed in many countries;[2] for instance a Brahman is forbidden to blow on a fire with his mouth. The relation of breath to fire in folk-lore and superstition is a very close one.[3] In Longfellow's "Hiawatha" it is described how Gitche Manito, the "Creator of the Nations", blew on to the trees so that they rubbed together and burst into flame. In the Old Testament breath is constantly associated with fire, and in the Hermetic writings it is stated that souls are made from "the breath of God and conscious fire". In the Mithra liturgy the creative breath proceeds from the sun, and in the Stoic philosophy the cosmic Divine Fire was identical with the atmosphere. Jung[4] and Silberer[5] quote a number of interesting passages from various sources that show the intimate association subsisting between the ideas of shining and sounding. It can therefore be said with certainty that in primitive thinking the ideas of *sound*, *heat* and *light* are as definitely interchangeable equivalents as the corresponding physical processes have been proved to be by the scientific doctrine of the transformation of energy.

[1] Frazer, *The Magic Art*, 1911, Vol. II, Ch. XV, "The Fire-Drill," and p. 233.
[2] Frazer, op. cit., p. 241. *Spirits of the Corn and of the Wild*, 1912, Vol. II, p. 254
[3] Frazer, *The Magic Art*, Vol. II, p. 239 et seq.
[4] Jung, op. cit., S. 206-8.
[5] Silberer, *Jahrbuch der Psychoanalyse*, Bd. II, S. 596-7.

We have now to inquire into the meaning of this association. Fire, or heat, is known to be one of the commonest libidinal symbols, and, as Abraham[1] has clearly shown, it is the equivalent of soma and sperma. This, however, obviously cannot be the original source of the association, for not only is the child ignorant of the existence of sperma, but it is relatively late before it learns to appreciate even that of fire. Years ago, in his Dora analysis, Freud[2] pointed out that in symbolic language, e.g., in dreams, the idea of fire replaced that of water, particularly urine; the association is partly one of contrast, from the mutual incompatibility of the two substances. In the psycho-analyses of patients I have also found that fire can symbolize not only urine, but also flatus, as for instance in phobias concerning gas-jets,[3] and further that the primary source of fire symbolism in general is probably to be explained in the following way. The infant's first experience of heat (as distinct from the warmth of the normal body temperature) is derived from the fact that all excretions are warmer than the external temperature of the body and in addition often produce, from their irritating and acrid nature (especially marked with young children), local burning sensations. When, now, the child becomes acquainted later on with other sources of heat, particularly burning heat, he inevitably forms an association between them and the causes of his earlier experiences. This happens so regularly that, for instance, with a phobia of fire at night one can predict with certainty that such a person will prove to be one who has incompletely overcome the infantile fear (and temptation) of bed-wetting. As we know that the child can express to itself the idea of sexual secretion only in terms of one or other excretion we can understand how it is that fire comes

---

[1] Abraham, *Traum und Mythus*, 1909.
[2] Freud, *Sammlung kleiner Schriften zur Neurosenlehre*. Zweite Folge, S. 80.
[3] This must have been so in the case described by Reitler, loc. cit.

to be such a general libidinal symbol, most often of urine, though sometimes of flatus. We must thus infer, on the principles enunciated above, that the association between fire and breath is a secondary one, replacing the earlier one between fire and flatus (and urine).

There is ample confirmation of this conclusion to be found in many spheres, but we shall confine ourselves mainly to the field of Greek philosophy, so as to extend our previous considerations on this subject. In the first place, it is striking that the idea of heat, or fire, played a part of central importance in the pneuma doctrine; Aristotle, for instance, maintained that the active element in the internal pneuma was of the nature of fire, identical with the principle of fertility in semen. According to Heidel,[1] "it is in the phenomena of fire as interpreted by the Greeks that we discover the best illustration of the processes of respiration and nutrition," and this is still the favourite method of introducing the study of chemical physiology. But the Greeks did not stay at the analogy; for them heat was the actual motive force that carried on these processes. Except among the Atomists, respiration was thought to proceed through the natural warmth of the body creating an expansion that mechanically draws in the colder air from without.[2] Similarly with nutrition. The native heat of the organism "digested" the food, i.e., converted it into pneuma, in which form it was conveyed all through the body. It was at first believed that the heat, or fire, worked no inner change in the food, merely comminuting it and so preparing it for absorption into the blood, but the hypothesis was carried by Aristotle to the further stage mentioned above, his views on digestion being accepted by Galen and most of the other later medical authorities.[3] A

[1] Heidel, op. cit., p. 142.
[2] Heidel, op. cit., pp. 136, 141.
[3] Heidel, op. cit., pp. 141-68.

great number of the Greek philosophers, however, just like the modern psycho-analyst, refused to be satisfied with the idea of fire as a self-sufficing primary agent, but broached the question of its nature and origin. They concluded, or rather accepted an age-old conclusion, that fire was sustained and fed by water in the form of vapour, the analogy being evoked of the sun drawing up or drinking moisture; since, however, the very production of vapour is dependent on the heat, it would seem as if a permanent cycle was posited, the primordial construction of which it was impossible to determine. It was believed that water was the primary nutrient element *par excellence*, though this was inactive without the influence of the fire which it itself fed. Presumably the ultimate source of the fire was the life-instinct itself, for the greatest attention was paid to the passage of heat from the mother to the child during pre-natal life, but if one asks for a more explicit account of it, particularly where it was supposed to reside, the only conclusion at all conformable with the different accounts seems to be that it was carried in a gaseous form, constituting thus the very essence of pneuma. In short, the Greek theory of nutrition, just as that of respiration, assumes the closest possible association between the ideas of heat (or fire) and of gas (or breath in the widest sense).

The idea of heat (or fire) played an equally prominent part in the Greek non-physiological conceptions, e.g., the philosophical and psychological ones. Some of the monists, such as Heraclitus, posited fire as their ἀρχή. The cosmic process, which, as was indicated above, was imagined in terms of respiration and nutrition, was supposed to depend on evaporation and precipitation, i.e., on an alternation of heat and cold; the continued existence of earth and sea was maintained through their emitting warm vapours and receiving back cooling showers.[1] The very word "psyche"

[1] Heidel, op. cit., pp. 134, 137-40.

itself is derived from the word ψύχω,[1] which has the double meaning of "I breathe" and "I cool",[2] and one of the favourite images in which it was described, as it still is in poetic diction, was that of a thin ascending flame. When the Neo-Platonic Plotinus rejected the Stoic doctrine of the material origin of the pneuma, he elaborated the following ingenious view: As the association of the soul with matter implies a degradation it cannot be placed in immediate contact with the body, so it makes use of a mediating element, a form of pneuma, in which to clothe itself and be guarded from a defiling contact; this aerial garb is of the nature of fire (!), in which the soul dwells and through which it moves the body.

Another example of the association between the idea of fire and the group under consideration is that to do with *speech*. Jung[3] has brilliantly demonstrated the symbolic equivalence of speech and fire, quoting numerous beliefs in which the former is primary to the latter, though I cannot agree with his conclusion[4] that "the origin of the fire-speech phenomenon seems to be the Mother-Libido". To the many passages he cites I might add one from the Upanishads[5] in which both speech and fire are identified with the Apâna, or down-breathing. Thus fire originates in speech, and both in pneuma, particularly the intestinal one: a conclusion which is in complete harmony with the one formulated above[6] on the basis of individual analyses which

---

[1] Prof. G. S. Brett was good enough to call my attention to Plato's sarcastic explanation of the word ψυχή=ἥ φύσιν ὀχεῖ καὶ ἔχει, "that which conducts the nature (vitality)". He adds: The word ὀχεῖ is not a natural one to use and is philologically connected with a number of words denoting (1) pipe, channel; (2) it is the technical word for "ride" and in the form 'οχεύω means to perform the sexual act.

[2] Roscher, *Ausfuhrliches Lexikon der griechischen und romischen Mythologie*, S. 3202.

[3] Jung, op. cit., S. 205-9.

[4] Jung, op. cit., S. 388.

[5] *Khandogya-Upanishad*, III, 13, 3.

[6] p. 292.

show speech to be an unconscious symbol for flatus (and sometimes urine also).

To the Assyrian Fire-God, Gibil, as to many others, was ascribed a Logos part,[1] and we have noted above the close association between speech and the Christian Trinity, particularly the Holy Ghost. It is therefore quite consistent that the Holy Ghost should be likened to fire. John the Baptist preached: "I indeed baptize you with water unto repentance: but he that cometh after me is mightier than I, whose shoes I am not worthy to bear: he shall baptize you with the Holy Ghost, and with fire" (Matthew iii. 11). To be purified with fire (i.e., re-born) is a familiar metaphor, even in common speech, and the gaseous origin of it, indicated also in this passage, has been explained above in connection with the theme of baptism. In the Acts of the Apostles we read further (ii. 3) the following description of the descent of the Holy Ghost: "And there appeared unto them cloven tongues, as of fire, and it sat upon each of them."

In reference to the mention of the *tongue* in the last passage quoted it will be convenient here to say a few words on this subject in so far as it relates to the present group of ideas. Symbolically the tongue is equivalent to the beak of the Dove, both having an evident phallic signification. Its physiological characters render it peculiarly adapted for this symbolism: thus, the facts that it is a red pointed organ, with dangerous potentialities, capable of self-movement, usually discreetly concealed but capable of protrusion (as in the defiant and forbidden exhibitionism of children), which can emit a fluid (saliva) that is a common symbol for semen.

In Bohemia a fox's tongue is worn by a timid person as an amulet to make him bold,[2] the meaning of which is

---

[1] Tiele, *Babylonisch-assyrische Geschichte*, 1886, S. 520.

[2] Grohmann, *Aberglauben und Gebrauche aus Bohmen und Mahren*, 1864, S. 54.

patent. The term "spit-fire", applied to anyone having a sharp tongue, is probably a relic of the belief in dragons, which emitted fire from both extremities of the body. In the Rig-Veda the fire-god Agni is called the "beautiful-tongued one"; his tongue, like the phallic magic rods, is so powerful that it can overcome all obstacles.[1] Fire, like the tongue, is said to lick ("lingua" and allied words come from the Sanscrit *lih* = to lick). The dangerous-weapon idea is well shown in a literal fashion in St. John's vision of the Being, of whom he writes (Revelations xix. 15) "And out of his mouth goeth a sharp sword" (another favourite phallic symbol); in another passage (Revelations i. 16) he describes the Son of Man as having a sharp two-edged sword proceeding from his mouth. The Holy Ghost was not the only divine spirit to descend to earth in the guise of a tongue, for precisely the same is narrated of the Egyptian God Ptah, who, like Yahweh, created by means of the Word.

Nor is the tongue bereft of connections with the alimentary group of ideas. It is, indeed, situate in the alimentary tract, and serves both for the taking in of food and for the spitting out of what may have to be expelled (bad food, phlegm, etc.); the Indians gave it the name of Atri, "for with the tongue food is eaten, and Atri is meant for Atti, eating."[2] It is also closely related to the gaseous ideas discussed above. In many languages, e.g., English and French, the same word is used to denote both tongue and speech, and the association between it and inspired speech or thought is indicated in the following passage from the Acts of the Apostles (ii. 4): "And they were all filled with the Holy Ghost, and began to speak with other tongues, as the Spirit gave them utterance." The association tongue

---

[1] Hirzel, "Gleichnisse und Metaphern im Rigveda," *Zeitschrift für Völkerpsychologie,* Jahrg. XIX, S. 356, 357.

[2] *Brihadâranyaka-Upanishad,* II, 2, 4.

—sexuality—speech is manifest in a number of nightmare superstitions collected by Laistner,[1] to which I will add one from Bohemia[2]—namely, that the tongue of a male snake, if cut from the animal on St. George's Eve and placed under a person's tongue, will confer the gift of eloquence; a similar explanation must hold for the well-known Irish belief of eloquence being conferred on whoever kisses the almost inaccessible Blarney stone. The tongue, therefore, is seen to be related to the ideas of fire, speech, sexuality, and divinity, a fact that will be commented on later when we discuss the idea of the combination of gas and an emitting organ.

6. *Odour*

This attribute differs from the preceding ones in being much more prominent with intestinal gas than with breath, and is on this account the more important for our purpose of elucidating the part played by the former. The essential relation of the sense of smell to coprophilia is well known to both ophresiologists and psycho-analysts, and it has been plainly shown that much of the interest attaching to agreeable perfumes and aromatics is a replacement of that taken by children, and by primitive peoples, in the odour of excretions; the adult attitude towards the latter odour has become as a rule, though by no means invariably, a negative one. For both these reasons it is legitimate to infer that where the sense of smell has played a part in the formation of complex-ideas these are more nearly related to the phenomenon of intestinal gas than to that of breath.[3]

[1] Laistner, *Das Rätsel der Sphinx*, 1889, Bd. I, S. 41, 42.

[2] Grohmann, op. cit., S. 81.

[3] It may be conjectured that the antiquity of this buried association is one reason for the mysterious affective power of odours, especially in the revival of forgotten experiences (as screen-memories); as Marlitt says in her story *Das Eulenhaus*, "Nichts in der Welt macht Vergangenes so lebendig wie der Geruch" ("Nothing on earth makes the past so living as does odour").

Even when the odour of breath itself is prominent it is probable that it is secondary to the other; bad breath is instinctively referred to digestive disorder. In the psycho-analysis of patients who have an excessive repugnance for the odour of bad breath it is always found that this has originated in the repression of pronounced anal-erotism. The same association is often manifested in popular sayings and beliefs; "to breathe on" was in Sparta a designation for the pederastic act,[1] and in Rome it was believed that the mouths of pederasts stank.[2]

We may begin with the part played in philosophical ideas. Heidel[3] says: "Aromatics, which possess the power of throwing off continuous streams of effluvia without perceptible diminution, had great significance for Greek thought, although it generally has been overlooked." This gives, for instance, the clue to the curious paradox that, although it is chemically pure water that is obtained by evaporation or distillation, the Greeks nevertheless held that it is through this process that various nutrient constituents pass from water to the inner fire and pneuma. They evidently seem to have regarded water not as a pure element, but as a liquid which contained in it all possible substances;[4] this belief points to an infantile origin in the idea of urine, the conception of which as an essence-containing liquid has proved fertile to many trains of thought.[5] The solution of the paradox is yielded by the observation that when a liquid evaporates the most volatile parts, not necessarily pure water vapour, are carried upwards, while the heavier, coarser parts are separated off and remain behind. The whole process, therefore, one of cardinal significance for the pneuma doctrine both of the

---

[1] Fehrle, *Die kultische Keuschheit im Altertum*, 1910, S. 86.
[2] Martial, *Epigrammata*, Lib. xii, 86.
[3] Heidel, op. cit., p. 125.
[4] *See* Heidel, op. cit., pp. 142, 143.
[5] *See* Chapter II, p. 51, 64 et seq.

individual and of the cosmos, was conceived as the evaporation and passing over of the volatile, quintessential elements, which were perceptible only to the sense of smell.
The closest association was thus formed between this sense
and the idea of essential constituent, one which is still
retained in our use of the word "essential" (cp. "an essential
oil", "an essential idea").

The importance of odour is shown in more direct ways
than in that just indicated. One thinks at once of the
extensive part played by incense in so many religions, and
this in all probability replaced the earlier idea of the "sweet
savour" of burnt offerings.[1] (Taste and smell were not
distinguished until relatively late in civilization and are
still popularly confounded to a remarkable extent; the
Greeks, for instance, for some time denoted both by the
same word ἡδονή.) The smell of the sacrifice was always
considered to be specially pleasing to the god. The Fountain
of Youth in Ethiopia, described by Herodotus, was aromatic
and so ethereal as to be almost comparable to a vapour-
bath, while the ambrosia on which the Gods fed had a
marvellous fragrance. Aromatics were quite generally
regarded in Greece as producing "enthusiasm" or possession
by the Godhead,[2] and inspiration altogether was connected
with the same idea; the Pythia, for example, Apollo's
priestess, derived her inspiration partly from the aroma of
the sacred laurel and partly from the vapours issuing from
her tripod.[3] It is interesting that in the Teutonic mythology
also poetic inspiration was attributed to the drinking of a
divine drink, Odrerir the "poet's drink" or "life-juice" of
Odin, which is psychologically equivalent to ambrosia,
nectar, soma, and semen. The sexual meaning of the drink
is plainly enough indicated in the myth that Odin won

[1] See Atchley, A History of the Use of Incense, 1909, pp. 18, 76, etc.
[2] Rohde, op. cit., Bd. II, S. 60 et seq.
[3] Bethe, "Die dorische Knabenliebe," Rheinisches Museum, Bd. LXII, S.
438-75.

possession of it by penetrating into a mountain in the form of a snake and so reaching the giant's daughter Gunnlod, whose love he of course wins; the Odrerir itself was generated by mixing honey with the blood of Kváfir, a man of wisdom who owed his existence to the mingling of two lots of saliva.[1] Customs of inducing inspiration by means of odours are very widespread; they are quoted by Frazer[2] from Bali, India, Madura, Uganda, etc. In Greece the foods partaken at the wedding feast and at the sacramental meal of the mysteries were all strongly pungent or aromatic, as were also the herbs laid beneath the dead at funerals.

On the homœopathic principle of "like repelling like" odoriferous substances have been extensively used to counteract unpleasant or dangerous influences. In Greece, according to Heidel,[3] "exhalations or effluvia of various kinds were the chief apotropaic and purificatory means employed in the most diverse circumstances." Heat and cold were thought of essentially as effluvia, so that it is little wonder that fire became the purifying and apotropaic agency *par excellence*, as possessing the most evident emanations; that these were concerned in the efficacy is testified by Plato's remark, "the demons love not the reek of torches".[4] Almost all cathartic simples known to the materia medica of the Greeks possess a strong odour, rank or aromatic; wines were diuretic, diachoretic, or constipating according as they were aromatic or not. The efficacy of olive oil as a daily unguent and at burial was

---

[1] Mogk, *Germanische Mythologie*, 1906, S. 46, 47.

[2] Frazer, *The Magic Art*, 1911, Vol. I, pp. 379, 383, 384.

[3] Heidel, op. cit., p. 126.

[4] Frazer (*The Magic Art*, Vol. II; *The Scapegoat* and *Balder the Beautiful*, Vol. I and II) gives many examples of the protection against evil influences, especially witches, by means of evil odours, smoke, fumigation, and so on. Luther divined the original sense of these procedures (*See* p. 288). In the Dark Ages evil spirits were exorcised by either purgation or by prayer and fasting; their departure coincided with the cessation of internal rumblings that goes with a state of internal emptiness (Private communication from Prof. G. S. Brett).

no doubt partly due to its aromatic properties; hence the use of it, or of wine, in the first bath given to the infant, and subsequently in Christian baptism. Nor should we overlook the extensive use of fumigations by Greek physicians, such as the internal fumigation of women after childbirth and as an emmenagogue.[1] But we need not go to the ancient Greeks for such examples. Oil at baptism and swinging censers are still universal in the Catholic Church; the fumigating powers of sulphur, alluded to by Homer, are still devoutly believed in by every house-wife, in spite of all proofs of their non-existence; no one places any faith in medicine that has no odour; the expelling of the demons of hysteria by evil-smelling asafœtida and valerian has not yet come to an end; and bacteriologists have had the greatest difficulty in dissuading surgeons from estimating the potency of a disinfectant by the strength of its smell.

We thus see that the idea of odour is interwoven with those of heat, fire, vapour, and speech (inspiration), that odorous gas was believed to further the fruitfulness of women,[2] herds, and land (*See* pp. 304-5), to be pleasing to the gods and to drive away evil spirits and disease. I would submit that this persistent over-estimation of the idea, in both folk-lore and early philosophy, may in a great measure be ascribed to the circumstance that it is a prominent attribute of that down-going gas which is so important in primitive thought. At all events no one would derive it from the upper breath, the odour of which is so much less a prominent feature.

---

[1] These three sentences are taken from Heidel, op. cit., p. 127.

[2] A poetical reference to this may be found in Milton's *Samson Agonistes*, who refers to Delilah as follows:

> "Who also in her prime of love,
> Spousal embraces, vitiated with gold,
> Though offer'd only, by the scent conceived
> Her spurious first-born, treason against me."

7. *Summary*

We may now briefly summarize our conclusions on the subject of breath symbolism. Starting from the consideration that the idea of breath has apparently played a part in the history of human thought disproportionate to the psychical significance inherently attaching to it, we inferred that it must have derived some of its importance by displacement from a still more primary idea. In the individual we had found by psycho-analysis that respiratory processes tend to be interpreted in the Unconscious in terms of alimentary ones, which phylogenetically they originally were and from the point of view of metabolic function still are, and which the erotogenic value of the corresponding sensations render of fundamental psychical significance in individual life. This conclusion is amply confirmed by a study of the ideas modelled on breath, the extensive material offered by Indian and Greek philosophy being specially chosen to illustrate this because of its accessibility and the prominence given there to such ideas. We found there that, just as in the child, the idea of respiration is secondary to that of alimentation; that breath receives much of its importance and interest from the conception of it as something which swallows, projects, and disseminates or expels food, besides intimately mingling with it in digestion to form vapour—the internal pneuma—which becomes the purveyor of nutrition to the system, the transmitter of both afferent and efferent nervous impulses, the generator of the fertilizing principle, of thought, intelligence, and the soul itself. *It is this internal pneuma, which arises from intestinal decomposition, and in the generation of which the inspired air may or may not be supposed to take part, that is the true "breath" largely responsible for all these secondary conceptions; and not solely, as is generally supposed, the inspired breath in the usual sense.*

In the ideas historically moulded on that of breath we recognize again what in the unconscious are symbolic equivalents of intestinal gas: thus, wind, fire, speech, music, thought, soul, etc. The idea that is symbolized seems to possess a peculiar facility for lending itself to the most refined forms of sublimation, a quality which is psychologically to be interpreted as a measure of the intensity of the repression to which the idea is subjected.[1] Attention may be drawn to two instances of this: the part played by incense and music, especially singing, in religion; and the prevailing conception of the soul. The latter is particularly striking and the different stages of its growth can be well traced in Greek thought. Beginning with the nutrient water, the source of all things, we see the coarser constituents being precipitated and discarded, while the finer elements, the essence of essences, are distilled over into vapour (pneuma), which in its turn is purified of any grossness still remaining and is rarefied into an aerial medium, ethereal and spiritual, intangible, invisible and indefinable—the psyche; such is the power ascribed to that magic laboratory, the intestinal tract. This extraordinary capacity for sublimation is probably the reason why the conception of the soul derived from the primitive "breath-soul" (*Hauchseele*) is definitely replacing that derived from the "shadow-soul" (*Schattenseele*), being better adapted to express the loftiest ideas of purity and spirituality.

It is highly probable that the sublimation of the original interest proceeded historically by a series of steps, as it does in the individual, and one might venture on the following description of these. Such an attempt must necessarily be schematic, for it is not to be supposed that the evolution in question takes place in the same order in all individuals, or in all races; a given sublimated interest, therefore, may

---

[1] *See* Freud on this correlation, *Sammlung kleiner Schriften zur Neurosenlehre*, Vierte Folge, 1918, S. 284.

represent one of the described stages in one respect, but perhaps not in others. To begin with we have the beliefs and interests in external phenomena that in a crude way nearly resemble the original personal ones: thus, the belief that hot evil-smelling vapours explosively issuing from the "bowels" of the earth lead to increased fertility and strength. The *first stage* in sublimation probably consisted in the replacement of disagreeable odours by agreeable ones, the stage of aromatics, ambrosia and incense. The *second stage* we may conceive as being brought about through the element of odour being eliminated altogether. Interest is then transferred to such ideas as those in which sound plays a prominent part, either in the form of noise (cries, savage instruments, "bull-roarer", thunder) or in that of music; the ideas of speech and the spoken "Word" also belong here. The *third stage* sees the removal of the attribute of sound, when we have developed the pneuma doctrine, theories of evaporation, and the idea of cosmic respiration. In the *fourth stage* moisture disappears, and interest gets concentrated on the importance of heat and fire, both as cosmic processes and as individual ones (respiration and digestion, refinements of the pneuma doctrine). With the *fifth stage* this also vanishes, and we are left with such ideas as "the breath of God", the winds and the outer air, and so on. The *sixth and final stage* finds even this notion of blowing movement too intolerable, as recalling, however dimly, the original idea. The complex has now been "purged of all material grossness", and is fit to render such lofty thoughts as those of "the rational soul", universal ether, and world-consciousness. Five of the six original attributes (odour, noise, moisture, warmth, and movement) have been eliminated by progressive processes of de-odorization, silencing, desiccation, cooling and calming, and there is left only the abstract conception of a fluid that is invisible, intangible, inaudible and odourless, i.e., imperceptible and inaccessible to any of the senses. As will be noticed, however, the sublimation has only in certain cases been carried through to its uttermost extreme, and all of the attributes find various expressions at the present time as well as in the past.

It should constantly be borne in mind that much of the importance which has been attached to the present topic owes its origin in the last resort not to physiological or philosophical speculation, but to the sexual interest and sensations of infantile life. For the young child, and for the adult unconscious, intestinal gas is before all a sexual material, the symbolic equivalent of urine and of the later semen. That it still retains some of this primary significance even in its conscious ramifications is indicated by the numerous beliefs referred to above in which the secondary ideas derived from that of breath, such as wind, speech, fire, etc., are treated as fertilizing principles, and have the capacity ascribed to them of leading to conception in the literal sense.

There are two answers to the question put at the beginning of this chapter, of why it was God's breath that was chosen to represent the fertilizing material in the Madonna legend, and they are of equal importance. One of them we reserve until some other features of the legend have been considered. The other is given by our analysis of the infantile source of the material in question, which has shown that this concerns a secretion that better than any other lends itself to de-sensualization.

IV. THE DOVE AND THE ANNUNCIATION

At first sight it would seem in the legend under discussion that the two figures of the Holy Dove and the Archangel Gabriel merely represent, in a duplicate fashion, the same idea, for both are divine agents that pour into the Virgin's ear, one breath, the other the Word; they have the further common attribute of being winged beings. There can be no doubt that they considerably overlap in their signification, but reflection shows that this doubling, as perhaps all symbolic reduplication, is of the nature of mythological "decomposition": in other words, the two figures represent attributes, dissociated from the main personality, which are closely akin, but not quite identical.

It is clear that the notion of a *messenger* in general is always based on this psychological process, which strictly speaking is a form of projection. A messenger represents one or more aspects of the main personality; for example, the king's thoughts on a given topic. Psychologically he may be called a part of the king, being an agent of his wishes in the same way as the king's hand or tongue might be. Otherwise expressed, he symbolizes the king, by representing one or other of his attributes. The primary conception of a messenger, well illustrated by the stories of the angels and of Satan in the Old Testament, was thus of an agent who carried out the king's wishes, rather than that of a mere conveyer of news. In ages when less attention was paid to the reality-principle this was clearly recognized, the messenger being treated as fully responsible for the news he brought and executed if this was bad. Even to-day we see—or did at least until before the War—indications of this early attribute in the special deference paid to ambassadors and other accredited representatives of power.

The same primitive attribute is also evident in the present legend, for the Annunciation is exactly synchronous with the conception; more than this, it may be said in a certain sense actually to effect it. And it is here that we can see the distinction between the parts played by the angel and the Dove. For while in older mythologies, e.g., the Greek, the Supreme Being wishing to impregnate a mortal

maiden appeared to her in the symbolic guise of an impregnating agent alone, a snake, a swan, or some other
phallic symbol, in the Christian myth He is not content
with this, but appears also in the guise of a man. The
Archangel Gabriel thus represents the Divine Being in
human form, or, more precisely, that aspect of Him which
wishes to effect a human act. This wish, the cause of the
act, is identical with the Annunciation, and since the
wishes of God, just like those of an obsessional patient, are
all-powerful, it is little wonder that we have a certain
difficulty at first in distinguishing between the part played
by the symbol of the wishing personality (the angel) and
that played by the symbol of the means of execution
(the Dove). The true significance of Gabriel is naïvely
revealed by St. Ephrem[1] thus: "The Archangel Gabriel
was sent under the form of a venerable aged man, lest so
chaste and so modest a maiden should be troubled, or
seized with any fear, at a youthful appearance."

In the Annunciation scene the Archangel Gabriel holds
a *flower*, usually a lily, in his right hand. Flowers have
always been emblematic of women, and particularly of
their genital region, as is indicated by the use of the word
"defloration" and by various passages in the Song of
Solomon. A flower in symbolic language signifies a child
(an unconscious equivalent of the female genitalia); the
association is formed through the origin of flowers in the
mother-earth, favoured by watering and manuring,[2] and is
represented in consciousness by the supposed innocence
and sexlessness of both—as fictitious in the one case as
in the other. The flower here, therefore, represents the

---

[1] *St. Ephrem*, De Divers. Serm., i, 600. In a Syriac tradition of the fourth
century (*The History of the Blessed Virgin Mary*, Edited by Wallis Budge,
1899, p. 22) I also read that "Gabriel appeared unto her in the form of a
venerable old man, so that she might not flee from him."

[2] The coprophilic association here hinted at is strengthened by the fact that
an attractive odour is one of the most striking attributes of flowers.

child[1] that the divine ambassador is promising and proffering—or rather giving—to the Virgin.

The *lily* was considered a special attribute of the Madonna, representing both her motherhood and her innocence, and before the fourteenth century was always depicted in the Annunciation scene at her side; later it was placed either between her and Gabriel, as in the accompanying picture,[2] or in the hand of the latter. Both aspects of the metaphor are expressed in the following description:[3] "Mary is the lily of chastity, but glowing with the flames of love, in order to spread around her the sweetest perfume and grace." A delightful odour was one of the Madonna's most prominent physical characteristics, and is constantly mentioned by the Fathers: thus, St. Chrysostom[4] calls her "the Paradise that is filled with the most divine perfume".

The lily is a flower with a long history in antiquity, and has always been especially associated with the idea of innocence. The very name comes from the Greek λείριον (= simple). The Romans called it Rosa Junonis, because it was supposed to have sprung from the pure milk of the Queen of Heaven. It was associated with the Chaste Susanna, the Hebrew name for lily being "shusham". (In other Semitic languages it is "susanna"; in Persia, from where the lily is said to have come, the ancient capital, Susa, was named after it.[5]) It was a favourite attribute of the youthful Aphrodite. The lily has also a close connection with the soul-idea. The Greeks, particularly the Athenians, strewed lilies on the graves of their dead. The Egyptians believed that the spirit-body in heaven transformed itself

---

[1] I have published an exact illustration of this connection (*Jahrbuch der Psychoanalyse*, 1913, Bd. V, S. 90, Fall III), the flower being there also, as it happens, a lily.

[2] *See* Frontispiece.

[3] Petr. Dam., *De Nat. Beat. Virg.*, iii.

[4] St. Chrysostom, *De Beatae Mariae Virg.*, vii.

[5] *See* Strauss, *Die Blumen in Sage und Geschichte*, 1875 S., 78-80.

into the celestial lily which the God Ra held to his nose.[1]

Turning now our attention to the other figure, the *Holy Dove*, we have two principal questions to answer: why was the Holy Ghost depicted in the form of a bird, and why particularly in that of a dove? Up to the present we have considered the idea of the Holy Ghost in its aspect as symbolizing the fertilizing principle, but from what has just been said it is plain that it symbolizes as well the agent that transmits this in obedience to the will of the Father.[2]

Birds have always been favourite baby-bringing symbols, and are still used for this purpose in the familiar stork legend;[3] winged phalli were among the commonest Roman

[1] Wallis Budge, *Osiris and the Egyptian Resurrection*, 1911, Vol. I, p. 111.

[2] In this essay the idea of the Holy Ghost is treated only in its masculine aspects, as is proper in Christian mythology. As is well known, the Christian Trinity is a distortion of the original one, as obtaining in all the older religions, e.g., the Babylonian, Egyptian, Greek, etc., where it comprised Father, Mother, and Son. The sternly patriarchal Hebrew conception banned the Mother to a subordinate part and the Son to a remotely distant future, but retained their original relationship. The Christian theology changed the Mother into the male Holy Ghost (combination of phallus and fertilizing principle), but in practice reinstated her importance. The attempt made by the Melchite sect in Egypt to retain the original Trinity of Father, Mary, and Messiah was crushed at the Nicene Council, though even the memory of it led Cardinal Newman to wax so ecstatic as to have his words termed "the very poetry of blasphemy" (Hislop, *The Two Babylons*, p. 82), Hebrew theology and Christian worship thus form the obverse of Hebrew worship and Christian theology in their attitude towards the Mother, who could not be completely abolished from either religion. It was reserved for Protestantism to make this final step in the evolution of a purely androgenic procreation myth, which has ended in a universal feminine protest in the countries professing this faith.

Now it is interesting to note that the idea of the Holy Spirit was intimately connected with that of a bird, and especially with that of a dove, even in its original maternal meaning. The passage in Genesis (i. 2), for instance, "And the Spirit of God moved upon the face of the waters" should really run "The Mother of the Gods brooded (or fluttered) over the abyss and brought forth life". According to Wallis Budge this Ruach is feminine and has descended from an earlier mythology (probably Babylonian) as the wife of God. The act of creation in Genesis is commonly portrayed (e.g., on a stained-glass window in the cathedral of Auxerre) as being performed by a dove, and we shall see that this bird was peculiarly emblematic of most of the supreme Goddesses.

[3] An exact analysis of this has been published by Otto Rank, *Die Lohengrinsage*, 1911, S. 55-8.

amulets.[1] The ways in which this association became forged are evident as soon as we consider the most striking characteristics of birds, which we will proceed to do in order.

1. *Power of Flight*

Certainly the characteristic of birds which has most impressed itself on the human imagination is the extraordinary power they have of rapidly ascending into the air at will, an idea the fascination of which may be measured by the appeal made by aviation. Psycho-analysis has revealed the underlying source of this interest—namely, that the act of rising in the air is constantly, though quite unconsciously, associated with the phenomenon of erection.[2] This characteristic of birds alone, therefore, would make them well suited to serve as phallic symbols.

Several religious similes are based, at least in part, on this association. Thus the upward flight of the bird was used to represent the aspiration of a soaring soul, and in the catacombs the idea of such souls being released from sin is depicted by birds escaping from their cages and flying upwards. In the same way the idea of a bird's flight came to represent that of resurrection, i.e., of arising again. Tertullian seems to have been the first to point out the resemblance between a flying bird with outstretched wings and the Saviour nailed to his cross, a fancy which was later much used in religious art; in most pictures, for instance, of St. Francis receiving the stigmata, the descending Saviour is portrayed, in cruciform fashion, as a bird with a human head.

---

[1] *See* Vorberg, *Museum eroticum Neapolitanum; Ein Beitrag zum Geschlechsleben der Romer*, Privatdruck. 1910.

[2] A fact first pointed out by Federn (Cited by Freud, *Die Traumdeutung*, 3 Aufl., S. 204).

2. *Form of Head*

The reptilian neck of birds, continued in a snake-like way into the head, the darting pointed beak, and the power of rapid protrusion, are all features that inevitably recall a snake, thus explaining why this part of the bird specially tends to be unconsciously conceived of in terms of phallic symbolism.

3. *Absence of External Genital Organs*

This strikes a boy's mind as strange after his experience of other animals, as well as of himself, and gives rise to a contrast association which is probably of a compensatory nature (denying the painful truth by excessive insistence); in a similar manner flowers, which are also popularly regarded as having no genital organs, are among the commonest of love-symbols. The importance of this observation, which will be discussed later, is that it leads to fancies being formed to explain it of such a kind as to link up with the infantile fancies of procreation we have considered previously, and which throw much light on the question of why a bird is chosen to depict the Holy Ghost.

4. *Power of Song*

This striking characteristic, almost unique in the animal kingdom, is so obviously related to love-making that it becomes associated with the series of symbolic equivalents discussed in the previous chapter. Reference may also be made here to the belief in the "thunder-bird" current among the North American Indians,[1] in which the sound element is emphasized in a connection that inevitably

[1] Eels, Annual Report of the Smithsonian Institute for 1887, p. 674; Boas, Sixth Report on the North-Western Tribes of Canada, 1890, p. 40.

reminds one of the thunder beliefs and thunder-weapons mentioned earlier.

5. *Relation to the Air*

It is only natural that the idea of air should play a prominent part in phantasies concerning birds, who show such a supreme mastery over this element, and similarly that birds should play a prominent part in symbolism relating to air; indeed the absence of a bird in such symbolism would need more explanation than its presence. In the examples mentioned earlier of the beliefs in the fertilization of animals by means of wind it is noteworthy that nearly all of them relate to birds; the idea of gaseous fertilization would thus seem to be readily associated with that of birds. The connection between the two ideas has been made use of in various cosmogonies. Thus the Polynesians describe the heaven- and air-God Tangaroa as a bird hovering over the waters,[1] and it is probable that this was the original sense of the reference in Genesis to the wind of Elohim brooding over the waters[2] (*See* Footnote, p. 326).

After what was said in reference to the previous characteristics it is not very surprising that they should become associated with the last-mentioned one, the head, neck and beak being then regarded as a phallic organ which expels the fertilizing gas. This is a more natural idea than it might at first sight appear, for, after all, whatever the nature of the fertilizing substance the male organ is the typical expelling agent. I have come across this phantasy several times in the course of individual psycho-analysis, the explanation being that the person has in childhood considered the male organ to be a continuation of the rectum

[1] Waitz, *Anthropologie der Naturvölker*, 1872, Bd. VI, S. 241.
[2] Cheyne, *Encyclop. Brit.*, Vol. VI, p. 447.

or its contents; the two corresponding part-instincts are always astonishingly closely connected in the unconscious.[1] The same association probably helps somewhat to explain the fondness that so many boys have for blowing whistles and trumpets (sound of course entering into the association); as well as the use of trumpets, to which attention was called above, for the purpose of raising the dead, i.e., of infusing life into them.[2] Noise, especially in the form of trumpet blowing, often plays an important part in initiation ceremonies, a matter which will be discussed later. The same association may also be found in erotic art, of which two examples may be mentioned: In a picture by Felicien Rops, entitled "Joujou", a nymph with satyr legs and a Phrygian cap is creating planets by blowing bubbles with the aid of a phallus which she holds to her mouth as a trumpet;[3] in one published in *L'Art de péter*, a cupid is depicted blowing bubbles through a tube with the mouth and at the same time with the anus.[4] The legend of Athene, who was born out of her father's head, the product of his "thought", has to be interpreted in the same way—to follow the hint from Plotinus mentioned above (p. 311). I would even suggest that this association[5] plays a part in determining a feature of our Madonna legend—namely, the notion that the fertilizing breath of God issues from the beak of the Holy Dove. In support of this the following examples may be cited. The unicorn (a purely phallic conception) was a recognized emblem of the Christian Logos, or creative Word of God; its symbolic meaning, and its close association with breath, becomes plain from an old

[1] *See* Freud, "Über Triebumsetzungen insbesondere der Analerotik," *Sammlung kleiner Schriften zur Neurosenlehre, Vierte Folge.* 1918.

[2] Compare the sexual significance of tongue and speech pointed out above.

[3] *Das erotische Werk des Felicien Rops,* 1905, Nr. 13.

[4] Reproduced in Stern's *Illustrierte Geschichte der erotischen Literatur,* 1908, Bd. I, S. 240.

[5] To this also may in part be attributed the use of such phrases as "inflated," "blown up", etc., as synonyms for excessive pride (narcissism).

German picture which was very popular at the end of the fifteenth century.[1] In this the Annunciation is represented in the form of a hunt. Gabriel blows the angelic greeting on a hunting horn. A unicorn flees (or is blown) to the Virgin Mary and plunges his horn into her "lap", while God the Father blesses them from above. A second example is even less ambiguous, for in it the passage of God's breath is actually imagined as proceeding through a tube; over a portal of the Marienkapelle at Würzburg is a relief-representation of the Annunciation[2] in which the Heavenly Father is blowing along a tube that extends from his lips to the Virgin's ear, and down which the infant Jesus is descending.

The extent to which the idea of a bird is connected with the attributes of bodily gas enumerated in the previous chapter is indeed remarkable: thus, with sound (singing), with invisibility (difficulty with which it is caught sight of, disappearance in the air), with heat (higher bodily temperature than any other animal, nearness to the sun), with movement and wind (rapid flight, mastery over air), and so on. Two further illustrations may be given of the way in which the idea of a bird enters into this circle of "gaseous" ideas. In the first place the soul is frequently conceived of in bird form[3] (especially in Christian art) and is then depicted, appropriately enough, as leaving the body after death by issuing from the mouth.[4] The second example, that of the phœnix, displays an extraordinary richness in the present

---

[1] Reproduced by P. Ch. Cahier, *Caractéristiques des Saints dans l'art populaire*, 1867.

[2] Reproduced by Fuchs, *Illustrierte Sittengeschichte; Renaissance; Ergänzungsband*, 1909, S. 289.

[3] Frazer (*Taboo and the Perils of the Soul*, 1911, pp. 33-5) gives examples from all parts of the world.

[4] As was hinted earlier in this essay, in this belief the mouth is probably in part a replacement of the other extremity of the alimentary canal; the original form of the belief sometimes comes to open expression, an example being in the fourteenth century farce "Le Muynier" (Dupuoy, *Medicine in the Middle Ages*, p. 84).

group of associations and epitomises most of the ideas we have up to here discussed, while of interest in the present connection is the circumstance that the early Christians adopted the legend of its life-history to symbolize the resurrection of Jesus.[1] The phœnix was a golden shining bird, sometimes described as a ray emanating from the sun. It prepares for its death by surrounding itself with cinnamon, myrrh and other aromatic spices, and by addressing to the sun a song that is "more beautiful than the sound of the nightingale, the flutes of the Muses, or the lyre of Hermes". It dies, amidst a blaze of fragrant perfume, in a fire created by the fanning of its wings, or—as was at other times believed—by the heat of the sun's rays. The first act of the young phœnix born from this fire is to carry the relics of its sire, in a casket of myrrh, to a sacred temple and pronounce over them a funeral oration.

The idea of a *rara avis*, usually a bird of fire, is common to many nations, being found in Egypt, China, and most oriental countries; the popular appeal of the idea is still witnessed by the success attending Maeterlinck's *L'Oiseau bleu*. A Slav fairy-tale tells how a certain Prince acquired a feather from the wing of Ohnivak, the Fire-Bird, and "so lovely and bright was it that it illumed all the galleries of the palace and they needed no other light"; he falls into a pensive decline and, summoning his three sons, says to them: "If I could but hear the bird Ohnivak sing just once, I should be cured of this disease of the heart."[2] In Namoluk, one of the Caroline islands, it is believed that fire came to men in the following way: Olofaet, the master of flames, gave fire to the bird "mwi" and bade him carry it to earth in his beak; so the bird flew from tree to tree

[1] Bachofen, *Versuch über die Gräbersymbolik der Alten*, 1859, S. 109.
[2] Harding, *Fairy-Tales of the Slav Peasants and Herdsmen*, 1896, p. 269 et seq.

and stored away the slumbering force of the fire in the wood, from which men can elicit it by friction.[1] In Shelley's "To a Skylark" most of the preceding associations are poetically illustrated. For example: soul (Hail to thee, blithe spirit—Bird thou never wert); fire (like a cloud of fire); invisibility (Thou art unseen, but yet I hear thy shrill delight); rising flight (thou scorner of the ground); voice (All the earth and air with thy voice is loud).

With all these associations it is plain that nothing could easily be better imagined than a bird to symbolize a bringer of a wonderful message from the air. Children keep a pretty reminder of them in the familiar saying "A little bird told me", meaning "whispered a secret to me".

The problem of why particularly a *dove* was chosen in the present instance is most conveniently approached by first considering some of the ways in which it has played a part in other mythologies. This part has been a rather extensive one, for the dove was a sacred animal among the Assyrians, Egyptians, and Hebrews, was an attribute of Astarte and Semiramis (who was supposed to have been transformed into one after her death), and was the favourite bird of Aphrodite, whose chariot was drawn by doves. At the Syrian Hierapolis, one of the chief seats of her worship, doves were so holy that they might not even be touched; if a man inadvertently touched one, he was unclean or taboo for the rest of the day.[2] Figures of doves played a prominent part in the decoration of Aphrodite's sanctuary at Old Paphos.[3] Frazer gives reason for thinking that the Cyprian custom of sacrificing doves in honour of Adonis dated from an older form of worship in

[1] Girschner, "Die Karolineninsel Namoluk und ihre Bewohner," *Baessler-Archiv*, 1912, Bd. II, S. 141.

[2] Lucian, *De dea Syria*, liv.

[3] A good description of this is given by Frazer, *Adonis, Attis, Osiris*, 1907, p. 29.

which a holy man, personifying the Goddess's lover, was sacrificed.[1]

The association of the ideas of dove and love has always been a close one, and is met with in different ages. The following is a love-charm used in Bohemia: A girl goes into the woods on St. George's Eve and catches a ring-dove, which must be a male one; early in the morning she carries it to the hearth, presses it to her bare breast, and lets it fly up the chimney (a well-known vaginal symbol), muttering an incantation the while).[2] In 1784 a mixed pseudo-freemasonry, the object of which was the pursuit of love, was formed at Versailles, the members being termed the "Chevaliers et Chevalières de la Colombe".[3]

The phallic symbolism of the dove is also unmistakable in the following examples. The Christian myth we are considering can be closely paralleled by the Greek one in which Zeus assumes the form of a dove in order to seduce Phtheia on one of his human expeditions, just as on other similar occasions he assumed other phallic ones, snake, bull, swan, and so on. When Catullus mentions Cæsar's salaciousness he does so by using the expression "columbulus albulus". According to Philo, the dove was the emblem of wisdom, which in mythology, as with the snake, unicorn, etc., is always a phallic attribute,[4] and Jesus himself brought it into a contrast association with the snake: "Be ye as wise as the serpent and as harmless as the dove" (Matthew x. 16). Von Hahn[5] relates three stories from modern Greek folk-lore in which the life of an enchanter or ogre is bound up with that of two, or three, doves; when they die, he dies also. The sense of this becomes

[1] Frazer, op. cit., pp. 114, 115.
[2] Grohmann, op. cit., S. 77.
[3] *Dictionnaire Larouse, Art.* "Colombe".
[4] *See* Chapter II, p. 44.
[5] Von Hahn, *Griechische und albanesische Märchen*, 1864, Bd. I, S. 187; Bd. II, S. 215, 260.

clear when it is compared with another variant in which the life of an old man is bound up with that of a ten-headed serpent; when the serpent's heads are cut off one after another, he feels ill, and when the last one is cut off he expires.[1] But the most unequivocal indication of the symbolic signification of the dove is to be found in the extra-canonical legend which relates that a dove escaped from Joseph's genital organ and alighted on his head (an unconscious symbol of the erect phallus) to designate him as the future husband of the Virgin Mary;[2] the story is weakened in the writings of the later Christian Fathers, who say that the dove escaped from Joseph's rod (!).

Appropriately enough it is a dove that furnishes Zeus with ambrosia (= soma), and in the legend of St. Remy brings the bishop the oil-flask to anoint King Clovis (oil being an equivalent symbol).[3] An interesting parallel to this is the legend that Aeneas was guided by two doves to the Golden Bough,[4] for Frazer has shown that the Golden Bough represents mistletoe growing on an oak-tree,[5] and mistletoe is as familiar a symbol of sperma (like ambrosia and oil) as the oak is of the male organ. French peasants think that mistletoe originates in birds' dung;[6] the ancients knew that it was propagated from tree to tree by seeds that have been carried and voided by birds, and Pliny[7] tells us that the birds which most often deposited the seeds were doves and thrushes.

According to Apollonius, a dove guided the Argonauts on their wanderings. The ideas of bringing, guiding and leading have much in common with that of "messenger",

[1] Von Hahn, op. cit , Bd. II, S. 23.

[2] *Protevang., St. Jacob.* Cap. 9; *Evang. infant St. Mariæ,* Cap. 8. Cited after Maury, *Essai sur les légendes pieuses du moyen-âge,* 1843.

[3] De Gubernatis, *Zoological Mythology,* 1872, Vol. II, p. 305.

[4] Virgil, Aen., VI, 190, 293 et seq.

[5] Frazer, *Balder the Beautiful,* 1913, Vol. II, pp. 285, 315-20.

[6] Gaidoz, *Revue de l'histoire des religions,* 1880, Vol. II, p. 76.

[7] Pliny, op. cit., XVI, 247.

335

and a well-known Greek legend of the dove is that in which it figures as the love-messenger carrying the *billets doux* of the poet Anacreon, who had been presented with it by Aphrodite in return for a song. Like most love-figures in mythology, including even Aphrodite herself, the dove could represent not only life, but also death; thus in the hymns of the Rig-Veda the dove (Kapota) is Yama's messenger of death.[1]

The dove was also associated with fire. When the Kapota touches fire, Yama, whose messenger he is, is honoured; in a Buddhistic legend Agni, the God of Fire, assumes the shape of a dove when he is being pursued by Indra in the shape of a hawk (the Sanscrit name of which, by the way, is Kapotâri, the enemy of doves).[2] In the "scoppio del carro" festival at Florence the holy fire is renewed every Easter Eve, and at the moment of celebrating High Mass a stuffed bird, representing a dove (called the dove of the Pazzi), is released from a pillar of fire-works in front of the altar, flies along a wire down the nave, and ignites the fire-works on the festive car that is waiting outside the door.[3] Maury quotes as a reason why the Holy Ghost appears sometimes in the form of fire, and sometimes in that of a dove, the circumstance that in the Orient the dove was the emblem of generation and of animal heat.[4] The association with heat is retained in Christian art, where the Holy Dove is always depicted surrounded by rays of light or flames of fire.

It is comprehensible that a bird symbolizing generation should also come to represent the ideas of re-birth, resurrection and salvation, which in the unconscious are practically equivalent.[5] De Gubernatis[6] quotes a number of

[1] *Rig-Veda*, X, 165, 4.
[2] De Gubernatis, op. cit., p. 297.
[3] Weston, "The Scoppio del Carro at Florence," *Folk-Lore*, 1905, Vol. XVI, pp. 182-4.
[4] Maury, op. cit., p. 179.
[5] *See* my *Papers on Psycho-Analysis*, Second Edition, 1918, Ch. X.
[6] De Gubernatis, op. cit., pp. 297-303.

stories from folk-lore, in which the dove warns or saves from danger. The dove was the messenger of salvation in the Deluge myth, which is now known to represent a glorified birth-phantasy; the meaning is brought to clear expression in a sketch found in the catacombs of Rome, in which Noah is seen floating in a little box that flies open at the appearance of the dove with its leaf.[1] It is perhaps significant that in another Old Testament birth-myth the name of the hero, Jonah, is the same as the Hebrew word for dove. It was a dove also that appeared to the three young Hebrews in the furnace at Babylon and announced to them their deliverance from the flames. The natives at Cape Grafton say that a dove brings the babies to mothers in their dreams.[2] To the same group of ideas belongs the association between the dove and the re-birth rite of baptism,[3] both in the New Testament and in ecclesiastical decorative art. Jesus himself, the figure of salvation and resurrection, is occasionally depicted in the form of a dove;[4] for example, in a lamp in Santa Caterina in Chiusi a dove is portrayed bearing an olive branch in its mouth and having a cross on its head. The dove is in the Catholic Church also an emblem of martyrdom, i.e., of attainment of eternal life through death.

In early Christian art the soul of a dying saint was depicted as escaping from the mouth in the form of a dove,[5] this being replaced in later art by the figure of a little child.

[1] Reproduced in Smith and Cheetham's *Dictionary of Christian Antiquities*, 1875, Vol. I, p. 575.

[2] Roth, cited by Rank, *Die Lohengrinsage*, 1911, S. 23.

[3] It is of interest that the German words for baptism and for dove (*Taufe* and *Taube*) are derived from the same root.

[4] We have seen in order the Holy Ghost as a symbol of the creative material, the creative agent, and the child created. (In later art he is often depicted in the form of a child instead of that of a young man, just as Eros became replaced by Cupid.)

[5] Many examples are cited by Didron, *Christian Iconography*, Engl. Transl. 1896, Vol. I, pp. 460, 461; and Maury, *Croyances et légendes du moyen-âge*, 1896, Vol. II, p. 266.

In this equating of dove—child—soul—breath we see another example of the infantile birth theory that was discussed earlier in this essay.

An equally plain illustration of the Logos association of the dove is furnished by its connection with the idea of inspiration (spiro = I breathe). In Lybia a dove communicated the sacred oracles, and in Dodona two doves performed the same function and were supposed to cry "Zeus was; Zeus is; Zeus will be; O Zeus, the greatest of the Gods". We noted earlier, in discussing the topics of speech and tongue, the important part played by the Holy Dove (Holy Ghost) in a similar connection. When St. Catherine of Alexandria confounded the learned doctors by her wisdom the Holy Dove kept flying over her head, and a dove, known to French art as the "colombe inspiratrice", is frequently depicted on the shoulder of a great saint, speaking into his ear and thus inspiring him.[1] The symbolic significance of this, which should be clear from the preceding chapter, may be further illustrated by quoting the following dream related by the Welsh poet Vaughan, in a letter written in 1694: "I was told by a very sober and knowing person (now dead) that in his time, there was a young lad father and motherless, and soe very poor that he was forced to beg; butt att last was taken up by a rich man, that kept a great stock of sheep upon the mountains not far from the place where I now dwell, who cloathed him and sent him into the mountains to keep his sheep. There in Summer time following the sheep and looking to their lambs he fell into a deep sleep; in which he dreamt, that he saw a beautifull young man with a garland of green leafs upon his head, and an hawk upon his fist: with a quiver full of Arrows att his back, coming towards him (whistling several measures or tunes all the way) and att last lett the hawk fly att him, which (he dreamt) gott into his mouth and

[1] Maury, op. cit., pp. 267-9; Larousse, loc. cit.

338

inward parts, and suddenly awaked in a great fear and consternation: butt possessed with such a vein, or gift of poetrie, that he left the sheep and went about the Countrey, making songs upon all occasions, and came to be the most famous Bard in all the Countrey in his time."[1]

Etymology fully sustains our view of the sexual connotation of the dove idea, indicating its association both with phallicism and with the group of "gaseous" ideas enumerated earlier. The word "dove" comes from the Anglo-Saxon "dufan" = to plunge into, and is probably allied to the Greek κολυμβίς = a diver; it is cognate with "dip", "dive", and "deep", the notion of penetration evidently being the fundamental one. The more generic word "pigeon" comes from the Greek πιπίζειν = to chirp; from the latter also comes the word "pipe", which has the meanings of a tube (cp. the Würzburg relief mentioned above), an instrument for making smoke, to chirp or sing, and, in slang, the male organ. A whole series of words are derived from the same root (probably of onomatopoetic origin), which mean "to blow", "the back parts", or "child", and Jung[2] has pointed out that the connecting link of these three apparently disparate ideas is to be found in the common infantile notion that children are born from the rectum. Thus: (1) "pop", "puff", "to poop" (= to pass flatus. Compare the French "pet" = flatus, the same word in English meaning darling, little dear, and the German "Schatz" = darling, treasure, which also comes from a vulgar word for defæcation); (2) French "poupée" and Dutch "pop", both meaning doll (German "Puppe"), Latin "pupus" = a child, "pupula" = a girl, and English "puppy" and "pupa", meaning the young of the dog and the butterfly respectively. That words of such widely

---

[1] This letter, which has never been published, is to be found in the MS. Bodleiana, Aubrey 13, Fol. 340. I am indebted to Mr. L. C. Martin for calling my attention to it and for giving me the opportunity of making use of it.

[2] Jung, op. cit., S. 230.

different signification as "pupil", "fart", "peep", "fife", "pigeon", "puff", "petard", and "partridge"[1] should all be derived from the same root illustrates the astonishing propagating power possessed by sexual words, to which Sperber[2] has recently directed special attention.

The choice of the dove for the purposes above mentioned was doubtless determined by many factors, perhaps by extrinsic ones as well as psychological ones: that it constituted a numerous genus and attracted much attention in ancient times is shown by the fact alone that there existed in Sanscrit some twenty-five or thirty names for pigeon.[3] It is generally said that its use in Christian symbolism was due to its association with the ideas of purity and immaculateness, but it is likely that cause and effect are here reversed; even its white colour cannot be cited in favour of this association, for most doves are not white, while other birds, e.g., swans, most often are. A more important feature is the tenderness they display in their love-relations, the activity of which must, as is evident from the extensive connotations related above, have vividly impressed itself upon the attention. Now this tenderness is chiefly manifested in a manner that is of particular interest to the present theme, in what is a very prominent characteristic of doves—namely, the soft, delightful cooing that plays a leading part in their love-making; we still use the expression "billing and cooing of turtle-doves" to denote a special relationship between lovers. In view of the extensive associations that subsist between the idea of birds in general, and of doves in particular, on the one hand and the group discussed in the previous chapter (sound, breath, sexuality, etc.) on the other, it seems to me probable that this striking feature of doves must have been a principal

[1] In view of the ancient belief that this bird could be impregnated by either the wind or the voice it is interesting that its name should enter into this series.

[2] Sperber, op. cit.

[3] Larousse, loc. cit.

reason for the choice of them to symbolize phantasies based on the idea in question. This suggestion may be illustrated by reference to the Christian belief that "the voice of the turtle-dove is an echo on earth of the voice of God".[1]

This peculiar tenderness in the love-making of doves is to be correlated with a feature in the associations surrounding the idea of them on which I have only lightly touched—namely, femininity. It would lead us too far to enumerate instances of this association, but it is a curiously extensive one, so that one is forced to say that of all phallic emblems the dove is one of the most gentle and effeminate. The significance of this to our main theme will be indicated in the following section.

V. THE EAR AS THE RECEPTIVE ORGAN

The infant's psychical interests and digital manipulations relating to the lower alimentary orifice are early transferred to the nostril, which, from its nearness to a less objectional part of the alimentary canal, its relation to the sense of smell, its size, its connection with breath and with mucoid secretion, is well adapted for the purpose. A patient of mine used even to impregnate himself in his phantasy by inhaling through the nose breath that had been exhaled from the mouth,[2] and in Genesis we read of Yahweh using a nostril for the same purpose in the creation of Adam, from which it is evident what the "dust of the ground" out of which Adam was moulded must have originally signified.[3]

By the time of the Christian era, however, a greater refinement had taken place, one corresponding with the increasing displacement that is to be observed in the progress of individual repression, and the nostril, which

[1] Conway, *Solomon and the Solomonic Literature*, 1899, p. 123.
[2] *Jahrbuch der Psychoanalyse*, 1912 Bd. IV, S. 598.
[3] I have elsewhere dealt with the symbolism of dirt at some length, *Jahrbuch der Psychoanalyse*, 1913, Bd. V, S. 90, Fall III.

can receive a palpable gas, is replaced by the ear, which can receive only impalpable sound—for instance the Word of God—a rarefied abstraction of the primitive gas idea. That in the Madonna legend[1] the ear symbolizes the lower alimentary orifice, and not the vagina, is a conclusion based not only on logic, for the idea of the vagina would be a meaningless intrusion into a series of themes that have nothing in common with it (they are all of infantile origin, while the infant knows nothing of the existence of the vagina), but through numerous analyses of persons in whom this orifice has acquired a symbolical significance; such habits as nose and ear-picking, for instance, invariably prove on analysis to be derivatives of, and substitutes for, anal masturbation. The exact symbolical equivalency of the two orifices, however, can be demonstrated quite apart from psycho-analysis.

In several of the medieval pictures of hell the devil is portrayed in the act of swallowing sinners (through the mouth, of course) and excreting them through the ear alone, the cloaca alone, or through both indifferently and simultaneously; instances of each of these in Florence alone are to be found in the Baptisteria, in Orcagna's fresco in the Santa Maria Novella, and in Fra Angelico's picture in the Academy. We see here a complete parity of the two orifices, one which can be matched by beliefs drawn from another part of the world, India: In the Ramayana[2] a sun-hero, Hanumant, is described as entering

---

[1] That in this legend the ear was thought of as the receptive organ in a quite concrete sense is clear from the evidence produced earlier in this essay, and is proved by consideration of such a presentation as the Würzburg relief alone. To the numerous passages already quoted from the early Fathers the following two may be added: "And because the devil, creeping in through the ear by temptation, had wounded and given death to Eve, Christ entering by the ear to Mary, dried up all the vices of the heart, and cured the woman's wound by being born of the Virgin" (St. Zeno: Epist. ad Pulcheriam Augustam); "None other was born of Mary, than He who *glided in through her maternal ear*, and filled the Virgin's womb" (St. Gaudentius, De diversis Capitulis, Serm. xiii).

[2] Frobenius, *Das Zeitalter des Sonnengottes*, 1904, Bd. I, S. 173, 174.

into the mouth of a sea-monster and emerging through the "other side" at the tail, evidently through the cloaca; in another part of the poem, however, he is made to emerge through the ear, the two orifices being again treated as equivalent. According to the Taitiriyaka-Upanishad,[1] the Apâna, or down-going breath, corresponds with the ear.

The ear figures as the receptive organ in other and earlier myths than the Christian one, which is doubtless derived from them. The Mongolian legend of Maya, who was impregnated through this orifice during sleep, has been referred to already (p. 272). Just as Eve, after having been seduced by the "serpent", tasted of the fruit of knowledge,[2] so Cassandra became a prophetess when the "serpent" licked her ear. The Sumerian word-sign for "ear" in its earliest form was written by the pictograph of a pair of ears, with the phonetic value of "wa" in the Sumerian and "uznu" in the Semitic-Akkalian or Assyrian; it is defined in the bilingual cuneiform of about 2000 B.C. and later as "the bent member".[3] In these glosses the Semitic "uznu" or "ear" is also defined as a title of the Mother-Goddess Ishtar, and particularly of her form as Antu, the Creatress and Goddess of generation, a usage which is explained as arising from the idea "bend down, bend over" in sexual intercourse.[4] This is perhaps the source of the large ears assigned to the woman in the presence of the Father-God as figured on the ancient Babylonian seals described by Pinches.[5] This word-sign for "ear" is moreover used as a synonym for the "cedar",[6] which through its ever-greenness was the "Tree of Life" of the Garden of

---

[1] I, 7, 1.

[2] i.e., the knowledge of sexual matters. *See* Ludwig Levy, op. cit.

[3] Prince, *Sumerian Lexicon*, 1908, pp. 1, 373; Barton, *Babylonian Writing*, 1913, p. 179.

[4] Prince, op. cit., pp. 338, 339.

[5] Pinches, *Proceedings of the Society of Biblical Archæology*, 1917, Vol. XXIX.

[6] Barton, loc. cit.; *See* also Muss-Arnolt: *Assyrian Dictionary*, p. 103.

Eden in the Hebrew legend[1] and an emblem of the Mother-Goddess Ishtar. In the Persian cosmogony the first man was created by the Divine Being inserting his "hand" into the ear of the female one; in another version, on which the preceding Babylonian myth throws light, it is his "main branch" that is inserted. This "main branch" is presumably the branch held in the hand of the Father-God in the archaic Babylonian seal-cylinders of the third and fourth millennium B.C.;[2] it may perfectly well be the origin of the modern expression "olive branch" for a child, since the olive came in Greece and Rome to replace the cedar as the special tree of the Virgin Mother-Goddess, Athene. In connection with the ancient Semitic-Babylonian hymn on the "Wailing of Ishtar" for the killing of her son-lover Tamnuz the origin of the wailing of the Jewish women of Jerusalem for Tamnuz is described by Ezekiel in a familiar passage,[3] but it would seem that the word usually translated as "cedar" might well mean "ear", when the stanza in question would read:

"Ah me, my child (now) far-removed!
My son-consort, the far-removed!
For the sacred *ear* where the mother bore him,
In Eanna, high and low there is weeping,
Wailing for the house of their lord, the women raise."[4]

A faint indication of the meaning of this symbolism is furnished in the pictures[5] where the Archangel Gabriel makes his appearance through a door at the *back* of the

---

[1] *See* Cheyne, *Traditions of Ancient Israel*, passim.
[2] Ward, *Seal Cylinders of West Asia*, 1910, pp. 96, etc.
[3] Ezekiel viii, 14.
[4] This rendering, based on Longdon's translation in his *Tamnuz and Ishtar*, is by Dr. Jyotirmoy Roy of Calcutta, who also kindly suggested to me several of the preceding points.
[5] Many examples are referred to by Mrs. Jameson, *Sacred and Legendary Art*, 1890 edition, Vol. I, p. 124.

Virgin, who is aware of his presence without seeing him. This expresses the same idea as the Kwakiutl myth of the hero who was conceived by the sun shining on the small of his mother's back.[1] We are not told whether Jesus was actually born, like Rabelais's Gargantua, through his mother's ear, as well as being conceived through it; the real passage is hinted at in St. Agobard's description (*See* p. 269) of how the holy fertilizing principle, after entering by the ear, emerges "through the *golden* gate".

That the danger of this form of conception is regarded by Catholics as not having entirely passed is shown by the custom with which all nuns still comply of protecting their chastity against assault by keeping their ears constantly covered, a custom which stands in a direct historical relation to the legend forming the subject of this essay.[2] This is the acme of chastity, for it protects even against the most innocent form of conception, one reserved for the most modest women. An Indian legend, which may serve as a pendant to the Persian one mentioned above, well illustrates this connection between aural conception and modesty. Kunti, the mother of the five Pandava princes, the great heroes of the Mahabarata, when still a virgin, made use of a *mantra* charm to test its alleged power of calling up the Gods. It worked, and the Sun God appeared to her. She became very confused and bade him go, but he said that as she had called him she could not refuse him a reward. On learning that the reward the God wanted was carnal knowledge she explained that she was a Virgin. To this objection the Sun God suggested sexual intercourse via the ear, and to this she consented, with the result that the hero Karna (whose name means ear) was conceived.[3] The same association with extreme

---

[1] Boas and Hunt, *Jesup Expedition*. Bureau of Ethnology, Vol. I, p. 80.

[2] *See* Tertullian, *De Virginibus Velandis*.

[3] *Mahabharat-Adiparva*, Ch. III, 1-20. I am indebted to Dr. Roy for calling my attention to this legend.

innocence is also indicated in the passage quoted above from Molière (p. 272, Footnote).

*   *   *

We may conclude the present topic by briefly considering an animal myth which offers interesting resemblances to the legend under discussion and which also possesses certain historical connections with it. The myth of the phœnix and other fire-birds, of which the aureole-surrounded Holy Dove is the lineal descendant, is paralleled by that of the salamander, the fabulous lizard born, like those, of fire. It would not be easy to imagine animals more unlike each other than a dove and a *lizard*, or *crocodile*, and yet the positions both have occupied in mythology and religion show a far-reaching similarity, one which should throw a new light on the legend of the Virgin Mary. The lizard has been an extensive object of worship, by the Slavs in Europe as late as the sixteenth century,[1] by the Egyptians in the form of the crocodile, by the Mexicans in that of the alligator; the crocodile is the protective totem of one of the chief Bechuanaland tribes.[2] It was specially sacred to the sun, and was, largely on that account, adopted by the Gnostics as a symbol of the Life-Giver; the Sun God Sebek was figured as a crocodile-headed man. On the other hand it was identified at Nubti with Set, one of the fore-runners of our devil, and—like most phallic animals, lion, dragon, serpent, etc.—it had to be overcome by the young God-Hero; thus at Adfou it was supposed to have been speared by the young Sun God Horus. In the Book of Gates the monster serpent Apep is described as being accompanied by a friend in the shape of a crocodile which had a tail terminating in the head of a serpent, its name being Sessi.

[1] Morfill, *The Religious Systems of the World*, p. 272.
[2] Bent, *The Ruined Cities of Mashonaland*, 1891, p. 15.

There seem to have been two principal associations between the idea of a lizard, or crocodile, and that of the Deity. One was the observation that "it veils its eyes with a thin transparent membrane which it draws down from the upper lid, so as to see without being seen, which is the attribute of the Supreme Deity" (Plutarch); this idea is naturally connected with that of the Sun-Father,[1] and in Egypt the crocodile was the chief symbol of Cheops, the "Ever-Existent Eye". A more important association, however, and one which is closely related to the group of ideas under discussion here, was that the crocodile was the symbol of silence, being "the only land animal which lacks the use of its tongue" (Pliny); "it is said to have been made an emblem of the Deity, as being the sole animal destitute of a tongue. For the Divine Reason stands not in need of voice, but walking along a silent path and rule guides mortal affairs according to justice" (Plutarch). Representing the silence of the wise, it became the emblem of the mind, of reason, of intelligence, and particularly of wisdom;[2] as such it figures on the breast of Minerva, the Goddess of Wisdom. The only instance of its use in this respect that I know of in Christian art is in Seville, where one dating from the Moorish occupation still stands over the portal of the entrance to the Cathedral leading from the Patio de los Naránjos; there is, of course, the well-known crocodile on St. Theodore's column in the Piazzetta in Venice, which doubtless had an apotropæic signification.

The attributes of the crocodile that have attracted interest thus appear to be mainly negative: it is an animal which has no visible genital organs, and is said to have no tongue and to be dumb—two ideas which, as we have seen earlier, symbolize impotence.

Side by side, however, with this conception of the croco-

---

[1] Cp. Chapter XII.
[2] For the symbolism of this *see* pp. 135, 334.

dile as an impotent animal, one having the most elementary defects, we find the precise opposite—namely, the idea that it represents a glorification of phallic power; consideration of this remarkable antithesis will prove highly instructive for the main theme of this essay. The phallic significance of the crocodile may be suspected from the circumstance alone that it is closely associated with the ideas of wisdom, the sun, and the snake, but grosser facts than these can be cited. In the text of Unas, written during the Sixth Dynasty, are passages expressing the desire that a deceased person may attain in the next world to the virility of the crocodile and so become "all-powerful with women".[1] At the present day in the Egyptian Soudan the belief is acted on that the penis of the crocodile eaten with spices is the most potent means of increasing sexual vigour in the male.[2] Both in Ancient Egypt and in the modern Soudan the belief has prevailed that the crocodile has the habit of carrying off women for sexual purposes. Two physiological facts concerning the animal probably contribute to these ideas: the copulatory act is unusually ardent and lasts a long time; and the male organ,[3] though never visible in the ordinary way—being concealed within the cloaca—is unusually large.[4]

The ancients, in pondering over the question of how the crocodile propagated its species, indicated consideration of both these opposite attitudes. They concluded that it must take place in some way that expressed the animal's independence of the ordinary means and, following the

[1] Budge, op. cit., pp. 127, 128.

[2] Bousfield, "Native Methods of Treatment of Disease in Kassala," *Third Report of the Wellcome Research Laboratories*, p. 274. Stanley, *Through the Dark Continent*, 1878, Vol. I, p. 253. Budge, op. cit., p. 128.

[3] It is perhaps of some interest in the present connection to note that this organ is situate in the rectal part of the cloaca, being separated from the anterior urinary chamber by a wide transverse fold. Of further interest in relation with the "gaseous" group of ideas is the circumstance that during the rutting period a pungent odour is emitted from the submaxillary glands of the creature.

[4] Gadow, *Cambridge Natural History*, Vol. VIII, p. 445.

path of associations indicated above, reached the belief that the female *conceived, like the Virgin Mary, through the ear.* According to this the crocodile would represent a force greater even than that of the Deity whose Word was all-powerful and all-creating,[1] for to execute its wishes it needed not even speech, being possessed of the still more potent Silence of the Wise. We have here, therefore, a beautiful example of the "omnipotence of thought", which is evidently higher than the "omnipotence of speech"; invisible and silent action is the highest limit of imaginable power. The ear is the orifice best designed to receive thought, even though this be inaudible to the uninitiated.

According to King,[2] it was this belief about the crocodile's natural history that later made it come to be regarded by the early Christians as "the type of the generation of the Word, that is, the Logos or Divine Wisdom". Plutarch (De Iside et Osiride) makes a similar statement about the cat: he refers to the belief that the cat "conceives through its ears, and brings forth its young through its mouth; and the Word, or Logos, is also conceived through the ear and expressed through the mouth". In the Egyptian Book of the Dead four crocodiles are said to reside in the four quarters of the world, and to attack the dead in order to seize the magic *words* on which they depend for existence in the Other World.[3]

The great characteristic on which I wish to lay emphasis in the preceding beliefs concerning the crocodile is their striking *ambivalency.* Herodotus[4] noticed that the creature was held sacred in some parts of Egypt and was slain as a noxious reptile in others, and the double attitude here indicated may be traced throughout Egyptian religion.

[1] Like, for instance, that of Ptah (First Dynasty).
[2] King, *The Gnostics and their Remains*, Second Edition, 1887, p. 107.
[3] Budge, op. cit., Vol. II, p. 239.
[4] Herodotus, ii. 69.

We have remarked above on the contrasting beliefs whereby the crocodile was endowed, now with absolute impotence, now with the maximum of procreative power.

*   *   *

Proceeding from this we may venture to develop a view that will afford a more complete answer to the question instituted at the beginning of the present inquiry—namely, why breath was chosen in the Virgin Mary legend to represent the fertilizing material. The view is that *the idea of gaseous fertilization constitutes a reaction to an unusually intense castration-phantasy*. It is one of the most remarkable of the various modes of dealing with the primordial Œdipus situation.

The idea of intestinal gas is inextricably associated with three others—of the father, of the male organ, and of power. We have already considered here and there each of these connections, so that only a few words need be added by way of summary.

Little need be said about the associations between the idea of *father* and the various "gaseous" ones discussed above, for in most of the examples quoted the latter have constituted attributes of the Heavenly Father himself, the Deity. The breath of a Maori chief (= father) is so powerful that he dare not blow on the fire, for a brand might be taken from the fire by a slave and so cause his death; or the sacred breath might communicate its qualities to the fire, which would pass them on to the pot on the fire, whence they would reach the meat in the pot, the future eater of which would surely die.[1] In the phœnix myth, one of the most characteristic of the whole series, the idea of piety to the father is of central importance, a sign of ambivalency. That this association applied not only to the more refined derivatives, but also to the gaseous

[1] Taylor, op. cit., p. 165.

notion itself, is indicated by the fact that oriental nations, and also Rome, worshipped a special Deity who presided over the function in question.[1] The connotations of intestinal gas are almost exclusively male and predominantly refer to the father, one reason for this being fairly obvious in the greater reticence displayed by women and the much greater openness by men in regard to the act concerned, especially during effort (e.g., coitus).

The association with the idea of the *male organ* has also been pointed out and explained above (pp. 329, 330). Something more may be added on the subject of initiation ceremonies, for it is now recognized that these are the expression of castration threats.[2] Throughout Australia women are strictly forbidden ever to see the bull-roarer (*See* p. 289), so essential is the relation of this to the idea of maleness; the Chepara tribe punish with death a woman who casts eyes upon it, or a man who shows it to a woman.[3] In Brazil also no woman may see the equivalent jurupari pipes on pain of death.[4] The association penis—gas (noise)—castration is well illustrated by the Kakian initiation ceremonies, the following account of which I abstract from Frazer.[5] The Kakian ceremonial house is situate under the darkest trees in the depth of the forest and is so built as to admit so little light that it is impossible to see what goes on within; the boys are conducted there blindfold. When all are assembled before the house the High Priest calls aloud on the devils, and immediately a hideous uproar is heard to proceed from the house. It is made by men with bamboo trumpets who have been secretly introduced into the building, but the women think it is made by the devils and are

[1] Bourke, *Scatologic Rites of All Nations*, 1891, pp. 129, 154-7.
[2] *See* Reik, *Probleme der Religionspsychologie*, 1919, Cap. 3, "Die Pubertätsriten der Wilden."
[3] Lang, op. cit., p. 34.
[4] Lang, op. cit., p. 43.
[5] Frazer, *Balder the Beautiful*, 1913, Vol. II, pp. 249, 250.

greatly terrified. Then the priests enter, followed by the boys, one at a time. As soon as each boy disappears within the precincts a dull chopping sound is heard, a fearful cry rings out, and a sword or spear, dripping with blood, is thrust through the roof of the house. This is a token that the boy's *head has been cut off*, and that the devil has carried him away to regenerate him. In some places the boys are pushed through an opening made in the shape of a crocodile's jaws or a cassowary's beak, and it is then said that the devil has swallowed them. The boys remain in the shed for five or nine days. Sitting in the dark, they hear the blast of the bamboo trumpets, and from time to time the sound of musket shots and the clash of swords. As they sit in a row cross-legged, the chief takes his trumpet and, placing the mouth of it in the hands of each lad, speaks through it in strange tones, imitating the voice of the spirits; he warns the lads, under pain of death, to observe the rules of the Kakian society.

The association with the idea of *power* has also been manifest throughout all the examples quoted above, and is an extraordinarily intimate one. To create or destroy with a word, a wind, a breath, or a vapour obviously implies a higher degree of power than to do so with an instrument of might, however wonderful and impressive this might be. With the primary idea (intestinal gas) the sense of power is in adult life usually manifested in the form of contempt; in many countries the passage of wind is regarded as the deadliest possible insult and in certain circumstances may involve such penalties as expulsion from the tribe or even death.[1] In an analysis, carried out from a different point of view, of two Old Testament myths, Lorenz[2] has shown how the might of God against his most

[1] Bourke, op. cit., pp. 161, 162.
[2] Lorenz, "Das Titan-Motiv in der allgemeinen Mythologie," *Imago*, 1913, Bd. II, S. 50-3.

desperate foes was displayed, in the one case by means of wind, in the other through the blowing of trumpets. The myths in question are those of the destruction of the tower of Babel and the walls of Jericho, and he shows, as I think convincingly, that both of these are variants of the Titan motive. In the first of them the destruction is brought about by a mighty *wind* that disperses the people by confounding their *speech*, in the second by God getting his chosen people to give a loud *cry* and to *blow their trumpets*.

The preceding considerations are in full accord with the conclusions I have reached on the basis of psycho-analytical experience with actual persons. In such study it becomes plain that the infantile complex concerned with gaseous fertilization is integrally related to the castration thoughts. The total complex is a characteristically ambivalent one, corresponding with the child's ambivalent attitude towards his father, and its manifestations express at once a denial of his power and an affirmation of his supreme might; his impotency and his omnipotence. Through the conception of the male organ as a flatus-emitting agency (*See* p. 330) these two opposite components become fused into a perfect unity.

Further psycho-analytic study throws still more light on the nature of this paradoxical attitude. It has elucidated the source of the two-fold attitude towards the father. The hostile and depreciatory one, the wish that he were impotent, originates in the rivalry between the boy and father over the possession of the mother. The admiration, which exalts the father's greatness, has a more personal source: it is a substitute for the primary narcissism and feeling of omnipotence which the child is unable to sustain in the face of experience, a failure which is largely contributed to by the presence of the obviously powerful Father. By transferring his own congenital sense of omnipotence[1] to the Father and identifying himself with him, he is enabled to maintain the feeling of power for some time longer, until the time comes for him to discover his Father's limitations also, when he has to repeat the same psychological process by substituting a heavenly for an earthly Father. There is a further important gain in both cases— namely, the reconciliation with a potentially hostile being, and the allaying of a sense of sin that arose from disobedient or hostile thoughts concerning him.

The curious way in which the attitude towards the Father is dealt with and reconciled in the compromise we have considered above, and even the specific form of this compromise, is also a mirror of changes within the individual himself, changes which are only secondarily transferred to the idea of the Father. For, in my experience, the particular group of phantasies that have constituted the main theme of this essay arise in persons who, chiefly on account of the incest barrier, have experienced a difficulty in passing from the pregenital stage of development to that of the genital one,[2] and who have thereby reacted by reverting to the former stage. In this earlier stage, which is principally composed of a combination of sadism and anal-erotism, the element most suitable for fusion with the genital attitude that could not be encompassed is that of the passing of flatus, with its close relation to the sense of power,[3] to expulsion and projection. As was pointed out above, the uniting of these elements to the actual genital one, in the phantasy of a flatus-expelling organ, fulfils all the wished-for conditions to an extent that one could hardly otherwise conceive. That the idea of supreme power is here recaptured under the guise of phantasies that

[1] *See* Ferenczi, op. cit., Ch. VIII, "Stages in the Development in the Sense of Reality."

[2] *See* Freud, *Sammlung kleiner Schriften zur Neurosenlehre*, Vierte Folge, Cap. III, "Die Disposition zur Zwangsneurose."

[3] *See* my *Papers on Psycho-Analysis*, 2nd Ed., p. 546.

have numerous feminine, anal, masochistic and homosexual implications—e.g., by means of the gentle dove—is in entire accord with the fundamental method of Christian salvation, so that further studies on these lines should lead to a deeper understanding of the psychology of this idea.

VI. CONCLUSION

If we now regard the theme as a whole, we cannot but be impressed by the ingenuity and fine feeling with which an idea so repellent to the adult mind has been transformed into a conception not merely tolerable, but lofty in its grandeur. In the endeavour to represent the purest and least sensual form of procreation that can be imagined, the one most befitting to the Creator Himself, the mind worked surely and on the soundest lines by reaching for its basis to the crudest and grossest idea obtainable; it is always through such violently extreme contrasts, as we know from the analytic study of literature, that the grandest psychological effects are achieved. Of all infantile theories of procreation that persist in the Unconscious there is perhaps not one more repellent than that described above, and no more astounding contrast could well be conceived than the original form of this and the form given to it in the legend here analysed. In the original one we have a Father incestuously impregnating his daughter (i.e., a son his mother) by expelling intestinal gas, with the help of the genital organ, into her lower alimentary orifice, one through which her child is then born. In the legend, the site of exit is completely omitted, and that of ingress is denoted by the receptive organ of music, an orifice with fewer sensual implications than any other in the whole body, than the navel, the mouth, or even the eye. What more innocent symbol exists than that gentle messenger of hope and love, the dove? And in the tender breath of the dove, reinforced by the solemn words of the Archangel, who would recognize the repulsive material thus symbolized, with its odour replaced by the fragrance of lilies, its moisture and warmth by the aureole of light and fire, and its sound by the gentle cooing—"the echo on earth of the very Word of God".

The Christian myth is perhaps the most gigantic and revolutionary phantasy in history, and its striking characteristic is the completely veiled way in which this phantasy is carried through to success under the guise of sacrificial submission to the Father's will. It is therefore entirely appropriate that such an important episode as the birth of the hero should be portrayed by symbolisms that signify a complete denial of the Father's power, and which at the same time, under the mantle of the Father, glorify the son's might in the most supreme terms imaginable.

Turning lastly to the accompanying picture by Martini[1] (*see* Frontispiece), painted over six hundred years ago, we see, although its marvellous colour cannot be here reproduced, that the whole theme which has occupied us is portrayed with a charm and fidelity hardly to be surpassed. One of our leading critics, Edward Hutton, writes of it: "Who may describe the colour and the delicate glory of this work? The hand of man can do no more; it is the most beautiful of religious paintings." To show how deeply the artist has reached for his inspiration I will call the reader's attention to one little detail, a trait characteristic of Martini's Annunciation pictures, though often copied from him later by other painters.[2] It has to do with the campanulas that stand between Gabriel and the Virgin. Our

[1] The picture is usually attributed to both Simone Martini and Lippo Memmi, but the latter painted only the setting and the angels at the side, which are not here reproduced.

[2] For instance, by Taddeo Bartoli (in the Siena Academy). A very clear hint of the function of the holy words is given by those painters who make them issue from the Archangel's mouth in the form of a *snake*. (An example of this is offered by the altar at Klosterneuburg, reproduced by Beissel, *Geschichte der Verehrung Marias in Deutschland während des Mittelalters*, 1909, S. 466.)

artist indicated, quite unconsciously, why the lily is the flower chosen for the present purpose. Of all flowers the lily is the most noted for the delicate fragrance of its odour: better than the luscious and half-lascivious rose, the heavy jasmine, or the fleeting wild flowers, the lily can serve as no other flower can to express the acme of purity that is necessary to conceal the exactly opposite original idea. In the picture, the artist makes the words of Gabriel, which are the counterpart of the Breath of God, pass through the lilies, as if to purify the fertilization principle of the last trace of early uncleanness, to cleanse it of any possible remaining dross.

In work done, as this must have been, under the direct inspiration of the unconscious, we realize the difference between true and pseudo-art. It also illustrates how happy was the union between Christian religion and art, before the divorce came with the decadence of the Renaissance and the reign of "Puritanism" in religion. The whole topic of this essay shows how important was the part played by æsthetic feeling in the elaboration of religious beliefs—the legend we have analysed may well be compared to an exquisite poetic conception—a fact that is throughout intelligible when we remember how intimate is the association between the unconscious roots of both. Religion has always used art in one form or another, and must do so, for the reason that incestuous desires invariably construct their phantasies out of the material provided by the unconscious memory of infantile corophilic interests; this is the inner meaning of the phrase "Art is the handmaid of Religion". The increasing separation between the two, and the diverting of art to other purposes, constitutes the first serious stage in the transformation of religion, and in the supersession of the pleasure-principle by the reality-principle.

357

XIV

A PSYCHO-ANALYTIC STUDY OF THE HOLY GHOST CONCEPT[1]

WHATEVER time may reveal about the historical personality of the Founder of Christianity, there is no doubt in the minds of those who have instituted studies into the comparison of various religions that many of the beliefs centring about Him have been superadded to the original basis, having been derived from extraneous Pagan sources, and the name of Christian mythology may very well be applied to the study of these accretions. As Frazer[2] puts it: "Nothing is more certain than that myths grow like weeds round the great historical figures of the past."

Some of the more important elements of this mythology have already been investigated by means of the psycho-analytic method by Freud.[3] According to him, the central dogma itself of the Christian religion—the belief that mankind is to be saved from its sins through the sacrifice of Jesus Christ on the cross—represents an elaboration of the primitive totemistic system. The essence of this system he sees in an attempt to allay the sense of guilt arising from the Œdipus complex, i.e., the impulse, gratified in primordial times, towards parricide and incest, there being good reason to think that this complex is the ultimate source of the "original sin" described by the theologians. This was the first great sin of mankind and the one from

[1] Read at the Seventh International Psycho-Analytical Congress, 27th September, 1922.

[2] Frazer, *Adonis, Attis, Osiris*, 3rd Ed., 1914, p. 160.

[3] Freud, *Totem und Tabu*, 1913, S. 142.

which our moral conscience and sense of guilt was born. The early history of mankind in this respect, the tendency towards this great sin and the moral reaction against it, is repeated by every child that comes into the world, and the story of religion is a never-ending attempt to overcome the Œdipus complex and to achieve peace of mind through atonement with the Father. Freud has pointed out that the most striking characteristic of the Christian solution as compared with others, such as the Mithraic, is the way in which this atonement is achieved through surrender to the Father instead of through openly defying and over-coming him. This surrender, the prototype of which is the Crucifixion, is periodically repeated in the ceremony of the Holy Mass or Communion, which is psychologically equivalent to the totemistic banquet. In this way the Father's wrath is averted and the Son takes his place as co-equal with Him. In the banquet is lived over again both the celebration of the original deed of killing and eating the Father and the remorseful piety which desires re-union and identification with him. It will be seen that, according to this view, the Christian reconciliation with the Father is attained at the expense of over-development of the feminine component.

The present communication will, it is hoped, afford confirmation of Freud's conclusions by a study on parallel lines. Some ten years ago I published in the *Jahrbuch der Psychoanalyse* an essay on the impregnation of the Madonna and what I have to present here is largely based on a recently written expanded edition of the essay which is to appear in English.[1] The research there pursued led incidentally to consideration of the following problem.

In the Christian mythology a startling fact appears. It is the only one in which the original figures are no longer present, in which the Trinity to be worshipped no longer

[1] Chapter XIII of this volume.

consists of the Father, Mother and Son. The Father and Son still appear, but the Mother, the reason for the whole conflict, has been replaced by the mysterious figure of the Holy Ghost.

It seems impossible to come to any other conclusion than the one just enunciated. Not only must the Mother logically constitute the third member of any Trinity whose two other members are Father and Son, not only is this so in all the other numerous Trinities known to us, but there is a considerable amount of direct evidence indicating that this was originally so in the Christian myth itself. Frazer[1] has collected some of the evidence to this effect and makes the conclusion highly probable on historical grounds alone. The original Mother, who was accepted by for instance the Ophitic sect as the third member of the Trinity, would appear to have been of mixed Babylonian and Egyptian origin, although there are not wanting indications to show that a misty Mother-figure floated in the background of Hebrew theology also. Thus the passage in Genesis (i. 2) "And the Spirit of God moved upon the face of the waters" should properly run "The Mother of the Gods brooded (or fluttered) over the abyss and brought forth life", a bird-like conception of the Mother which must remind us not only of the Holy Dove (i.e., the Holy Spirit that replaces the Mother), but also of the legend that Isis conceived Horus while fluttering in the shape of a hawk over the dead body of Osiris. While the sternly patriarchal Hebrew theology, however, banned the Mother to a subordinate part and the Messiah-Son to a remotely distant future, it nevertheless retained the normal relationship of the three. It is probable, therefore, that any eludication of the change from Mother to Holy Ghost would

[1] Frazer, *The Dying God*, 1911, p. 5. [Ewald Roellenbleck, in his *Magna Mater im alten Testament*, 1949, has made a comprehensive study of this matter and shown conclusively that indications of the original Mother Goddess are strewn throughout the Old Testament, even if many are in a veiled form.]

throw light on the inner nature of the psychological revolution betokened by the development of Judaism into Christianity.

The mode of approach here adopted will be by considering the circumstances of the conception of the Messiah. This approach is justified on two grounds. In the first place, as is well known, the figure of the Holy Ghost appears in the myth only as the procreative agent in the conception of the Son, and as an ambrosial benediction poured out on to the Son when the latter undergoes the initiatory rite of baptism (later on also in connection with the followers of the Son). In the second place, Otto Rank[1] has long ago shown that the tendencies of a myth are revealed already in its earliest stages, in what he has termed the Myth of the Birth of the Hero. Consideration of the Christian myth makes it probable that this law holds good here also, so that a study of the conception of Jesus may throw light on the main tendencies and purposes of the whole myth.

To begin with, the very idea of a conception being induced by a supernatural and abnormal means yields a clue to the mythical tendency. It tells us at once that there is some conflict present in the attitude towards the Father, for the unusual route of impregnation implies, as we know from other studies, a wish to repudiate the idea of the Father having played any part in it. There may or may not be present as well the opposite tendency to this—the desire to magnify admiringly the special power of the Father. This ambivalency is clearly seen in the primitive belief that children are begotten not of their Father, but through impregnation of the Mother by the particular clan totem, for the totem is simply an ancestral substitute for the Father, a super-Father. It is thus not surprising to learn that the Christian myth must, like most

[1] Otto Rank, *Der Mythus von der Geburt des Helden*, 1909.

other religious myths, be concerned with the age-old struggle between Father and Son.

It will be remembered that the conception of Jesus took place in a most unusual manner. As a rule, whenever a god wishes to impregnate a mortal woman, he appears on earth—either in human form or disguised as an animal with specially phallic attributes (a bull, a snake or what not)—and impregnates her by performing the usual act of sexual union. In the Madonna myth, on the other hand, God the Father does not appear at all, unless we regard the Archangel Gabriel as a personification of Him; the impregnation itself is effected by the angel's word of greeting and the breath of a dove simultaneously entering the Madonna's ear. The Dove itself, which is understood to represent the Holy Ghost, emanates from the Father's mouth. The Holy Ghost, therefore, and His breath play here the part of a sexual agent, and appear where we would logically expect to find a phallus and semen respectively. To quote St. Zeno: "The womb of Mary swells forth by the Word, not by seed"; or, again, St. Eleutherius: "O blessed Virgin . . . made mother without co-operation of man. For here the ear was the wife, and the angelic word the husband."

It will be seen that our problem is immediately complicated. To find that the mysterious figure replacing the Mother is a male being, who symbolizes the creative elements of the Father, only adds a second enigma to the first. Before taking this up, however, it is necessary to consider more closely the details of the impregnation itself.

A comparative analysis of these leads to an unexpected conclusion. When we seek to discover how the idea of breath could have become invested in the primitive, i.e., unconscious, mind with the seminal connotation just indicated, we find that it does so in a very circuitous way.

As I have shown in detail in the work referred to above, the idea of breath does not have in the primitive mind the narrow and definite signification we now give to it. A study of Greek and Hindu physiological philosophy in particular shows that breath used to have a much broader connotation, that of the so-called pneuma concept, and that an important constituent of this concept—probably the greater part of at least its sexual aspects—were derived from another gaseous excretion, namely that proceeding from the lower end of the alimentary canal. It is this down-going breath, as it is termed in the Vedic literature, which is the fertilizing element in the various beliefs of creation through speech or breath. Similarly, analysis of the idea of the ear as a female receptive organ leads to the conclusion that this is a symbolic replacement, a "displacement from below upwards", of corresponding thoughts relating to the lower orifice of the alimentary canal. Putting these two conclusions together, we can hardly avoid the inference that the mythical legend in question represents a highly refined and disguised elaboration of the "infantile sexual theory", to which I have elsewhere drawn attention,[1] according to which fecundation is supposed to be effected through the passage of intestinal gas from the Father to the Mother. I have also pointed out why this most repellent of sexual phantasies should lend itself better than any other to the conveyance of the most exalted and spiritual ideas of which the mind is capable.

Now there are certain characteristic features accompanying this infantile theory which we can discover by means of individual psycho-analyses of persons holding it, as well as from a study of the comparative material in association with it. Superficially considered it would appear to imply a denial of the Father's potency and to represent

[1] *Jahrbuch der Psychoanalyse*, 1912, Band IV, S. 588 et seq.

a form of castration wish, and no doubt this is in part true. Yet, on the other hand, one is astonished to find that throughout all the numerous associations to the idea of creation in connection with wind there is nearly always implied the very opposite idea of a powerful concrete phallus which expels the wind. Thus in most of the beliefs attaching in all parts of the world to the idea of divine creative thunder there is also present some sort of thunder-weapon, the best-known and most widely spread of which is the bull-roarer. Further than this, the idea of impregnation by means of wind itself would seem to be regularly regarded by the primitive mind as a sign of peculiarly great potency, as if the power to create by a mere sound, a word or even a thought, were a final demonstration of tremendous virility. This reaches its acme in the notion of conception without even sound, by a silent thought alone, such as in the belief cherished by various nuns in the Middle Ages that they had conceived because Jesus had "thought on them".

An excellent example of this complex of ideas, interesting from several points of view, is afforded by certain Egyptian beliefs about the crocodile. They also bear directly on the present theme, for the crocodile was taken by early Christians to be a symbol for the Logos or Holy Ghost; moreover, the creature was believed to impregnate his mate, just like the Virgin Mary, through the ear. Now on the one hand the crocodile was notable to the ancients for having no external genital organs, no tongue and no voice (symbolic indications of impotency), and yet on the other hand—in spite of these purely negative qualities (or perhaps just because of them)—he was regarded as the highest type of sexual virility, and a number of aphrodisiac customs were based on this belief. The crocodile was an emblem of wisdom, like the serpent and other phallic objects, and as such figures on the breast of Minerva, so that the ancients seem to have reached the conclusion that the most potent agent in all creation was the Silence of Man, the omnipotence of thought being even more impressive than the omnipotence of speech.

We know that this over-emphasis on paternal potency is not a primary phenomenon, but is a transference from personal narcissism in response to the fear of castration as a punishment for castration wishes. We thus come to the conclusion, which is amply borne out by individual psycho-analyses, that a belief in a gaseous impregnation represents a reaction to an unusually intense castration phantasy, and that it occurs only when the attitude towards the Father is particularly ambivalent, hostile denial of potency alternating with affirmation of and subjection to supreme might.

Both of these attitudes are indicated in the Christian myth. The occurrence of impregnation by *action à distance*, merely through messengers, and the choice of a gaseous route, reveal an idea of tremendous potency, one to which the Son is throughout subjected. On the other hand, the instrument employed to effect the impregnation is far from being a specially virile one. Though the Dove is evidently a phallic symbol—it was in the guise of a dove that Zeus seduced Phtheia, and doves were the amor-like emblems of all the great love-goddesses, Astarte, Semiramis, Aphrodite and the rest—still it plainly owes its association with love principally to the gentle and caressing nature of its wooing. We may thus say that it is one of the most effeminate of all the phallic emblems.

It is thus clear that the Father's might is manifested only at the expense of being associated with considerable effeminacy. The same theme is even more evident in the case of the Son. He attains greatness, including final possession of the Mother and reconciliation with the Father, only after undergoing the extremity of humiliation together with a symbolic castration and death. A similar path is laid down for every follower of Jesus, salvation being purchased at the price of gentleness, humility, and submission to the Father's will. This path has logically led in extreme cases to actual self-castration and always leads in that direction, though of course it is in practice replaced by various acts symbolizing this. There is a double gain in this. Object-love for the Mother is replaced by a regression to the original identification with her, so that incest is avoided and the Father pacified; further the opportunity is given of winning the Father's love by the adoption of a feminine attitude towards him. Peace of mind is purchased by means of a change in heart in the direction of a change in sex.

We return at this point to the problem raised above of the psychological signification of the Holy Ghost. We have seen that He is composed of a combination of the original Mother-Goddess with the creative essence (genital organs) of the Father. From this point of view one approaches an understanding of the peculiar awfulness of blasphemy against the Holy Ghost, the so-called "unpardonable sin", for such an offence would symbolically be equivalent to a defilement of the Holy Mother and an attempted castration of the Father. It would be a repetition of the primordial sin, the beginning of all sin, gratification of the Œdipus impulse. This is in complete harmony with our clinical experience that neurotics nearly always identify this sin with the act of masturbation, the psychological significance of which we now know to be due to its unconscious association with incestuous wishes.

So far the figure of the Holy Ghost may be held to correspond with the terrible image of the phantastic "woman with the penis", the primal Mother. But the matter is more complicated. On union of the Mother with the Father's creative agent all femininity vanishes, and the figure becomes indisputably male. This reversal of sex is the real problem.

For the reasons given above this change in sex must have something to do with the act of begetting, and here we are reminded of another curious change in sex connected with the same act. In his brilliant researches into the initiation rites and couvade ceremonies of savages Reik[1] has shown that the most important tendency permeating these is the endeavour to counter the Œdipus-complex—i.e., the wish for Father-murder and Mother-incest—by a very peculiar and yet logical enough device. Acting on the deeply-seated conviction that the foundation of the fatal attraction towards the Mother is the physical fact of one's having been born by her, a conviction which has some real basis, savages enter upon various complicated procedures the essential aim of which is so far as possible to annul this physical fact and to establish the fiction that the boy has been at all events re-born by the Father. In this way the Father hopes to abrogate the incestuous wishes on the one hand and to bind the youth more closely to him on the other, both these aims diminishing the risk of parricide. Put in terms of the instincts this means that an incestuous heterosexual fixation is replaced by a sublimated homosexuality.

When we reflect how widely spread is this tendency —the rites themselves, as Reik remarks, are found in every part of the world—it would not seem too bold to ascribe to it also the substitution of the male for the female sex in the case under discussion. I would therefore suggest that *the replacement of the Mother-Goddess by the Holy Ghost is a manifestation of the desirability of renouncing incestuous and parricidal wishes and replacing them by a stronger attachment to the Father*, a phenomenon having the same signification as the initiatory rites of savages. Hence

[1] Reik, *Probleme der Religionspsychologie*, 1919, Ch. II and III.

the greater prominence in Christianity, as compared with Judaism, of personal love for God the Father. In support of the conclusion may further be quoted the extensive part played by sublimated homosexuality throughout the Christian religion. The exceptional precept of universal brother-love, that one should not only love one's neighbour as oneself but also one's enemies, makes a demand on social feeling that can be met, as Freud has pointed out, only from homosexual sources of feeling. Then the effeminate costume of the priests, their compulsory celibacy, shaven head, and so on, plainly signify deprivation of masculine attributes, being thus equivalent to symbolic self-castration.

The figure thus created represents an androgynic compromise. In surrendering some elements of virility it gains the special female prerogative of child-bearing, and thus combines the advantages of both sexes. The hermaphroditic ideal offered to the world by Christianity has proved of tremendous importance to humanity. We have in it a great reason for the enormous civilizing influence of Christianity, since the civilizing of primitive man essentially means the mastery of the Œdipus complex and the transformation of much of it into sublimated homosexuality (i.e., herd instinct), without which no social community can exist. We realize also why a real conversion to Christianity is typically described as being "re-born of the Holy Ghost", and why immersion in water (a birth symbolism) is the official sign of it; we have here, further, the explanation of the curious finding, which I have pointed out previously,[1] that the baptismal fluid is lineally derived from a bodily fluid (semen, urine) of the *Father*. It should, incidentally, be no longer strange that the most vivid forms of religious conversion are seen either at puberty, i.e., the homosexual phase of adolescence, or, in adult life,

[1] Chapter II, p. 71, etc.

with drunkards; it will be remembered that drunkenness is a specific sign of mental conflict over the subject of repressed homosexuality.

The conclusions thus reached accord well with those reached by Freud along other lines regarding the connection between Christianity and totemism. Christianity constitutes in large part both a veiled regression to the primitive totemistic system and at the same time a refinement of this. It resembles it in the sharpness of the ambivalency towards the Father, though in it the hostile component has undergone a still further stage in repression. It also agrees with the tendency of the primitive initiation ceremonies as disclosed by Reik, but it indicates a progress beyond these inasmuch as the shifting of procreative importance from the female to the male sex is put backward from the time of puberty to that of birth, just as, incidentally, the initiatory rite of baptism subsequently was. Instead of the maternal birth being nullified by a symbolic paternal rebirth at the time of puberty, the birth itself is mythologically treated on these lines.

In discussing the fate of the original Mother-Goddess and her transformation into the Holy Ghost we have passed by a very obvious consideration. Although in the Christian Trinity itself the Holy Ghost is the only figure that replaces the primal Mother, nevertheless there is in Christian theology a female figure, the Virgin Mary, who also plays an important part. It would thus be truer to say that the original Goddess has been "decomposed"—to use a mythological term—into two, one of which goes to make the Holy Ghost and the other of which becomes the Madonna. To complete our analysis a little should be said about the latter figure.

By a divine Father or Mother, i.e., God or Goddess, we mean, from a purely psychological point of view, an infantile conception of a Father or Mother, a figure invested

with all the attributes of power and perfection and regarded
with respect or awe. The decomposition in question, therefore, signifies that the divine, i.e., infantile, attributes of
the original Mother image have been transferred to the
idea of the Holy Ghost, while the purely human, i.e., adult,
attributes have been retained in the form of a simple
woman. Apart from the change in sex that occurs in the
former case, which has been considered above, the process
is akin to the divorce that normally obtains during the
years of adolescence, when the youth, following the dicho-
tomy of his own feelings, divides women into two classes—
human accessible ones and unapproachable forbidden
figures of respect, the extreme types being the harlot and
"lady" respectively. We know from countless individual
psycho-analyses that this splitting is simply a projection
of the dissociation that occurs in the feelings originally
entertained by the boy for the Mother; those that have
been deflected from a sexual goal become attached to
various figures of respect, while the crudely erotic ones are
allowed to appear only in regard to a certain class of
woman, harlot, servant, and so on. Both the "lady" and
the harlot are thus derivatives of the Mother figure. So we
infer that the division of the original Goddess into two
figures in Christianity is a manifestation of the same
repression of incestuous impulses.

Light is thrown on the part played by the Virgin Mary
both by these considerations and by comparison of the
woman in Christian mythology with the woman of other
Trinities. For this purpose we may select the three that
have been so fully studied by Frazer, three which seriously
competed with Christianity in its early days and which
were the sources of some of its most prominent elements.
I refer to the three Saviour-Gods Adonis, Attis and Osiris.
With all these we have a Son-Lover who dies, usually
being castrated as well, who is periodically mourned,

chiefly by women, and whose resurrection betokens the welfare or salvation of humanity. Two of these contrast with the third in the following interesting respect. With Adonis and Attis the Mother-Goddess, Astarte or Cybele respectively, towers in importance over the young Saviour; Osiris on the other hand is at least as distinguished and powerful as Isis. Frazer writes:[1] "Whereas legend generally represented Adonis and Attis as simple swains, mere herdsmen or hunters whom the fatal love of a goddess had elevated above their homely sphere into a brief and melancholy pre-eminence, Osiris uniformly appears in tradition as a great and beneficent king." Later on,[2] however, he suggests that "This . . . seems to indicate that in the beginning Isis was, what Astarte and Cybele continued to be, the stronger divinity of the pair". Thus, in the series: Astarte, Isis, Mary we have a gradation in the diminishing greatness of the primal Mother. Although Mary retains the attributes of perfection, she has lost those of divine and unapproachable grandeur and becomes simply a good woman. This subordination of the primal Mother, and her deprivation of the infantile conception of divinity, would seem to accord well with the view expressed above of the tendency in the Christian myth to exalt the Father at the expense of the Mother. The significance of this is, as has been indicated, to counter the incest wish by instituting a closer bond with the Father.

Reflection on the history of Christianity shows that its object has been gained only in part, that the solution provided of the Œdipus complex was not one of universal applicability, and that the age-old conflict between Father and Son has continued to lead to further efforts to solve it. The transition from the Mother to the Holy Ghost was not accomplished without a struggle even at the beginning,

[1] Frazer, *Adonis, Attis, Osiris*, 1914, pp. 158, 159.
[2] Ibid., p. 202.

as might have been expected in a community always accustomed to Goddess worship. Several sects tried to maintain the divinity of Mary, the obvious successor of Isis, Hera, Astarte, Aphrodite and the rest, and the Melchite attempt to retain the original Trinity of Father, Mary, and Messiah was crushed only at the Council of Nice. For a thousand years matters proceeded quietly, perhaps because of the astounding syncretizing activity of those years in assimilating Pagan mythology of all kinds, including most of that pertaining to the earlier Mother-Goddesses. After this time, however, voices were increasingly raised in favour of according the Virgin Mary a loftier part in the hierarchy. This tendency won the day in the Catholic Church and may be said to be still proceeding, for it is hardly more than half a century since the last step was taken of pronouncing that she herself was also conceived immaculately.[1] The human need for a Mother to worship was too strong, so that She had to be reinstated. Christianity here, therefore, as in so many other respects, effected a compromise between the Hebraic tendency towards an androgenic conception and the Classical tendency towards acknowledgement of the Mother-Goddess as a central figure.

The peculiarly Christian solution, which was later adulterated by Catholicism, was thus a lineal descendant of the Hebraic tendency. The Protestant Reformation was clearly an attempt to reinforce the original solution and to carry it to its logical conclusion by abolishing all traces of Mariolatry from religion; only those who have witnessed the horror with which the "Red Woman" is mentioned among the extreme Protestant sections of the community can fully appreciate the strength of this impulse. It is interesting, further, to note that the more completely is this process carried out the less necessity is there to adopt a homosexual attitude in religion; the extreme Protestant

[1] While this is in the press comes the doctrine of the corporeal assumption.

ministers not only marry, but discard all special costume and other indications of a feminine rôle, whereas all the self-castrating tendencies are more evident where Mariolatry is highly developed. One might perhaps say that the Protestant solution of the Œdipus complex is the replacement of the Mother by the Woman, while the Catholic one consists in the change of the masculine to the feminine attitude.

INDEX

374

INDEX

Unconscious, 2–4, 8, 118, 122–3, 126, 143, 183–4, 186, 193, 200, 226–7, 229, 237, 240, 245–6, 275, 293, 320, 336
Unicorn, 330–1
Urine, 64, 308, 315, 322

Vaerting, 145
Vaughan, 338
de *Vaux*, 281
Vergil, 283, 335
Virgin Mary, 210–11, Chapter XIII, 369–70, 372
virility, 142, 348
Vorberg, 327

Waitz, 329
Wake, 118
Waldron, 28
wealth, 62
weather, 258
wedding ceremony, 80, 92
wedding cake, 92
Wells, H. G., 250, 261
Wernicke, 41
Westermarck, 153, 155, 171

Weston, Jessie L., 168, 336
Westropp, 118
westwind, 280, 284
Wheeler, 75
Willsford, 37
Winterbottom, 152
wisdom, 23 et seq., 294, 334, 347–8
witchcraft, 112
Witzschel, 284
von *Wlislocki*, 60, 91
word-deposits, 98
Wordsworth, 140
Wohler, 231
Wright, A. R., 6, 29
Wundt, 274, 294
Wuttke, 24, 28, 30–32, 35, 37–8, 52–3, 61, 67, 86, 91, 101–3

Yahweh, 287, 341
Yama, 336
Yoni, 88

Zacharias, 291
Zeus, 208, 287, 289, 293, 334–5, 338, 365